I wish you
all the best in
everything you do!
Tony Alessandra
3/91

"Alessandra and O'Connor have hit a real home run with *People Smart*. It's the best thing I've ever seen written in this area! It is a must read for anyone who wants to learn more about themselves and others—easy to read, but powerful in content. *People Smart* will make you more aware and more effective from the moment you finish reading it."

Kenneth Blanchard, Ph.D.
Co-author, *The One Minute Manager*

People Smart
Powerful Techniques for Turning Every Encounter into a Mutual Win

Tony Alessandra, Ph.D.
and
Michael J. O'Connor, Ph.D.
with
Janice Alessandra

KEYNOTE
PUBLISHING
COMPANY
La Jolla, California

First Printing 1990
Second Printing 1990

Although the authors and publisher have made every effort to ensure the accuracy and completeness of information contained in this book, we assume no responsibility for errors, inaccuracies, omissions, or any inconsistency herein. Any slights of people or organizations are unintentional.

Library of Congress Cataloging-in-Publication Data

Alessandra, Anthony J.
   People Smart : powerful techniques for turning every encounter into a mutual win / Tony Alessandra and Michael O'Connor with Janice Alessandra
      p.   cm.
   ISBN 0-9625161-0-4 : $19.95
   1. Inspirational relations.   I. O'Connor, Michael J.
II. Alessandra, Janice.   III. Title.
HM132.A354   1990
302—dc20   89-71069
                                   CIP

Dedications

From Tony and Janice:

To each other and our children, Justin and Jessica

From Michael:

To Mary Ann, my loving wife and my greatest teacher, and to my children Kevin and Kara, for their patience, tolerance, and appreciation of my life's work

Acknowledgments

Writing this book has become more and more a team effort as we have progressed from one stage to the next. Some people contributed content, either directly or indirectly; others gave helpful comments about the manuscript; some recharged our batteries when the going got rough; and some reached seemingly unreachable deadlines to keep the project going on time.

With this in mind, the authors would like to thank Carl Jung, David Merrill, Larry Wilson, and Myers and Briggs for their pioneering research and observations; and Jim Cathcart whose long-standing and valued partnership was instrumental in development of the terminology and core concepts presented here. Those who gave valuable feedback on the manuscript include Rick Barrera, Sheila Murray-Bethel, Don Cipriano, Judy Zitzloff, Marcia Feener, Charles Boyd and Jay Lewis.

Many others contributed input on their particular personality types—Ron Friedman, Holli Olson, Paula Cathcart, Danny Colleran, Colleen Alessandra, John Lee, Catherine Carpenter, Mary Faith Reading, Stan and Melody Leopard, Mikala Limbrecht, Seymour Myers, and Jessica and Justin Alessandra. Their insights especially enlivened the chapters on romance and family.

Thanks to Gary Alessandra for his tireless dedication in getting several days of copy ready today, Linda Brown and Lynda London for transforming text into graphics, and Melody Leopard for making the format "reader friendly." Dee Jones and Catherine Carpenter made sure everything was organized and sent off to the right people at the right time.

Additionally, the authors wish to thank and acknowledge Carlson Learning Company and its Performax Network Division for their support in supplying information on the needs model of behavior (DISC). For further information on their learning instruments and related materials, please write or call Carlson Learning Company, Carlson Parkway, P.O. Box 59159, Minneapolis, MN 55459-8247; (612) 449-2856.

Contents

PART TWO
WORKPLACE APPLICATIONS

PART THREE
PERSONAL APPLICATIONS

PART FOUR
CUSTOM-FITTED PERSONAL PATTERNS

12 *Keys to Unlocking Personal Effectiveness* **. . . 331**
  Self-managing your fears and anxieties
  How you can help all 15 classical patterns behave
   more productively
  How each of the 15 classical patterns can in-
   crease their effectiveness
  More on how each pattern can increase its ef-
   fectiveness

Introduction

Everybody is interested in finding out more about themselves—and how to deal with others more effectively. If you're like most people, you want to improve your interactions with others. This book shows you a simple, yet proven, way to positively influence others.

The purpose of *People Smart* is threefold: to give you a conscious awareness of what people do, to help you predict what people are likely to do and why they do it, and to accept yourself and others as worthwhile so you can adapt and successfully relate.

Managers want to know how to maximize productivity and efficiency from their staff, salespeople need to build better rapport with customers, employees want to get along with their peers and managers. It's natural for people to aspire to success in business organizations. Those in helping professions want to provide better care for their patients and clients.

Entertainers seek to reach a larger audience and more effectual agents, while speakers want to leave their audiences with something to grow on. Engineers want to fit into their workplace as they turn out more quality products. Diplomats and public officials desire to influence varying groups so they can improve communication—whether internationally, nationally, or locally. And, of course, it's important for parents to relate well with their children—and vice versa. In short, virtually everyone is fascinated with making their working and living relationships better.

People Smart will not only help you become a better you, it will help you behave more maturely and productively by teaching you how to focus on your goals instead of your fears. Then you can develop and use more of your natural strengths, while recognizing, improving upon, and modifying your weaknesses. This book does not deal with values or judgments. Instead, we concentrate on individuals' needs and fears—our natural tendencies that cause us to do the things we do.

Every person has his or her own special way of doing things and an identifiable and predictable behavioral type. Behavioral type is a pattern, or group of recurring habits, resulting from the way you typically do things—the way you deal with people and situations. It's your comfortable method of behaving, most of the time, when you relax and just *act yourself.*

Often, when we do what comes naturally we alienate others without realizing it. Why? Because that same behavior may not be natural for them. If we want to get along with our colleagues, employees, bosses, friends, and families, it's essential we become aware of our natural tendencies—and their natural preferences! Then we can defuse extreme behaviors before we sabotage ourselves. We do this by temporarily using behavioral modification to change only our own behavior so the other person feels comfortable. When this happens, tension lessens and cooperation zooms.

Your technique of interacting with people succeeds when you receive and heed their external signals; it fails when you ignore and cross them. Of course, everyone experiences the same basic human needs, but each of us ranks some needs higher than others.

When you understand something about your own habitual style and how it differs from others' styles, you can modify your approach to get on the same wavelength with them. The ideas you present don't change. But you can change the way you present those ideas. And people will teach you how to treat them if you're willing to discover their unique signals.

For example, one type of person measures his success by results. He heads for the finished product and the bottom line. He'll do whatever it takes, within reason, to get the job done. In fact, his natural response to what he views as other people's lack of accomplishment is, "Don't just sit around wasting time! Get busy!" He needs achievements.

Another type places high value on recognition and measures success by the amount of acknowledgment and praise she receives. Consequently, she typically follows that route to attention and applause. She gravitates toward friendliness and enjoyment, popularity and prestige—while consciously avoiding rejection, negativism, and arguments.

Then we have the steady, cooperative type of person who needs close relationships. He places a high value on sharing and trust, but bases his feelings about people and things on concrete evidence. He wants the security and predictability found in daily routine—so he resists sudden, unplanned changes and needs stable, predictable environments. He thrives on the familiar. Changes or surprises make him uncomfortable.

The last type concerns herself more with content than with congratulations. She wants to know how things work so she can evaluate how correctly they function. At the extreme, this tendency toward perfectionism can result in *paralysis by analysis*. Because she needs to be right, she prefers checking processes herself. Concerned with appearances, she focuses on the process—how to perform a task—while complying with established rules and regulations. As the most cerebral of the four types (in terms of how they deal with people and situations, not I. Q.), tasks win over people and a slow pace prevails.

People Smart will help you connect with people in the workplace and in your personal life. For example, Part One, "Understanding People Smarts," helps you to identify and better deal with virtually everyone. In "The Platinum Rule," we show you more about treating others the way they want to be treated, not the way you want to be treated—without being phony or under-handed. In "I Know Who You Are, But What Am I?", we describe each behavioral style and help you determine which one you are. Next, we assist you to identify other people's natural styles. The Adaptability chapter, includes both versatility and flexibility characteristics and helps you to determine how adaptable you are in life's varying situations.

Part Two deals with "Workplace Applications." The chapters here help you identify and appropriately respond to the four basic types in a work environment. And we show how the different types typically lead and want to be managed. The sales and service chapter covers how the four types prefer to sell—and be sold.

"Personal Applications" is the thrust of Part Three. "The Social Scene" depicts each type behaving with friends and acquaintances, while the family chapter describes the four types at home with spouse and children. And the romance chapter portrays each type in dating situations.

In Part Four, we delve into more specific behaviors, combination patterns that more accurately describe you and others. Then we summarize all 15 commonly combined patterns and show you what they specifically want, need, and fear.

This is a reader-friendly book, with lots of charts and graphs to summarize and explain the text. The reader can use and reuse it as a constant companion for dealing with difficult people and stressful situations. *People Smart* shows clearly how to understand both your own unique strengths and inherent shortcomings and those of others. It gives you the tools to get what you want in various life situations. This reference equips you with the power and knowledge to cash in on these insights through more positive and productive exchanges with others. You can realistically take charge of improving all your relationships and this book shows how.

Part One

Understanding People Smarts

Chapter I
The Platinum Rule

Personality clash or instant rapport?

In your dealings with others, have you ever experienced a personality conflict? (If you haven't, check to see if you're still breathing like the rest of us mortals). No matter how much you may try, your teeth clench and your adrenalin pumps faster when you're with this difficult character. Whatever you may want to call the process, you clash. You're not tuned in on the same wavelength.

When we clash with someone, we often move towards the extreme of avoiding that person, no matter what. Or the other extreme of telling him exactly what we think of his unacceptable behavior. Or we may tell everyone else how distasteful we find him. Or just grit our teeth and tolerate him. Whatever our initial reaction, we feel uncomfortable because we have a personality conflict.

On the other hand, we'll bet you can think of somebody you liked immediately. You had instant rapport, immediate chemistry. "Ann is so down-to-earth, I feel as though I've known her for years." After ten minutes you felt like you'd known Mr. or Ms. Wonderful for half a lifetime. Here was a soul mate who clicked with you from word one. Her personality *felt right* and you also felt good about yourself when you were near her. You felt relaxed and comfortable with this person. Chemistry prevailed, and Ann made your Top Ten list of favorites.

What could possibly account for these two extreme variations in the human species? Certainly, our unique sets of experiences coupled with the genes passed down by Mom and Dad ensure we're all different. Everyone's idea of a person to avoid versus a best friend varies. Given these subjective differences, the way people communicate can result in conflict or chemistry. So how do you go about interacting with all those fascinatingly diverse, sometimes difficult, people out there?

How to deal with difficult people

This book will teach you how to treat people in a way which allows them to feel comfortable with you, so there'll be less tension between you. When tension goes down, positive outcomes—trust, credibility, creativity, cooperation, respect, commitment, and productivity—go up. How do you get results with people? By communicating with them on their level so they're at ease. Because challenging relationships are a fact of life, we'd like to show you how to:

- *understand* your own style, its strengths and weaknesses, and how your behaviors communicate that style to others.
- *identify* someone else's style by quick, easily learned techniques so you'll know how to *read people* and treat them the way they'd like to be treated.
- *adjust* your behavior to make all kinds of people more at ease with you, and you with them!

Bending the Golden Rule

We contend that you can create much more chemistry and far less conflict in all your relationships—work, social, dating, and family—based on how well you practice the Golden Rule. If you exercise the Golden Rule appropriately, you'll create much more relationship chemistry. But if you fail to understand the true spirit of the Golden Rule, you'll create many more personality conflicts. Just to make sure you have the proper perspective, what is the Golden Rule?

It's simply, "Do unto others as you would have them do unto you." Not the managerial version—"The person with the gold makes the rules,"—or the skeptical interpretation—"Do unto others before they do unto you."

"So," you say? "How could people get in trouble if they practiced that truth? Living by the Golden Rule should result in more harmonious relationships, not create conflict!" You're right. The problem lies with practicing the Golden Rule verbatim and not understanding its true intent. When you misapply it, you stand a much greater chance of triggering conflict over chemistry.

Let's explain. When you treat others as you want to be treated, you can end up offending others who have different needs, wants, and expectations from you. So when you apply the Golden Rule verbatim, there's a much greater chance of triggering conflict over chemistry. Yes, you heard it right. If you literally apply, "Do unto others as you would have them do unto you," you'll make problems for yourself with up to 75% of the types of people you meet. Following the Golden Rule verbatim means treating others from your point of view. That means you naturally tend to speak in the way you are most comfortable listening; or sell to others the way you like to be sold; or manage the way you want others to direct you.

When you treat people as you seek to be treated, it can cause tension. Why? Because the other person may not like your way. Perhaps you fill your own needs instead of his or hers. Or speak in a way that's easy for you to follow, but hard for the other person. That brings us to the second reason the Golden Rule can actually damage relationships. It implies all people want to be treated the same when, in fact, our preferences are not all alike. So application of this principle varies from one individual to the next based on their personality differences.

Margaret treats you as she wants to be treated

The Golden Rule would work only in a perfect world where all of us were identical. But we're not. For instance, Tony's mother devoutly practices it, but it backfires. She treats everybody alike. The world population is part of her extended

Italian family. To understand her, try picturing the women in the Italian family from the hit movie *Moonstruck*. You'll have a sense of what she's like . . . only more so.

Tony's mother is an exceptionally people-oriented, outgoing person. She's so gregarious, she makes Bruce Willis look like an introvert. Anyway, when she goes to a restaurant, she greets the hostess and other patrons as though they're in her kitchen. Anyone who makes eye contact with her is fair game.

As she approaches a table of complete strangers, she typically says, "Hello? My name is Margaret. What's yours? Are you an Italian girl? No? Too bad . . . " And on and on. She joins in other people's conversations. She doesn't mind being asked personal questions. Readily and willingly misapplying the Golden Rule, she asks other people personal questions—whether they want to answer or not. "What is the special occasion?" Or, "What do you do for a living?"

"I'm an actuary."

"An actuary. Is that a religious society or something? And what do you do as an actuary?"

"I calculate rates for insurance companies."

"Do you make good money? Yes? How much? " (She also likes to prospect for her daughter Linda.)

If we take a poll at that restaurant, half the people will probably think that Margaret Alessandra is wonderful. "Boy, I wish my mother acted like that," or, "The woman is a national treasure." The rest of them are likely to react or think differently. "I enjoy my privacy when I go out to eat," or even, "Who let her loose?" As well-meaning and people-oriented as she is, she often unintentionally steps on people's toes. She doesn't want to, but . . .

What has happened? Margaret puts the Golden Rule into action and, by doing so, impresses some people and depresses others. Well, maybe she doesn't exactly depress them, but heightens their tensions. By acting the way she likes to be treated, there are mixed reviews. When behaving from only her own perspective, she doesn't take others' preferences into account. Why not? Simply because it's okay if strangers approach her and ask about her intimate, private thoughts; so she naturally figures it's okay for her to do the same thing.

It's true for the rest of us. If we don't think first of the other person, we run the risk of unintentionally imposing a tension-filled win/lose or lose/lose relationship on them.

The Platinum Rule

We believe in refining The Golden Rule to take into consideration the feelings of the other person. Notice we don't say break the rule. We redefine it into the Platinum Rule— "Do unto others as they want to be done unto." Treat others the way they want to be treated. By platinum, we don't mean to imply *better*. We simply want to capture the true spirit or actual intention of the Golden Rule so we consider and respond appropriately to the other person's needs. We can learn to treat different people differently, according to their needs, not ours. That leads to greater understanding and acceptance.

Doing what comes naturally

Imagine Bruce Willis of MOONLIGHTING trying to motivate Mr. Spock of STAR TREK—with both of them practicing the Golden Rule. The problem that inevitably surfaces is Bruce will try to inspire Spock as he himself would like to be inspired. "Hey, this new plan is incredible!" Spock's typical reaction would probably be, "This does not compute." He wants concise, factual, accurate information. "Where's the proof? Can you document that?" while Bruce prefers to deal with the bigger, more generalized picture.

When we treat another person from our perspective, the result is often tension, whether it's expressed or not? In Neil Simon's THE ODD COUPLE, Felix and Oscar represent opposites. Oscar perceives himself as a *real* man—rough and tumble; Felix sees him as what he sometimes refers to as a slob. Felix thinks he's a *model of perfection*; Oscar figures Felix is an uptight worrywart. Whenever Felix approaches Oscar with his own expectations based on his needs—tidiness, punctuality, and moderation—Oscar explodes. Even though the two characters exaggerate many behaviors that we're likely to encounter, they represent clear examples of how we can turn people off when we *act naturally* en route to meeting only our own needs. While watching them clash may be entertaining for us, it's not so much fun in the daily lives of the real, although less dramatic, Felixes and Oscars around the world.

A steady dose of conflicting needs can end a promising relationship unless we treat the other person appropriately! If Felix and Oscar made the effort to understand each other's needs, they could begin to gain greater appreciation of and learn more about their differences. Then they could find practical, optional ways of solving their own naturally occurring conflicts. The two of them collide when they expect each other to act like clones of themselves.

Archie Bunker says:

"Edith do you know why we can't communicate? Because I'm talking in English and you're listening in dingbat!" Well, maybe Archie could benefit from learning how to communicate in *dingbat*! Then, he could mentally change places with Edith to understand her expectations instead of just his own.

Every day we face the potential for conflict or success with different types of people. Conflicts are inevitable, but the outcome from how you handle dissension are much more controllable. At the very least, you can manage your end of it. You can choose to treat somebody from his perspective, the way he wants to be treated by modifying your own behavior; or you can choose to meet only your own needs—facing consequences such as dissatisfaction, frustration, confusion, and distress. It's up to you.

Modify your spots

"Modify my behavior? Hey, I don't want to change! And I hate phonies!"

We're not talking about changing a leopard into an elephant. We mean acting in a sensible, successful way. When someone wants to move at a faster pace, move at that pace. If others want more facts and details, provide them.

But wait? Isn't it phony to act in a way that isn't natural for you? We think acting in a way that is responsive to Japanese behavior patterns in a Japanese environment is more likely to be appreciated and accepted there. The result is greater success! It helps dispel the "Ugly American" stereotype that has been associated with some tourists who *act themselves* and expect others to do likewise. Of course, anything that's new feels strange at first, until you get more comfortable with it through repeated practice.

People learn to become more adaptable through education, experience, and maturity. We simply have to allow the opportunity for appropriate behaviors to surface. As we've mentioned, if you're able to put yourself in the other person's position, you become more open-minded in dealing with him or her. When you understand the way the other person feels comfortable communicating, you can modify your approach to get on the same wavelength. You haven't changed your own natural personality. You've merely added to it still other consciously learned, behavioral insights and strengths for dealing with different types of people and situations. The best part is that people will teach you how to communicate with them if you're willing to learn their signals by *reading* and then appropriately responding to them.

A suggestion for Felix and Oscar

Felix Unger and Oscar Madison, television's ODD COUPLE, have known each other for years. But they don't always choose to apply what they know. When each considers only himself, he unconsciously tends to plunge ahead towards meeting only his own needs. When they do this, they ignore the signals of how to allow each other to meet their own needs.

Imagine this more productive exchange:

"Oscar, your room is a mess. Here, I'll help you straighten it up by throwing away these old newspapers."

"Okay, but don't touch anything else in my room without my approval, Felix. You'll ruin my personal filing system."

Oscar's housekeeping is intentionally looser than Felix's. If Felix can tolerate a more "lived in" look and Oscar can learn to pick up after himself, they'll become more successful at meeting each other's needs. Regarding the housekeeping issue, Felix needs orderliness while Oscar needs freedom. With this realization in mind, they can communicate more effectively by letting each other know they've received these two signals. Then they can explore ways for satisfying both types of needs.

One option is trading off. Oscar can keep his room as sloppy as he wants as long as the door is closed and their common living area is neat. Or they can collaborate by cleaning Oscar's room together.

"Oscar, I know you like your freedom to do what you want, but your room is so filled with personal expressions you seem to be a prisoner in it. (How does he find his bed?) I'd like to help you organize your room so that it's more comfortable for you and for me."

(Ha! Felix would probably throw everything out if it was his room.) "I like it the way it is, but I'll go along with your idea if you don't throw anything away without asking me first."

There! Felix and Oscar have reached a naturally acceptable solution based on understanding and accepting each other's needs. Good for them!

Background of behavioral types

People have been both frustrated and fascinated with each other's differences for thousands of years. The earliest recorded efforts to explain our differences were made by astrologers who recorded the positions of the heavens. The twelve signs in four basic groupings—Earth, Air, Fire, and Water—are still used today.

In ancient Greece, Hippocrates' concept of four temperaments followed—Sanguine, Phlegmatic, Melancholy, and Choleric. He viewed personality as shaped by blood, phlegm, black bile, and yellow bile. As unpalatable as this might sound to us, people accepted these physical or bodily causes for varying *humors* for centuries. Respected figures from medical/ physical sciences, metaphysics, mathematics, and philosophy observed these four temperaments—including Aristotle, Empedocles, Theophrastus, and, in Roman times, Galen. References to Hippocrates' Big Four can be found in Shakespeare's plays. We still use these terms, especially in the SAT college admissions test and in reference to babies and young children. "Jason looks so serious and melancholy for a one-year-old," or "Jennifer has a sanguine, ruddy-faced disposition."

In 1923, Dr. Carl Jung wrote his famous *Psychological Types*, at that time the most sophisticated scientific work on personality. In it, he again described four behavioral styles —the Intuitor, Thinker, Feeler, and Sensor.

This basic, four-type model spans all cultures? East and west, north and south. For instance, contemporary Japan still studies behavior and physical composition. Advice on *How to Form a Good Combination of Blood Types*, a best-seller by Toshitaka Nomi, claimed 100,000 documented cases of cross-referencing personalities with blood types. Nomi indicated that 40 percent of Japan's population has Type A blood. He associated this with the conscientious, hard-working behavior expected of engineers and technicians. He hypothesized that this explained Japan's emphasis on high-technology excellence.

Four styles with a difference

Today's Information Age features more than a dozen varied models of our behavioral differences. But they all have one common thread—the grouping of behavior into four categories.

Most of these explanations of behavioral styles have focused on internal characteristics leading to external behaviors. *People Smart* focuses on patterns of observable, external behaviors which each style shows to the rest of the world. It also demystifies those lesser known, but scientifically proven, internal forces which are the motivating clues behind our behaviors. In other words, this book will help you understand why you do what you do. Because we can see and hear these external behaviors, that makes it much easier for us to *read* people. Therefore, our model is simple, practical, easy to remember and use, and extremely accurate.

Our model divides people into four natural, core behavioral types:

— The Dominant Director
— The Interacting Socializer
— The Steady Relater
— The Cautious Thinker

So . . . which are you?

Chapter 2

I Know Who You Are, But What Am I?

So how do you identify your behavioral type? Here's how! You begin by choosing those traits that most and least describe you from a list of one-word possibilities. At first, you might think, "All these sound like me," or "None of them do," but select your personal traits from these commonly found choices with a clear focus in mind. Your reward will be in arriving at one behavioral type that is more descriptive of you than any of the others.

Any of us occasionally may behave like each of the four types, but we behave in predominantly one style more of the time. The most familiar place where you operate most comfortably is called your core behavioral type—your own unique personality style. This is most evident when you just act yourself. This natural tendency appears when you don't think about how to act. It's where you're found when your mind is on automatic pilot. This type of core behavior is your home base. To discover your behavioral type, read the instructions carefully and answer accordingly.

PERSONAL ASSETS INVENTORY *

INSTRUCTIONS FOR RESPONDING & SCORING

1. In the space provided below, identify those behaviors which have typically been MOST-TO-LEAST characteristic of you. Working left to right, assign "4" points to the MOST characteristic, "3" to the next most characteristic, then "2" and finally "1" to your least characteristic behavior.

EXAMPLE

__3__ DIRECTING   __4__ INFLUENCING   __1__ STEADY   __2__ CAUTIOUS

2. **Total** the numbers in each of the **four** columns. Place the **total** number for **each** column in the **blank** at the bottom of the column.

3. **Check** the accuracy by **adding** all the columns together. When **all four** columns are **added** together, they will equal 50.

COLUMN 1	COLUMN 2	COLUMN 3	COLUMN 4
——— Directing	——— Influencing	——— Steady	——— Cautious
——— Decisive	——— Optimistic	——— Patient	——— Restrained
——— Daring	——— Enthusiastic	——— Stabilizing	——— Analytical
——— Competitive	——— Talkative	——— Accommodating	——— Precise
——— Forceful	——— Charming	——— Easygoing	——— Curious
——— TOTAL	——— TOTAL	——— TOTAL	——— TOTAL

HOW TO DETERMINE YOUR "CORE" STYLE

If your highest column TOTAL is under **column 1**, you are a **Dominant Director.**

If your highest column TOTAL is under **column 2**, you are an **Interacting Socializer.**

If your highest column TOTAL is under **column 3**, you are a **Steady Relater.**

If your highest column TOTAL is under **column 4**, you are a **Cautious Thinker.**

IT'S YOUR PICK . . . AFTER ALL, IT'S REALLY <u>YOU</u>!

This personal inventory is a realistic measure of your actual behaviors. Think of your personal traits across the variety of environments and periods of your life. In other words, complete this inventory as you see yourself. To do this, start asking yourself, *"Is this or isn't this really me?"*

Look at the overall results to determine which of the four *behavioral patterns* you see as the single MOST and LEAST characteristic of you. Also notice the *specific behaviors* within the inventory which you may have identified as MOST or LEAST characteristic of you. Later, you may want to use the same instrument to help you reevaluate your own and others' pattern(s) in four major settings--work, social, family, and romance.

The Personal Assets Inventory

This inventory is designed to help you take stock of those personal assets related to the goals and results which are important to you in different settings. It is a valuable personal resource for identifying: 1) your already developed personal characteristics and 2) other potential strengths you can further develop. These potential strengths can be especially helpful. So you can learn to adapt your style to handle different types of situations, even those more *difficult* ones we don't prefer, but must manage in the real world laboratory of life.

It's your pick . . . after all it's really you!

This personal inventory is a realistic measure of your actual behaviors. Think of your personal traits across the variety of environments and periods in your life. In other words, complete the inventory as you see yourself. "Is this or isn't this really me?"

An Overview of the Four Types

The Dominant Director:
Look at My Accomplishments!

Goals and Fears

Dominant Directors, driven by the inner need to lead and be in personal control, take charge of people and situations so they can reach their goals. Since their key need is achieving, they seek no-nonsense, bottom line results. Their motto is: "Lead, follow, or get out of the way." They want to win, so they may challenge people or rules. Similarly, Dominant Directors also accept challenges, take authority, and go head first into solving problems. Closely related to Dominant Directors' goals are their fears: falling into a routine, being taken advantage of, and looking *soft*. So they may go to extremes to prevent those fears from materializing. They may act impatient, but they make things happen.

"Do as I say"

Since Dominant Directors need to have control, they like to take the lead in both business and social settings. The song *Don't Fence Me In* may have been written for this type, because they behave almost claustrophobically if they perceive someone is trying to stymie them. As natural renegades, Dominant Directors want to satisfy their need for autonomy. They want things done their way or no way at all.

Strengths and weaknesses

They often prefer strong directive management and operational tendencies and work quickly and impressively by themselves. Dominant Directors try to shape their environments to overcome obstacles en route to their accomplishments. They demand maximum freedom to manage themselves and others, using their leadership skills to become winners. Additionally, Dominant Directors often have good administration and delegation skills. This matches their motivating need. In fact, if they could delegate their exercise regimens or visits to the dentist's office, they probably would.

These assertive types tend to appear cool, independent, and competitive. They opt for measurable results, including their own personal worth, as determined by individual track records. Of all the types, they like and initiate changes the most. We symbolize this personality type with a lion—a leader, an authority. At least, they may, at least, have the inner desires to be #1, the star, or the chief.

Less positive Dominant Director components include stubbornness, impatience, and toughness. Naturally preferring to take control of others, they may have a low tolerance for the feelings, attitudes, and *inadequacies* of co-workers, subordinates, friends, families, and romantic interests.

From general to specific

Dominant Directors process data conceptually by using deductive reasoning—from general to specific information. They are more comfortable using the left brain more than the right. When combined with their need for control, this helps us better understand the emphasis on getting down to the bottom line results.

Masters of "mind control"

They may use various *mind control* techniques to help them focus on one task priority at a time. For instance, some are adept at blocking out distractions when they immerse themselves in projects. They don't hear voices, sirens, or doorbells. They seem to channel all their energies into specific jobs. Similarly, in a summer biology class, the instructor, Dr. Rains, seemed oblivious to the smell (and the grumbling) when his students dissected decomposed fish. While the class choked and hurried from their desks to the windows to gulp for air, Dr. Rains instructed them like the odor were an everyday occurrence. No big deal. Not to him, anyway.

Venting relieves their tension

Under pressure, Dominant Directors are likely to rid themselves of anger by ranting, raving, or challenging others. They naturally react to tense situations with a fight response. This tendency reflects the Dominant Directors' natural blind spots concerning other people's views and feelings. Although this venting allows the relief of their own inner tensions and hostilities, other personality types may feel intimidated by this natural, (for them!) stress reducing practice. But the Dominant Directors' barks usually exceed their bites, and they may soon forget what specifically upset them in the first place.

"Watch this performance"

Dominant Director musicians and performers typically seek to simultaneously command the stage and awe their audience. They envision themselves rising above their admirers and peers and moving into the position of number one, the best ever. Frank Sinatra, Evel Knievel, Reggie Jackson, Mike Tyson, and Jane Fonda all fit into this competitive category that tends to welcome any and all challenges.

Vince Lombardi, the former coach of the Green Bay Packers, coined this typical Dominant Director statement: "Winning isn't everything; it's the only thing." And who can forget that confrontational baseball coach, Billy Martin! Other famous Dominant Directors include Barbara Walters, Margaret Thatcher, Mike Wallace, General George Patton, Telly Savalas as KOJAK, Ed Asner as LOU GRANT, and Bea Arthur as MAUDE or as Dorothy in the show GOLDEN GIRLS.

Dominant Director territory

Two cultures which have produced many Dominant Directors are northern, industrialized Germany and South Africa. These examples are not meant to over-generalize or stereotype individual behavior; instead, they help us understand how cultures tend to socialize or group people into patterns of behavior which are more consistent with past customs and expectations. In this regard, it's easier for us to understand the more natural Dominant Director behaviors. These have emerged as the expected norms or preferred behavioral patterns over the long, colorful histories of both Germany and South Africa. How often have you described people you know of German or South African background by the following behavioral descriptions of the Dominant Director temperament mentioned throughout this chapter?

* take charge—naturally seek direct control and want to run things their way
* controlling—fear losing personal power or status?
* competitive—want to win
* motivated to be #1—seek being first or *on top* whether other people approve or not
* task-focused—strive to get the job done, often less aware or oblivious to others' feelings—which may make them appear insensitive
* *no nonsense*—view life in terms of overcoming the obstacles to their successful achievement of desired results
* strong-willed—once they make up their minds, preferring to stick to their ideas; even becoming headstrong, especially under stress
* impatient—expect other people to help them get results, ASAP!!!

Action Plan . . .

**DOMINANT DIRECTOR
CHARACTERISTICS**

SO YOU. . .

Concerned with being #1 — Show them how to win, new opportunities

Think logically — Display reasoning

Want facts and highlights — Provide concise data

Strive for results — Agree on goal and boundaries, then support or get out of their way

Like Personal Choices — Allow them to "do their thing", within limits

Like changes — Vary routine

Prefer to delegate — Look for opportunities to modify their work-load focus

Want others to notice accomplishments — Compliment them on what they've done

Need to be in charge — Let them take the lead, when appropriate, but give them parameters

Tendency towards conflict — If necessary, argue with conviction on points of disagreement, backed up with facts; don't argue on "personality" basis

- fast-paced—often somewhat involved with many projects simultaneously; may even exhibit *workaholism* tendencies

The Interacting Socializer: Hey, Look at Me!

Outgoing, Supporting, Interacting Socializers

He-e-e-ere's the Interacting Socializer!—the person who likes to go where the action is. Typically, he is outwardly energetic or fast-paced, and relationships tend to naturally take priority over tasks. The Interacting Socializer tries to influence others in an optimistic, friendly way focused on positive outcomes, whether in the social or work environment. In other words, if he shows others he likes them, he figures others will be more likely to reciprocate by responding favorably towards him. Since recognition and approval motivate him, he often moves in and around the limelight and hub of activity.

Goals and Fears

He wants your admiration and thrives on acknowledgment, compliments, and applause. "It's not just whether you win or lose . . . it's how you look when you play the game." People's admiration and acceptance typically mean more to this type than to any other. If you don't talk about him, he may spend considerable time talking about his favorite subject—himself— to gain the acceptance he wants. His biggest fear is public humiliation—whether appearing uninvolved, unattractive, unsuccessful, or unacceptable to others. These frightening forms of social rejection threaten the Interacting Socializer's core need for approval. Consequently, he may go to extremes to avoid public humiliation, lack of inclusion, or loss of social recognition.

Strengths and weaknesses

Interacting Socializers' primary strengths are their enthusiasm, persuasiveness, and friendliness. They are idea people who have the ability to get others caught up in their dreams.

With great persuasion, they influence others and shape their environments by building alliances to accomplish results. Then they seek nods and comments of approval and recognition for those results. If compliments don't come, Interacting Socializers may invent their own. "Well, Harry, I just feel like patting myself on the back today for a job well done!" They are stimulating, talkative, and communicative. This type can be represented by a porpoise—playful, sociable, and talkative.

Their natural weaknesses are too much involvement, impatience, being alone, and short attention spans. This causes them to become easily bored. When a little data comes in, Interacting Socializers tend to make sweeping generalizations. They may not check everything out, assuming someone else will do it or procrastinating because redoing something just isn't exciting enough. When Interacting Socializers feel they don't have enough stimulation and involvement, they get bored and look for something new again . . . and again . . . and again. When taken to an extreme, their behaviors can be seen as superficial, haphazard, erratic, and overly emotional.

Talk, talk, talk . . .

Picture Willard Scott, the smiling weatherman on the TODAY show. He strikes up conversations with everyone from Iowa pig farmers to visiting dignitaries. He smiles and laughs with most people he meets, somehow managing to sandwich in a few comments about the day's weather forecast. We believe Willard when he wishes a *beautiful 100-year old darling* a happy birthday or endorses a pecan pie as "the best I've ever had."

Irrepressible Willard alternately dazzles us with his footwork and baffles us with his homespun corn. But we can't help liking him. He seems so genuinely moved by his fans' gifts—moose hats with antlers, lop-sided cakes, and one-of-a-kind T-shirts—that both his co-workers and we catch ourselves smiling as we think, "What a warm person he is!" This man would probably talk as naturally to the President as he does to anyone else. Willard Scott epitomizes the down-to-earth, person-to-person, Interacting Socializer tendency which minimizes role, status, and familiarity differences among people.

"Let me entertain you!"

If they pursue the entertainment field for careers, Interacting Socializers typically allow their natural, animated emotions to show and flow. They become stimulated by the movement and reactions of the audience, trying to get the audience to figuratively fall in love with them by acting charming and friendly. They want viewers to feel, "He (or she) is fabulous!" Interacting Socializer performers who mesmerize and win over their fans include Dolly Parton, Mickey Rooney, Tracy Ullman, Muhammad Ali, Bill Cosby, Tony Danza, Dom DeLuise, Eddie Murphy, Carol Burnett, Sammy Davis Jr., David Brenner, *Magic* Johnson, and Liza Minnelli.

Two countries brimming with Interacting Socializers

Every country, culture, and sub-culture socialize their society's members into typical daily patterns of behavior. In this respect, both Ireland and Italy are often mentioned as settings where this Interacting Socializer type seems quite commonplace. Globally, people refer to them as highly emotional people who tend to "wear their hearts on their sleeves." The Irish are known for their animated, interactive storytelling and neighborhood socializing. In fact, many areas of the Northeastern United States have become settled as Irish-Italian communities by these immigrants with similar lifestyles.

Italians' Interacting Socializer attributes have made them world-famous in the performing arts, restaurant and hospitality fields, and other person-to-person areas such as fashion and sales. How often have you described a native Irishman or Italian you have met by the following general description of the Interacting Socializer tendencies?

- optimistic—prefer to view life's positives; often block out negative situations, facts, concerns
- fast-paced—talk, move, and do most activities rather quickly

Action Plan . . .

INTERACTING SOCIALIZER CHARACTERISTICS

SO YOU . . .

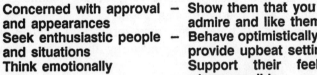

Concerned with approval and appearances	— Show them that you admire and like them
Seek enthusiastic people and situations	— Behave optimistically and provide upbeat setting
Think emotionally	Support their feelings when possible
Want to know the general expectations	— Avoid involved details, focus on the "big picture"
Need involvement and people contact	— Interact and participate with them
Like changes and innovations	— Vary the routine; avoid requiring long term repetition by them
Want others to notice THEM	— Compliment them personally and often
Often need help getting organized	— Do it together
Dislike conflict	— Act non-aggressively and avoid arguing directly on a personal bases
Look for action and stimulation	— Keep up a fast, lively, pace
Surround themselves with optimism	— Support their ideas and don't poke holes in their dreams; show them your positive side
Want feedback that they "look good"	— Mention their accomplishments, progress and your other genuine appreciation

- emotional—readily show their own feelings and respond to others' feelings
- approval-seeking—look to others for acceptance and re-energizing; want people to approve of and like each other, too
- fun-loving—seek an upbeat, positive, casual atmosphere and love a good party, especially with friends
- excitable—show emotions and become enthusiastic, at best; rattled, at worst—when pressured or tired
- spontaneous—behave impulsively; dislike planning or dealing with follow-through details
- expressive—at times, they may forget and divulge secret information; or they may say too much to the wrong people

The Steady Relater: Notice How Well-Liked I Am

Goals and fears

This type, as sung by Aretha Franklin in her hit record, may privately want a little *R-E-S-P-E-C-T*, as demonstrated by your sincere personal attention and acceptance of them. Steadiness and follow-through actions characterize these people. They prefer a slower and easier pace: "It's not whether you win or lose . . . it's the friendship that counts." They focus on building trust and getting acquainted because they aim for long-standing personal relationships. Pushy, aggressive behavior secretly irritates them.

Steady Relaters strive for security. Their goal is to maintain the stability they prefer in a more constant environment. To Steady Relaters, while the unknown may be an intriguing concept, they prefer to stick with what they already know and have experienced. *Risk* is an ugly word to Steady Relaters. They favor more measured actions, like keeping things as they have been and are, even if the present situation happens to be unpleasant. Related to their goal of keeping things very similar is their accompanying fear of change and disorganization. Consequently, any disruption in their routine patterns can cause distress in Steady Relaters. Fearing sudden changes, they are naturally concerned with what may happen. A general worry is that the unknown may be even more unpleasant than the present. They need to think and plan for changes. Finding the elements of sameness within those changes can help minimize their stress by identifying the specific assurances required to cope with such demands.

Strengths and weaknesses

America's favorite *Uncle*, Walter Cronkite, is a classic example of a low-keyed, sincere-acting, Steady Relater. He visited millions of homes each week night via TV for decades. People still reminisce about his soothing voice and comforting delivery. Whether the news was good, bad, or indifferent, his manner had a unique way of adding a sense of stability, calmness, and reassurance to the evenings at the end of our busy workdays.

Like *Uncle Walter*, other Steady Relaters also naturally *wear well* and are an easy type to get along with. They prefer stable relationships which don't jeopardize anyone, especially themselves. Steady Relaters can be represented by the koala with its accompanying slower, steady pace; relaxed disposition; and appearance of approachability and warmth. Steady Relaters have a tendency to plan and follow through. This helps them to routinely plug along. But they have their own type of unique difficulties with speaking up, seeming to go along with others or conditions, while inwardly, they may or may not agree. More assertive types might take advantage of this Steady Relater tendency to give in and avoid confrontation. Additionally, Steady Relaters' reluctance to express themselves can result in hurt feelings. But if Steady Relaters don't explain their feelings, others may never know. Their lack of assertiveness can take a toll on this type's health and well-being.

Take it slow

Steady Relaters yearn for more tranquility and security in their lives than the other three types. They often act pleasant and cooperative, but seldom incorporate emotional extremes such as rage and euphoria in their behavioral repertoire.

Unlike Interacting Socializers, Steady Relaters usually experience less dramatic or frequently-occurring peaks and valleys to their more moderate emotional state. This reflects their natural need for composure, stability, and balance.

"*Just plain folks*"

Picture Edith Bunker of the classic sitcom ALL IN THE FAMILY. She lends a tone of continuity, coziness, and *motherliness* to virtually every scene in which she appears. Edith mothers everyone around her. With her easygoing manner, she projects a genuine liking and acceptance of her family, friends, and acquaintances. She's a comfortable person to watch and listen to who emanates that "I'm just a regular person" modesty. She puts on no airs and projects contentment with present conditions—just as they are and always have been.

"*May I entertain you?*"

In the same respect, Steady Relater celebrities tend to give predictable deliveries. Both the audience and performer may seem to merge because the Steady Relater feels so in tempo with his or her viewers. Typical audience responses may include: "He's truly one of us!" Or, "It's like being with a member of the family or my closest friend!" Steady Relaters welcome group participation, and their performances reflect their natural give and take. Steady Relaters that we know and are fond of are: Perry Como; Kenny Rogers; Mr. Rogers; Mary Richards (THE MARY TYLER MOORE SHOW); Elise Keaton (FAMILY TIES); MARCUS WELBY, M. D. (in vintage reruns with Robert Young in the title role); Mother Theresa; Pope John Paul II; Gary Collins; David Hartman; John Denver; Hugh Downs; Ed Sullivan; and Martina Navritilova.

Two countries with many Steady Relaters

Two Steady Relater countries that seem to have emphasized this lifestyle as a cultural norm resulting in a disproportionate number of such individual styles, are Poland and Spain. Both cultures have historically found ways to get along with foreign elements while methodically plodding forward in the direction expected, even though that direction has often been dictated by others in the short run. The Polish people are world famous for their friendly, hard-working perseverance despite the obstacles which may confront them. And, the Spanish people (those beloved Latins) make others feel at home while practicing such distinctive customs as their renowned midday siestas. Taking siestas actually allows them to go home to their families during the work day. This is consistent with the preferred slower lifestyle of this temperament, without disrupting the differing customs of guests in their homeland.

Citizens of both countries are known in their native lands and in the United States for their neighborhood restaurants and extensive group social activities. Compare the following distinguishing characteristics of this Steady Relater type which describe people you know who've been influenced directly by their own ethnic, social group, or cultural roots:

- easygoing—calm, measured, low-key behavior and outlook
- slower paced—wait until they know the steps or guidelines before acting, then move forward in a pre-set manner
- patient—tend to define themselves by their desire for stable relationships with others; often view problems or concerns as workable
- predictable—favor routine and stable conditions and practices
- persevering—likely to stick to a project for longer periods of time or at least until the concrete results have been produced
- modest—less likely to blow their own horns, but are often appreciative when others sincerely acknowledge their contributions
- accommodating—like to get along with others through predictable role relationships
- neighborly—prefer friendly, pleasant, helpful working relationships

Action Plan . . .

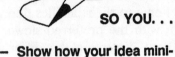

**STEADY RELATER
CHARACTERISTICS**

SO YOU. . .

Concerned with stability	– Show how your idea minimizes risk
Think logically and facts	– Show reasoning
Want documentation	– Provide data/proof
Like personal involvement	– Demonstrate your interest in them
Need to know step by step sequence	– Provide outline and/or one-two-three instructions as you personally "walk them through"
Want others to notice their patient perseverance	– Compliment for their steady follow-through
Avoid risks/changes	– Give them personal assurances
Dislike conflict	– Act non-aggressively, focus on common interest or needed support
Accommodate others	– Allow them to provide service or support for others
Look for calmness and peace	– Provide relaxing friendly atmosphere
Enjoy teamwork	– Provide them with a cooperative group
Want sincere feedback that they're appreciated	– Acknowledge their easy going manner and helpful efforts, when appropriate

The Cautious Thinker:
Have You Noticed My Efficiency?

Goals and fears

Cautious Thinkers concern themselves more with content than with congratulations. They prefer involvement with the performance of products and services under specific, and preferably controlled, conditions so the process and the results can be correct. Since their primary concern is accuracy, human emotions may take a back seat with this type. After all, emotions are subjective and tend to distort objectivity. Cautious Thinkers biggest fears of uncontrolled emotions and irrational acts relate to their goals. More precisely, Cautious Thinkers fear that these illogical acts may prevent goal a-chievement. Similarly, they fear emotionality and irrationality in others. This type strives to avoid embarrassment, so they attempt to control both themselves and their emotions.

Strengths and weaknesses

Cautious Thinker strengths include accuracy, dependability, independence, clarification and testing skills, follow-through, and organization. They often focus on expectations (e.g., policies, practices, and procedures) and outcomes. They want to know how things work so they can evaluate how correctly they function. We picture a fox as an appropriate symbol for Cautious Thinkers—cagey, resourceful, and careful. Because they need to be right, they prefer checking processes them-selves. This tendency toward perfectionism, taken to an extreme, can result in "paralysis by overanalysis". These overly cautious traits may result in worry that the process isn't progressing right, which further promotes their tendency to behave in a more critical, detached way.

Complex and serious

They prefer tasks over people, clearly defined priorities, and a known pace which is agreeable to them, especially where task time lines and deadlines are involved. Other types typically live life through a single predominant time orien-tation—past, present, or future. But Cautious Thinkers are apt to be concerned about all three, as one aspect of their complex mental makeup. They tend to see the serious, more complicated sides of situations as well as the lighter—or even bizarre side—which accounts for their natural mental wit.

As the most cerebrally-oriented of the four types, Cautious Thinkers concentrate on making decisions in both logical and cautious ways to ensure that they take best available action. (This cerebral quality refers to the way they process information and experiences, and does not relate to I.Q.) "It's not whether you win or lose . . . it's how you play the game" —the more technically perfect, the better.

Think deeply

Visualize Woody Allen, the quiet, unassuming director, actor, and clarinet player who covets his privacy. In most of his movies, either he or his characters agonize over what to do next, what and how their feelings operate, and how to ultimately do the right thing. He typically puts his emotions under a microscope where he analyzes and reanalyzes them. In Hannah and Her Sisters, for instance, Woody Allen's character thinks repeatedly about his *wrong feelings* for his sister-in-law, while viewing his wife Hannah as a saint. He mentally vacillates between the two women for the duration of the film. Like Woody Allen's Cautious Thinker characters, this type can even become overwhelmed by indecision when pressure builds.

Due to compliance to their own personal standards, they demand a lot from themselves and others and may succumb to overly critical tendencies. But Cautious Thinkers often keep their criticisms to themselves, hesitating to tell people what they think is deficient. They typically share information, both positive and negative, only on a need-to-know basis when they are assured that there will be no negative consequences for themselves.

When Cautious Thinkers quietly hold their ground, they do so as a direct result of their proven knowledge of facts and details or their evaluation that others will tend to react less assertively. So they can be assertive when they perceive they're in control of a relationship or their environment.

Having determined the specific risks, margins of error, and other variables which significantly influence the desired results, they will take action.

The "mystery" First Lady

Visualize Jacqueline Kennedy Onassis, the private, yet national figure who is consistently on *The Ten Most Admired Women in America* list. She is and was impeccably groomed and has subsequently made dozens of lists of *Best Dressed Women*. Her mystique and personal style have captivated Americans since the days of *Camelot* when John F. Kennedy was President. She even received an Emmy award for the perfection of her televised tour of the White House. Many people remember her obvious grief, but refusal to cry, at her husband's funeral.

Cautious Thinkers entertain uniquely

Cautious Thinker entertainers want to move beyond the audience, since they are motivated to deliver a one-of-a-kind, captivating, near-perfect performance. They want spectators to think, "What a unique performance" or "Nothing else is quite like it!" When they take their varied stages, Mikhail Baryshnikov, Neil Diamond, Barbra Streisand, Katharine Hepburn, Larry Bird, and Wayne Gretsky have meticulously prepared themselves to provide a memorable experience with each intense performance—a key reason why they seem more emotionally drained from their own efforts. Other well-known Thinkers include: Meryl Streep, Dr. Joyce Brothers, Dick Cavett, Albert Einstein, Henry Kissinger, Dustin Hoffman, STAR TREK's Mr. Spock, and Sherlock Holmes. And, of course, Jack Webb from the vintage DRAGNET series, the now classic *patron saint* of Cautious Thinkers—"The facts, Ma'am . . . just the facts."

Cautious Thinker countries

Under adverse political and geographic conditions, two Cautious Thinker countries have historically figured out creative, intuitive ways to survive. Both Sweden and Switzerland have harsh winter climates, but they've mastered the art of survival. Switzerland, especially, boasts a substantial corner on the market of world finance. For a small country, it controls a disproportionate amount of the world's money. And Sweden, long known as a land which appreciates beauty, continues to have a worldwide impact in exporting its aesthetic talents, products, and services resulting from cultivated efforts.

Whether watching a professional tennis match or beauty contest, we frequently see a representative from sparsely-populated Sweden in the running for top honors. And, whether shopping for distinctive items—such as Scandinavian sweaters, needlework, furniture, crafts or other unique objects—or tasty and eye-catching bakery goods, the artistic flair of the Swedish heritage has universal appeal.

Which of the following Cautious Thinker characteristics listed below match individuals you know with cultural roots similar to those discussed above?

- careful—methodical and cautious; don't jump into things initially
- precise—need to be accurate, so they check and re-check in their effort to find the right or best available answer
- proper—more formal, discreet, and inclined to allow others to be in their own space, expecting the same for themselves
- private—keep thoughts to themselves; do not willingly disclose their own or others' thoughts and feelings
- reserved—somewhat formal and cool; take time to get to know them—they have few close relationships
- logical—process-oriented seekers of reason
- inventive—like to see things in new or unique ways; often have a unique perspective that includes or addresses both themselves and others
- contemplative—introverted and reflective, they ponder both the why and how elements in situations

Four types, just acting themselves

With the natural differences among the four behavioral types in mind, pretend that you want to give four people 15-20 minutes to make three simple decisions:

Action Plan ...

CAUTIOUS THINKER CHARACTERISTICS	SO YOU ...
Concerned with their aggressions controlling	– Approach them in a indirect, non-threatening way
Think logically	– Show your reasoning
Seek data	– Give it to them in writing
Need to know the process	– Provide explanations and rationale
Utilize caution	– Allow them to think, inquire and check-out before they make decisions
Prefer to do things themselves	– When delegating, let them check on others' progress and performance
Want others to notice their accuracy	– Compliment them on their thoroughness and correctness when appropriate
Gravitate toward quality control	– Let them assess and be involved in the process when possible
Avoid conflict	– Tactfully ask for clarification and assistance you may need
Need to be right	– Allow them time to find the best or "correct" answer , within available limits
Like to contemplate	– Tell them "why" and "how"

1. Where the next meeting will take place
2. When it will happen
3. The theme of the meeting

Quite by accident, your group consists of one Steady Relater, one Cautious Thinker, one Dominant Director, and one Interacting Socializer who all believe in practicing The Golden Rule. Do you think they'll get the job done? Perhaps, or perhaps not, depending on how each responds to one another in handling the simple task. Let's see why this may not work out. As they walk into the room, the Dominant Director typically speaks first. "Here's my plan . . . "

The Interacting Socializer says, "Hey! Who died and left you boss?"

The Cautious Thinker says, "You know there seems to be more here than meets the eye. We might want to consider some other relevant issues and break into sub-committees to explore them."

The Steady Relater smiles and says, "We may not get this done if we don't work as a team like we have before."

If you think that we're stacking the deck, consider putting all four of one behavioral type into the room to make those decisions. They'd get the job done, wouldn't they? Not if they follow the Golden Rule verbatim!

What do you call it when you send four Dominant Directors into the same room? War!

Or four Cautious Thinkers? A laundry list full of questions!

And four Steady Relaters? Nothing! They sit around smiling at each other: "You go first."

"No, why don't you go first. By the way, how's the family?"

When four Interacting Socializers walk out, try asking them if they've gotten the job done. "Get what done?" They've had a party and instead come out with 10 new jokes and stories.

We admit that we may be exaggerating to make a point, but in some cases, not by much. Dominant Directors tend to have the assertiveness and leadership initiative to get tasks started. They may then delegate to others for follow-through, enabling the Dominant Directors to start still other new projects which interest them more.

Cautious Thinkers typically are motivated by their planning and organizational tendencies. If we want a task done precisely, find a Cautious Thinker. Of the four types, they're the most motivated to be correct—the quality control experts.

Steady Relaters have persistence, people-to-people strengths —patience, follow-through, and responsiveness. When we have a problem, we may choose to go to a sympathetic-appearing Steady Relater because he or she listens, empathizes, and reacts to our feelings.

Interacting Socializers are natural entertainers who thrive on involvement with people. They also love to start things, but often do not finish them. In fact, they may pick up three balls, throw them in the air, and yell, "Catch!" Emotional, enthusiastic, optimistic, and friendly, Interacting Socializers usually pep up an otherwise dull environment.

A behavioral knight-time story

Here is a story to reinforce the differences between the four basic behavioral types:

Four of King Arthur's knights, each representing a different behavioral type, were convicted of a crime and sentenced to death by decapitation. On execution day, they mounted the stairs together to position their heads in a custom-made, four person guillotine. (For you skeptical types who may be wondering why King Arthur uses a French product, maybe it's a gift from King Louis.) The Lord High Executioner swings his royal ax, the rope snaps, and the blade comes down—stopping inches from their necks. King Arthur interprets this as a sign of innocence, so he pardons all four men. They all rejoice—some noisily, some silently—with everyone reverting to his own type of instinctive response.

Almost immediately, the Dominant Director knight turns to the others and yells, "You see! I told you I'm innocent!"

The Interacting Socializer knight screams, "Let's eat, drink, be merry . . . and party, party, party!"

The Steady Relater knight walks up to the executioner and says, "I want you to know that I don't hold this against you. You were just doing your job and I know you're a good person at heart. Would you like to join me for dinner sometime?"

The Cautious Thinker knight pauses, looks up at the mechanism, scratches his head, and says, "Hmmm, I think I see the problem."

Pick a type . . . any type

After our general introduction to the basic four, core behavioral types, you may already know which one is most like you. Did you also recognize other people you know? Besides deciding which type is most like you, you may have thought of people who sounded quite similar to one or more of the personality types in this chapter—those you harmonize with and those who tend to rub you the wrong way. Now that you know which type *you* are, you can better determine *other people's* types. Integrating what you know about yourself with what you can observe and learn about others reveals valuable information to help you relate more effectively with them. The next chapter explains how to determine other personality types by focusing on specific verbal, vocal, and visual signals they provide. So get ready to become a people reader in Chapter 3.

Remember . . .

TASK ORIENTED	PEOPLE ORIENTED
Cautious Thinker	Steady Relaters
Dominant Director	Interacting Socializers

FASTER PACED	SLOWER PACED
Dominant Directors	Steady Relaters
Interacting Socializers	Cautious Thinkers

WHO SEEKS WHAT?

Dominant Directors ... Power & Control
Cautious Thinkers .... Accuracy & Precision
Interacting Socializers .. Popularity & Prestige
Steady Relaters ...... Sincerity & Appreciation

KIND OF DECISION MAKER

Dominant Director .... Decisive
Cautious Thinker .... Deliberate
Steady Relater .... Conferring
Interacting Socializer .... Spontaneous

Chapter 3

How Will You Know One When You Meet One?

Now that you're familiar with your core behavioral type, how can you recognize other types when you meet them? Since relationships depend on your appropriate interactions with each behavioral type, the immediate question is, "How can I identify someone's behavioral type and how can I do it quickly?"

Two important dimensions for recognizing another person's behavioral type are Directness/Indirectness and Supportingness/Controllingness. We all exhibit a range of these characteristics in our expressed, observable behaviors. But we need to focus on how people act in order to determine their core type.

"Excuse me, Mr. Smith, but would you mind giving me some information about how Indirect or Direct and how Supporting or Controlling you are so I can figure out your behavioral type?" definitely won't do. Neither will guesswork, but that approach is seldom necessary because people give so many clues, if you just know what to look for. To identify someone's type, observe what he does by tuning in to both his verbal, vocal, and visual behaviors.

Verbal, vocal, and visual clues

The verbal channel of communication includes the words people use to express themselves—the content. The other two areas convey the intent of the message—how people want to say it. The vocal channel includes all the subtle aspects of voice intonation—volume, speed, resonance, pitch, inflection, and rhythm. The visual channel includes all the aspects of body language—the range of movements and positions—from the subtle raising of an eyebrow to the precise movements of the trained actor.

We have assembled a range of verbal, vocal, and visual characteristics into a list of observable behaviors for each type. But beware! These descriptions refer to actions you can see, not value judgments you may be tempted to make about them. If you see a woman hopping up and down, is it because she is throwing a temper tantrum, has stepped on a nail, has a foot that has fallen asleep, or is very excited? All you can say is she is hopping up and down. Finding out why requires more observable verbal, vocal, and visual clues.

Is the person more Direct?

Directness, the first of two dimensions in our expressed behavior, is the amount of involvement a person uses to meet his needs by more directly seeking to influence people and situations. Directness means the tendency to move forward or act outwardly by expressing thoughts, feelings, or expectations. Direct people come on strong, take the social initiative, and create a powerful first impression. They tend to be assertive, fast-paced people who make swift decisions and take risks. They can easily become impatient with others who cannot keep up with their pace. As active people who talk a lot, they appear confident and sometimes dominant. Direct people tend to express opinions readily and make emphatic statements. Such individuals try to shape their environment and relationships—"Tell McCullough that I want to talk to him ASAP." Indirect people typically act in a more measured way—"I'll get back to you about McCullough, Jack."

Direct people are faster paced, more assertive, and more competitive. At worst, these tendencies can transform into hastiness, combativeness, or lower awareness of others' needs. More outspoken, talkative, and dominant, Direct people are extroverts who focus their attention on interests in their environment. In other words—action! They tend to work and play faster. When at a social gathering, they're the ones who introduce themselves as a natural way of seeking to influence others in their surroundings.

They prefer to make rapid decisions, becoming impatient when things don't move fast enough or don't go their way. Checking for errors is something other people can do. It's too time-consuming and self-involving for Direct people. Instead of checking, they busily rush into new areas where the more Indirect may fear to tread. In fact, they rush into so many new areas that their time seems to evaporate into thin air. That's one reason why they have difficulty consistently being prompt—because something comes up at the office or somewhere else. Meanwhile, their more punctual, Indirect friends learn to busy themselves with time killers, such as projects or magazines, while waiting for their more easily side-tracked companions.

Direct people may enjoy risks and want results now, or yesterday. Risks are a way of life with them. Not only are they less worried about rocking the boat, they'll often tip it over and splash around in the hot water they find themselves in. They crave excitement, so they do as much as possible to get it.

This type feels if they throw enough against the wall, something has to stick. Who cares if the output isn't perfect! Quantity beats quality (within limits known only to them) most days of the week. So they're likely to tolerate a higher error rate than their Indirect counterparts to gain a higher number of trial opportunities, even if their success ratio is lower. They generally figure that the number of successes is more important than the percentage of successes.

Anyone involved in telemarketing or outside sales realizes that the road to success is littered with setbacks. Direct people excel in these arenas because they're able to take no's; they simply go out to find more prospects. Aware the yes's are out there somewhere, they're determined to unearth them. "The odds are definitely in my favor now. I'm due for a big hit!" Indirect people tend to take those no's as personal rejections, responding by examining other alternatives which force them to go out again. "Maybe if I send out a direct mail letter first, then follow-up by phone, I'll increase my chances of getting a *yes*.

Direct people point, finger jab, or otherwise more observably express themselves in methods ranging from open arms to forearms—literally, a hug or a shove. They are verbally intense. "Tough toenails! This is the way it is, so get used to it." They emphasize their points of view with confident-sounding vocal intonations and assertive body language.

They speak with conviction. "This bozo got an advanced degree from a diploma mill!" Fast-talking, Direct people like to tell, not ask, about situations. If you want to know the answer, just ask them. They can even become brutally blunt—"That's supposed to be a custom suit? It looks more like a horse blanket."

Impatient and quick-paced, they jump into things, so they get into more iffy situations than their indirect counterparts. Just as the songs of the sirens lured sailors to their doom, the *windows of opportunity* beckon Direct people. Entrance sometimes nets them huge results and sometimes slaps them with dramatic disasters. Wherever inclination takes them, their natural tendency is to do their own thing.

When the windows of opportunity crack open, the Direct types can't wait to tell somebody. So they seek willing listeners—usually of the Indirect variety—and they say, "I've found a gray area."

What sort of feedback do you suppose the Indirect types probably provide? It sounds interesting, but it also raises a lot of questions. Have you asked anyone else for their opinion? Your boss, for instance?"

"Ask my boss? Forget it! He might say no! Then what do I do? My hands would be tied."

This more Direct person's motto in these cases is, "It's easier to beg forgiveness than seek permission." When in doubt, do it anyway. You can always apologize later.

Or Indirect?

On the opposite side of the Directness spectrum, Indirect people are more quiet and reserved. They are seen as more easygoing, or at least more self-contained. Indirect people ask questions and listen more than they talk. They typically reserve their opinions. When asked to take a stand, they may make tentative statements. They often appear more objective, quiet, and indecisive. When taken to an extreme, these positive traits can be viewed as negative ones—wishy-washy, tight-lipped, unassertive behaviors. Indirect people are also less confronting, less demanding, less assertive, and less socially competitive than their Direct counterparts. They're team players who allow others to take the social initiative. For instance, when they want to go to the movies or a restaurant, they might think to themselves, "Gee, I'd really like to see that new Kevin Kline movie." Then they wait for someone to invite them to go instead of outwardly expressing interest to others.

They tend to be more security-conscious—moving slowly, meditating on their decisions, and avoiding bigger risks. As a result, they often avoid taking bold chances or spontaneous actions. After all, what's the best way to keep from failing? One way is to do nothing until you're satisfied it will be an improvement. In other words, do only sure things. Those sure things result in a higher success ratio, so they are more natural for Indirect people. Number of successes divided by number of tries equals success. In a given month, they may try 10 things. Nine may be successfully completed, one not— for a success ratio of 90%.

When Indirect people flop, they tend to take the setback personally. They are likely to internalize or privately think about it, often wondering if there's something wrong with them. "How could I have been so stupid?" Just give them a hint that something is going wrong, and reserved folks may engage in negative self-talk for days.

Indirect people tend to move at a slower or more measured pace. For them, sooner or later is good enough. They speak and respond more slowly since they are more cautious or stability-focused when considering change. If the behavior becomes too measured, detractors (usually Direct people) can view this as dragging their feet, or even lacking interest.

Predictability is more important to such Indirect people, so they tend to consider the pros and cons, attend to details, and fact-find. Caught in a gray area with no clear-cut guidelines, they usually ask for clarification or permission before they take action. They seek to meet their needs by accommodating the requirements of their environment. Generally they operate according to established formats and rules, so when you make an appointment with an Indirect person, you can expect him to show up on time, or possibly wait for you!

Indirect people tend to communicate by asking instead of stating. Their questions clarify, support, or seek more information—"By that, do you mean . . . ?" They prefer qualified statements—"According to my sources, the candidate received an advanced degree from a non-accredited university." They speak more tentatively and take a roundabout or step by step approach—"It seems to me that this is so." If they don't like something, they respond subtly—"Well, I think your other suit looks better." They reserve the right to express their opinions or keep them to themselves. But, they can also act like impregnable rocks when they don't want to crack.

Some are more, some less

It is important to realize that people vary in their location on this scale of Direct to Indirect behavior. Bob Newhart and Mary Tyler Moore both portray Indirect individuals on their long-running sitcoms, but Mary Richards exhibits comparatively more Direct behavior than Bob. Similarly, although they're both Direct, Ronald Reagan is much more Indirect when compared to Archie Bunker of ALL IN THE FAMILY.

Think of someone you know who irritates you. Now that you know about Direct and Indirect characteristics, have you figured out which trait best describes him or her? One important consideration is to determine the person's preferred pace. Pace refers to natural rate of speed—whether he does things quickly or slowly. Bearing in mind pace and other trait descriptors for Direct and Indirect people, let's determine whether that person is more Direct or Indirect. Nobody fits exactly in the middle.

You may be wondering which are better—Direct traits or Indirect ones. We can answer with an unqualified, "It depends." Sometimes it's better to act more Direct and sometimes it's better to act more Indirect. Comparing the two is like evaluating San Diego and New York City. Each is very different, yet we could build a strong argument in either one's favor.

Appropriateness depends on the requirements of a situation. The real question isn't which is better, but how to best use the positive aspects of each trait while recognizing accompanying less developed attributes. Since each of our lives involves a variety of situations requiring differing responses, remember there is no one best personality type. The idea is to maximize people's natural traits while understanding and trying to minimize their accompanying drawbacks.

Survey of Directness Versus Indirectness

This is an informal survey designed to provide you with a general description of how you see others in daily situations. Answer as objectively as possible. This is a non-judgmental assessment—there are no right or wrong answers. Choose one person you know (socially, personally, or at work) and answer these nine questions in terms of how you see that person most of the time, in most situations. This will help you determine if this person is more Direct or Indirect. For each number, choose the one statement that best applies to the person you are evaluating.

Is the Person More Direct or Indirect?

1. (I) A less frequent contributor to group conversations OR
   (D) A more frequent contributor to group conversations
2. (I) Tends to keep personal thoughts or feelings private, sharing only when asked and necessary, OR

(D)   Tends to express personal thoughts or feelings about things, whether asked to or not

3. (D)   Frequently uses gestures, facial expressions, and voice intonation to emphasize points, OR

   (I)   Less likely to use gestures, facial expressions, and voice intonation to emphasize points

4. (D)   More likely to make statements: "That's the way it is!" or, "I feel . . . ", OR

   (I)   More likely to ask questions or speak less assertively: "How does this fit?" or, "As I understand it . . ."

5. (I)   More likely to wait for others to introduce him (or her) at social gatherings, OR

   (D)   More likely to introduce self at social gatherings

6. (I)   Tends to remain involved with known situations, conditions, and relationships, OR

   (D)   Tends to seek out new experiences, situations, and opportunities

7. (D)   Likely to express own views more readily, OR

   (I)   Likely to reserve the expression of own views

8. (I)   Tends to react more slowly and deliberately, OR

   (D)   Tends to react more quickly and spontaneously

9. (I)   Likely to respond to risk and change in a more cautious or predictable manner, OR

   (D)   Likely to respond to risk and change in a more dynamic or unpredictable manner

Total number circled: D's____   I's____
                           (Directness)   (Indirectness)

Supporting or Controlling

Besides Direct to Indirect behaviors, we've also found that people tend to be either Supporting or Controlling—the other major dimension which describes our daily actions. Basically, the Directness and Indirectness describe people's observable behavior—how others see and hear us behaving. The second behavioral scale explains the motivating goal behind these daily actions. Why we do the things we do in the way we do them. When combined, these two scales explain both the tendency to reveal our thoughts and feelings plus the degree we tend to support other people's expressions of their thoughts and feelings.

Is the person more Supporting?

If he talks with his body, uses more vocal inflection, makes continual eye contact, and speaks in terms of feelings, then he's projecting more Supporting than Controlling behaviors. Other Supporting cues that show greater responsiveness include animated facial expressions, much hand and body movement, a flexible time perspective, and immediate non-verbal feedback. Supporting people also like to tell stories and anecdotes and make personal contact.

Supporting people are more open to responding to digressions than Controlling personalities are. They need to make conversation more enjoyable, so they look favorably upon straying from the subject to discuss personal experiences. As long as it's in the ball park, they figure it's probably relevant. "That reminds me of the time Uncle Jed got stuck on the Garden State Freeway for five hours . . . " And exaggeration of details just adds interest by fully depicting their experiences.

Supporting types are also more negotiable about time. Their time perspective is organized around the needs of people first and tasks second, so they're more flexible about how others use their time than the Controlling types. "I'm sorry I'm late for work today, but my son was crying this morning because Jason broke his science project. So I had to write a note to the teacher and cheer him up before I dropped him off at school."

Of course, like any behavior that's overused, these same Supporting characteristics can also drive people up the wall if they get out of hand. For example, self-disclosure can be seen as neediness, digression as inattention, animation as melodrama, acquiescence as weakness, and friendliness as patronization. As with Direct to Indirect tendencies, too much of anything can become a liability.

Or Controlling?

If Supporting types seem more like open books, then Controlling ones tend to be more *poker faced*. Controlling individuals prefer to play their real cards closer to the vest— increasing the probability of getting the upper hand and decreasing the probability of appearing foolish. They usually like to keep their distance, both physically and mentally. They don't touch you and you don't touch them. People often say this about a Controlling person they know: "Once you get to know him, he's a really great guy." But you must become acquainted by breaking through that exterior shell that he erects. Consequently, Controlling people tend to stand further away from you, even when shaking hands. They have a strong sense of personal space and territory, so make sure you don't take anything from their desks. At home they might set traps with a rug or a sofa cushion to see if someone used them when they weren't supposed to. You know—the tiny fold in the rug or the perfectly aligned pillow on the couch. "You sat on that couch today, didn't you? I asked you not to go in my room when I'm not there. I have proof that someone walked on that rug and sat on that couch."

Controlling people show little facial expression, use controlled or limited hand and body movement, and adhere to a more time-disciplined agenda. They push for facts and details, focus on the issues and tasks at hand, and keep their personal feelings private. They don't touch, and they tend to respond coolly if anyone touches them. Unlike their Supporting counterparts, they give little non-verbal feedback.

By contrast, Controlling types place higher priority on getting things done. They prefer working with things or through people—rather than with or for them. "I can't talk now, Frank. I have a two o'clock deadline to meet," or "I'll let you know when I have time to do that," are characteristic comments of this pattern.

Controllers like structure, since they expect results within that structured environment. When negatively motivated, these types of individuals can be viewed as coercive, restrictive, or overbearing. They prefer to stick with the agenda, at least their own. As more naturally independent workers, they need to control the conditions around their tasks—either in terms of input and output (Directness) or the process itself (Indirectness). These more self-contained people make use of either key talent or key procedures to meet their goals. Thus, they view the planning and supervision processes as ways of reaching goals. The Direct individuals need to control people while the Indirect types need to control their environment.

Because time equals money to Controllers, they're more disciplined about how other people use their time. In part, this explains their tendency not to show, discuss, or willingly listen to thoughts and feelings like Supportives. Controllers are more matter-of-fact, with more fixed expectations of people and situations. Just as facts place second for Supportives, feelings take a back seat for Controllers. You might say that Supportives experience life by tuning in to the concerns or feeling states (of themselves and others) and then reacting to them. Controllers focus on the points or ideas in question.

Controllers like to know where a conversation is going. Idle, non-directed chitchat is not for them. If Supporting types stray from the subject, Controllers find a way to bring them back on track. They usually need clarity before they move on to the next topic. If you get off the subject, they're likely to ask, "Can you sum that up for me?" or, "What is the key point you're trying to make?"

Because of their different priorities, Controlling types can perceive more Supporting ones as time-wasting or wishy-washy. And Supportives may view these Controllers as cold, unsympathetic, or self-involved. As a result, misunderstandings can quickly grow out of proportion when we don't discern and respond to these types of differences. You may still wonder which is better—Supporting or Controlling behavior? And again, the answer is, "It depends." As with Directness and Indirectness, circumstances determine the appropriateness of any type of behavior. Our awareness of potential pitfalls for each personality pattern can save multitudes of problems for ourselves and others as well as for our workplace, social groups, and organizations.

Whereas Supporting people may feel any attention is better than no attention at all, Controllers tend to be more selective about whom they associate with. They feel more comfortable retaining firm control over their emotions.

Ranges of behavior

Whether a person is more Supporting or Controlling, remember there are degrees of these characteristics that vary from individual to individual. These range from the more Direct Captain Kirk character on STAR TREK to the more Indirect, less talkative, and more reserved Mr. Spock. Bruce Willis (of MOONLIGHTING) and Bill Cosby are both Supportive, but Willis gives his openness more free rein. And then, of course, there's Vanna White, the best-known card turner in the country. Everyone from toddlers to octogenarians seems to relate to her warmth as she roots for all the contestants on WHEEL OF FORTUNE.

Controllers, too, cover a wide range of less-than-open behaviors. When we compare Charles Bronson's characters to MAGNUM P. I.'s Higgins, Higgins is more open. Again, both are Controlling, but Bronson is usually more so. Other Controlling TV personalities include MURPHY BROWN and Julia Sugarbaker on DESIGNING WOMEN.

When the chips are down, Supportives tend to spare others' feelings at the expense of completing a task. Controllers want to get things done, even though feelings may get hurt as part of the emotional cost of accomplishment. This doesn't necessarily mean that Supportives don't believe in responsibly doing their work; it just means that people are a higher concern. Similarly, it doesn't mean Controllers don't value other people. They simply think the best way to deal with people is by a more controlled style of behavior.

Survey of Supporting
Versus Controlling Behaviors

Follow the same guidelines for this set of nine questions as you did for the Direct and Indirect ones earlier in this chapter. Focus on the same person that you did previously.

Is the Person More Supporting or Controlling?

1. (S) More open to getting to know people better and establishing new relationships, OR

   (C) Exerts more control over who you get involved with, including how well you get to know them

2. (C) Focuses conversations on tasks, issues, business, or subject at hand, OR

   (S) Allows conversations to take the direction of interest of the parties involved, even though this may stray from the business or subject at hand

3. (C) Tends to make decisions based on objectives, facts, or evidence, OR

   (S) Tends to make decisions based on feelings, experiences, or relationships

4. (C) More likely to expect and respond to conflicts, OR

   (S) Less likely to expect conflict and more motivated to personally deal with conflicts when they arise

5. (S) More likely to accept others' points of view (ideas, feelings, and concerns), OR

   (C) Less likely to accept other people's points of view (ideas, feelings, and concerns)

6. (C) Tends to focus mostly on the idea, concept, or outcome, OR

   (S) Tends to focus primarily on the interest level, persons involved, and process

7. (S) More open about own time involvement with others, OR

   (C) Less open about own time involvement with others

8. (C) Likely to stick with own agendas and concerns while tuning in to the power motives of others, OR

   (S) Likely to tune in to others' agendas and concerns while minimizing any conflict or disagreement

9. (C) Prefers to work independently or dictate the conditions as it involves others, OR

   (S) Prefers to work with and through others, providing support when possible

Total number circled: C's_____   S's_____
                       (Controlling) (Supporting)

To identify a person's behavioral style

Simply use the process of elimination. If the person is more Direct than Indirect, then you can eliminate the Steady Relater and Cautious Thinker types (the two Indirect styles). If the person is also more Supporting than Controlling, then eliminate the Dominant Director (the more Controlling type). Now you arrive at the remaining style, in this case, an Interacting Socializer.

Which type is this?

You have an appointment with a client whose secretary sets the time for exactly 10:10 a.m., not 10:00 or 10:30. After acknowledging you in the reception area with a fixed, polite smile, she gives several detailed instructions to her secretary. Gathering behavioral clues, you notice that she dresses impeccably. She again smiles politely at you and asks you to follow her into the office. She tells you where to sit, checks her watch, and actually says, "You have exactly 15 minutes. Go."

During your presentation, the client remains as expressionless as a statue in a museum. No emotion shows. She asks for highly specific facts, assesses your responses, and then extends the discussion in areas of interest to her. She invites you to stay longer and literally closes the sale herself after getting specific answers to her time, schedule, and cost questions.

There are many clues to help you determine the behavioral style of this client. First, look at her Direct versus Indirect behaviors. You can be fairly sure of placing her as Direct: She directs the conversation, confronts the issues head-on, controls both you and the situation (when to begin, where to sit, what to discuss), and closes the sale herself. That's Directness!

Next, look at her Supporting or Controlling tendencies. By nature of her time discipline, fact and task orientation, formality, and expressionless face, she is fairly easily to classify as Controlling.

When you put together the two aspects which determine behavioral style, you have a combined rating of high Directness/low Supportingness. These two classifications tell you that the client is a Dominant Director.

One more time

You conduct a seminar which begins at 8:30 a.m., following an 8:00 coffee and doughnut session. When you arrive at 7:45, the first participant is already seated in the room, pad and pencils neatly lying in front of her. She says nothing until you approach. Then she politely shakes hands. She is totally noncommittal. You ask a few questions and receive polite, short answers.

Around 8:15, with several other people in the room, a person stops hesitantly at the door and softly asks, "Excuse me. Is this the training seminar for salespeople?" When he hears yes, he breathes a sigh, walks in, takes a cup of coffee, and mentions how interesting he hopes the seminar will be, saying it really could be helpful in business and at home. He asks a few questions, listening intently to other's remarks. He expresses some concern for role-playing in front of a group.

At this moment, another participant strides in, loudly asking, "Hey, is this the sales seminar?" Upon hearing yes, this person dramatizes relief and asks where the coffee is, explaining that he *can't function without that black poison.* He has overheard the role-playing comments and leaps in on the conversation to say how he likes doing those things. He follows this with a tale of how he embarrassed himself in the last role-play session he attended.

Which style is the first person? The second? The last?

The first person's apparent disinterest in conversation and restrained gestures identify her as Indirect. This narrows the possible choices to either a Steady Relater or Cautious Thinker. She is also clearly in control of her emotions and the setting—Controlling, as opposed to Supporting. Another name for an Indirect/Controlling person is a Cautious Thinker.

The second participant speaks with a soft voice, requests clarification, and hesitates before starting the seminar. All these clues add up to an Indirect behavior pattern (Cautious Thinker or Steady Relater). He volunteers information about personal feelings and gives rapid feedback with his sigh and comments. These are Supporting characteristics. This person shows a Steady Relater style.

Participant number three demonstrates Directness through his speed of response, fast movements, and high quantity of conversation (Dominant Director or Interacting Socializer). He also shows Supporting behaviors by telling stories and responding quickly. These are traits of the Interacting Socializer.

How Will You Know a Dominant Director When You See One?

At the office

When entering a Dominant Directors' offices, look around. The overall tone suggests authority and control. Their desks may be covered with projects and papers, stacked in neat piles. Both their in- and out-baskets typically bulge with busywork. They tend to surround themselves with trophies, awards, and other evidence of personal achievement. Virtually everything about the place suggests hustle, bustle, formality, and power. This type is the one that often favors a large chair behind a massive authority structure known as a *power desk.* Besides non-verbally announcing, "I'm important," the desk separates them from visitors, literally keeping them at a distance.

Notice the walls

The walls may include diplomas, commendations, and other evidence of success. One wall may have a large planning sheet or calendar on it . . . the better to juggle with, my dear. If Dominant Directors have family photos, they may hang behind them or someplace where they don't readily see them. To this type, their offices are places of business and the fewer distractions they have, the better.

Hustle, bustle, and busywork

Dominant Directors like constant activity, so you'll seldom catch them idle. Between existing tasks, they pick up new ones. They perk up when competing and appear to thrive with a pressure cooker schedule. They often squeeze you onto their calendars and let you know that their time is limited, either by telling you outright or by showing you. Looking at a watch or clock, they frequently shift their gaze elsewhere, or make and take phone calls while you sit in their office.

They walk fast in pursuit of a tangible goal, so Dominant Directors may not notice people around them or may just hurriedly grunt something to acknowledge them. They often act both brisk and brusque without realizing it. When under stress, impatience emerges and they may push others aside to reach their goal—completing a report, getting served first, or running out the door to make an appointment. When pressure intensifies, Dominant Directors often rise to the occasion. Under time constraints, they may concede to impatience and rely on educated guesses, even their own hunches.

Power symbols

Dominant Directors tend to dress comfortably and typically pay less attention to their appearance than the other types. They may program themselves primarily for work results, so wardrobe tends to play a secondary role in most fields of work. They may be candidates for a time-saving personal shopper or tailor who can choose or measure outfits for them in the privacy of their own offices. Dominant Directors gravitate toward authority symbols, so they may wear navy blue or charcoal gray *power* suits.

Dominant Directors may like to let people know they've *made it* without having to tell anyone about it, so they often prefer possessions that emit success and authority messages— like a black or steel gray Mercedes or BMW. Someone once suggested they'd buy a Sherman tank, if they could.

Observable Characteristics of Dominant Directors

Verbal	Vocal	Visual
States more than asks	More vocal variety	Firm handshake
Talks more than listens	More forceful tone	Steady eye contact
Primarily verbal, not written,	Communicates readily	Gestures to emphasize points

communication		
Makes strong statements	High volume, faster speech	Displays impatience
Blunt and to the point	Challenging voice intonation	Fast moving body language

How Will You Know a Dominant Director by Phone?

When speaking on the phone to a Dominant Director, treat her the same way as a person-to-person contact. Think of the ABC's: Keep it abridged, brief, and concise. Then we prepare our delivery with the bottom-line in mind: "The trend in your industry is toward computer-generated graphics. The research we've conducted with other typesetters in your area indicates increased profits of 20 to 30% over two years. I'd like to meet with you for 10 minutes to show you the numbers and see if this concept interests you."

They waste no time

It's not unusual for a Dominant Director to call someone and, without saying hello, launch right into the conversation. "You've got to be kidding; the shipment from Hong Kong will kill us . . . by the way, this is Jack." When other people can't keep up with their speed, they may view them as incompetent.

On the telephone, determine whether the person sends power signals. Dominant Directors want to pick the time and place to meet. They often speak in a sort of shorthand—concisely and pointedly—and sound cool, confident, and demanding. When Dominant Director Dennis phones, he actually says: "Janice? Dennis. Tony there?" Talking to him is like speaking to a human telegram. He reduces the concept of *brief and to the point* to another dimension. As commanding speakers who tend not to listen to others, they naturally want to direct the conversation toward their goals. Under stress, they can become defensive and aggressive, attacking others personally to show who's in control. They dislike using *touchy -feely*, emotional terms and prefer sensible *thinking* terminology. "I think we'll implement this plan tomorrow," or, "I think this discussion is over."

Their letters are brief and to the point

A letter from a Dominant Director tends to be brief, forceful, and to the point. They may mention highlights of conversations or materials, but they don't belabor them. They may give specifics for your follow-through or raise questions they want answers to now. "The Mulvany account needs to be reworked. I hear he's got a new partner and a different address. Track him down and get the data we need so we can let him know that we've studied his account and we know our stuff."

Even notes and cards take on abbreviated forms and may show little or no indication of feelings. "Todd, hope you're doing well. I'm working hard . . . " We know more than one Dominant Director who signs personal birthday and Christmas cards with no closing, not even *Sincerely*, but with just their names. Steady Relaters and Interacting Socializers gravitate more toward *Warmly*, *Fondly*, or *Cordially*. But Dominant Directors, perhaps in their efforts to get as many things accomplished as possible, tend to opt for brevity.

Pick a Dominant Director co-worker

Think of a co-worker who is a strong Dominant Director in the workplace. What characteristics does he or she exhibit that reveal those Dominant Director traits? How do you get along with this person? Why?

How Will You Know an Interacting Socializer When You See One?

At the office

When you enter the working area of an Interacting Socializer, look around his office. What does it look like? Even if you've never been to this type's office before, you may recognize it from across the room. Remember Oscar Madison?

He and other high Interacting Socializers may strew paperwork across their desks, sometimes trailing it along the floor, too. They react to visual stimuli, so they like to have everything where they can see it. Consequently, their desks often look cluttered and disorganized. If anyone comments, "How do you find anything?" they like to say that they're *organized in their disorganization.*

And the walls?

Interacting Socializer walls may sport prestigious awards. They may be broad, liberal arts degrees, motivational or upbeat slogans, generalized personal comments, or stimulating posters. You may see notes posted and taped all over the place with little apparent forethought, rhyme, or reason. Overall decor reflects an open, airy, lively atmosphere that often reveals the personality of its occupant. Likewise, the furniture arrangement tends to indicate warmth, openness, and contact. An Interacting Socializer seldom sits behind a desk when he talks. He often opts for comfortable, accessible seating, enabling him to meet his goal of getting to know people better. He prefers to sit next to us at a table or on a couch so he can see and hear us better and get a feel for how we respond to him. He talks a lot and shows emotion with both his body language and speech.

Feelings take priority

Interacting Socializers have a natural preference for talking and listening in *feeling* terms. Unconsciously, they may become uncomfortable when talking to a person who, instead, uses *thinking* words. (The opposite also is true). Statements like, "I feel that we should have been consulted about moving our office," or, "I feel good about what we've accomplished today," tend to put this people-oriented type more at ease.

They like glitz and pizzazz!

The way Interacting Socializers dress often relates to their need for recognition. Since they like others to notice them, they may dress in the latest style. *Look at me* Socializers like bright colors and unusual clothes that prompt others to compliment them. Many Interacting Socializers even prefer negative comments to none at all. "Are you dressed for Halloween today, Rhonda?" At least she's getting the attention she craves.

In an informal poll taken by Tony at his many seminars, red ranks number one with Interacting Socializers as their color choice for clothes or for a sports car or convertible. They like glamour, flash, and excitement . . . and their purchases often express their preferences. Musical choices even include energizing songs like *Celebration* or *Fame*.

Observable Characteristics of Interacting Socializers

Verbal	Vocal	Visual
Tells stories, anecdotes	Lots of inflection	Animated facial expressions
Shares personal feelings	More pitch variation	Much hand/body movement
Informal speech	More variety in vocal quality	Contact-oriented
Expresses opinions readily	Dramatic	Spontaneous actions
Flexible time perspective	High volume	
Digresses from conversation	Fast speech	

How Will You Know an Interacting Socializer by Phone?

"What's up?" or "What's happening?" are usual Interacting Socializer opening lines. They are sometimes so animated that their gestures can be transmitted via the phone lines. How? By their varied, emotional vocal inflections/intonations and their colorful choice of words that may tend toward exaggeration. "Really? That's fantastic!" or, "You have to be kidding me!" The telephone can be a favorite toy that enables them to both prolong conversations and re-charge themselves, especially when no one else is physically around. "I just called because I'm bored." You may also detect background noise when you speak to individuals of this type. They sometimes put on the TV or radio just for the sound, visual stimulation, and activity.

On the phone, Interacting Socializers speak rapidly and emotively. "I feel that if we go through with this plan, the community will resent us as anti-environmentalists," or, "I feel that I've contributed enough to this organization over the years to allow me to talk about this." Other styles may more naturally use *thinking* words, instead.

Say it with feeling

Typically, you'll notice a wide range of vocal inflection and intonation and a tendency to want to know your reaction. "Do you feel that way, too?" They liven up conversations with personal anecdotes and may keep you on the phone longer than you had anticipated. If you need to extricate yourself from an extended monologue, try something like, "Well, Don, it's been great talking with you. I'm really looking forward to our appointment on Monday!" If you say it with feeling, the Interacting Socializer may already eagerly anticipate your meeting.

By Letter?

Letters, too, can reveal the Interacting Socializer behind the correspondence. Often, this type overuses exclamation points, underlining, and bold highlighting. You can almost hear her emphasizing those picturesque adjectives and adverbs. Just as the Interacting Socializer tends to speak in a stimulating, energetic way, so does she write. She may also throw in an image-provoking personal anecdote or reference to some mutually satisfying experience. "I'll never forget our adventure on the freeway en route to Los Angeles—in rush hour, of course!" When she's finished a letter or note, she may add a postscript (P.S.), a P.P.S., or even a P.P.P.S.

Caution: Again, these tendencies may not as readily reveal themselves if the Interacting Socializer has learned to tone down her natural flair while conducting business. And there's always a possibility that the secretary *cleans up* her copy before typing it out, especially if she is a more exacting, less animated behavioral type.

How Will You Know a Steady Relater When You See One?

Office memorabilia

When you enter a Steady Relater's office, be alert for conservatively framed personal slogans, group photos, serene landscapes and posters, and other personal items. Since they seek close relationships, also look around for tell-tale family pictures and mementos, usually turned so they can view them from their desk chair. They often favor nostalgic memories of stabilizing experiences and relationships in our increasingly high tech world. These remembrances of a pleasant, uncomplicated past allow them to transform their offices into an environment of friendly, warm ambience. They prefer to arrange seating in a side-by-side, more congenial, cooperative manner. No big power desks for them! If they do have one, though, they'll typically come out from behind it to *reach out* by opting for a more personal touch.

Service certificates

Their educational background often includes more specialized areas of attention and interest within their professions. You may also see certificates recognizing volunteer hours for various hands-on activities in their community. While other behavioral types may contribute in other ways—such as gifts of money—Steady Relaters typically enjoy giving their time for causes they feel strongly about. Besides the possibility of meeting more potential friends, this also helps satisfy their need to see for themselves: (1) what's really going on (2) where they fit into the group effort, and (3) how they can get meaningful, concrete results.

Steady Relaters are natural listeners

You can recognize Steady Relaters by their natural listening patterns and slower, lower-key delivery. Their questions often focus on concrete topics and experiences. "What did you say the terms for payment were again?" They walk casually, acknowledging others and sometimes getting side-tracked by chance encounters.

Nothing too loud for them

Steady Relaters dislike calling attention to themselves, so they tend to wear subdued colors and conservatively cut clothing, favoring conventional styles that don't stand out too much. Their cars also reveal these preferences. They often like beige or light blue station wagons or vans, factory recommended tires, and in the best of all worlds—no horn. To Steady Relaters, using a horn is like yelling at somebody. Steady Relaters often tell us they like most songs by Lionel Ritchie or Barry Manilow. Both have more predictable, Steady Relater styles of performing mellow, soothing, easy listening music.

Observable Characteristics of Steady Relaters

Verbal	Vocal	Visual
Ask more than state	Steady, even-tempered delivery	Intermittent eye contact
Listen more than talk	Less forceful tone of expression	Gentle handshake
Reserve opinions	Lower, quieter volume	Exhibit patience
Less verbal communication	Slower rate of speech	Slower moving body language

How Will You Know a Steady Relater by Phone?

"How are you?" or "I'm glad to hear from you again," are typical Steady Relater greetings. Like those telephone company TV commercials, their warmth can seem to transcend the limitations of the phone lines. Although they prefer more personal interactions with people, they will also settle for indirect contact—especially if the person is pleasant and non-threatening. They project this people orientation by phone and like to build a personal, first-name relationship with callers. Even if they don't know you, they may say, "You don't have to be formal. Just call me Alice." They may project a desire to know you personally or provide you with good service.

They communicate with steady, even vocal intonations to convey friendliness, comfort, and a sense of relaxation. Steady Relaters tend to be naturals at listening to others' ideas and feelings, whether on the phone or in person. They tend to be interested in the blow-by-blow, point by point description of what you did yesterday or the sequential pattern of how to complete a certain task. You're probably talking to a Steady Relater if you notice slower than average speech patterns, more moments of listening than of speaking, and references to actual, real-life experiences regarding either products or mutual acquaintances.

"I'll look it up for you"

Steady Relaters tend to express themselves in a rather tentative manner in both their face to face and telephone conversations. "I'll need to consult Mrs. Adams before I can make that decision," or, "I'm not sure we can do that, but I'll get back to you as soon as I find out." As in other aspects of their lives, they often defer to the more human, proven way things have always been done. They typically feel more comfortable making decisions based on conferring with others rather than by themselves. "What do you think?" and "How do you feel?" and "What do you recommend?" are all common questions this type may ask.

When They Think About Someone, They May Drop a Line

In their written correspondence, Steady Relaters may send letters just to keep in touch or to let you know they're thinking of you. Of the four personality types, this one is likely to send thank you notes for almost anything—inviting them to a party, driving them to the dry cleaners, or saving coupons for them. They may even send a thank you note to acknowledge your thank you note. Again, they are likely to organize their letters, writing as they do their other *to do* task lists—probably in sequential *in-out* order. Since they tend to write in a slower, more methodically paced manner, their work tends to follow a systematic outline pattern.

Visualize a Steady Relater friend

Picture a friend of yours who best typifies the Steady Relater. What does he or she do that fits the type? How do you tend to interact with him or her?

How Will You Know a Cautious Thinker When You See One?

At the office

Cautious Thinkers often carry their organizational tendencies into their work environments. Environmental clues include neat, highly organized desks with cleared tops so they can work unimpeded by clutter—clean, shipshape, and professional with everything in the appropriate place. Charts, graphs, exhibits, models, credentials, and job-related pictures are often placed neatly on their office walls or shelves. Cautious Thinkers favor a functional decor that will enable them to work more efficiently. They tend to keep most objects within reach, readily available when needed. Where appropriate, you may notice state of the art technology to further enhance efficiency.

Cautious Thinkers ask pertinent questions

People of few words, Cautious Thinkers tend to ask pertinent questions instead of making statements. They typically speak more carefully and with less expression than the other types. Reluctant to reveal personal feelings, they often use *thinking* words (like the Dominant Director), as opposed to *feeling* words. "From what I've read, I think Product X may be better for our situation than Product Y because of its superior filtration system," or, "I think that Jones is overreacting in this matter."

Formality is more comfortable

Cautious Thinkers are non-contact people who prefer the formality of distance. This preference is reflected in the functional, but uninviting arrangement of their desks and chairs, usually with the desks physically separating you and them. They generally are not fond of huggers and touchers, and prefer a cool handshake or a brief phone call. When Cautious Thinkers walk, they usually move slowly and methodically toward a known destination.

Noticeably understated

Picture Felix Unger, the neat, perfectionistic one on television's THE ODD COUPLE. Like Felix, Cautious Thinkers tend to wear more conservative clothes, but with unique, often perfectly matched accessories. While the Interacting Socializer may draw attention to himself with glitz and glitter, Cautious Thinkers usually prefer a more understated, faultlessly groomed look with nary a hair out of place. But their taste may differ from the people around them.

They like expressions of individuality and creativity, but within guidelines. For some reason, male Cautious Thinkers with beards seem to prefer short, well-manicured ones. If they smoke, they often prefer pipes—perhaps, someone noted, this is because taking a puff from a pipe gives them more time to think before they answer. Since they may prefer exploring life's complexities, they may enjoy the intricacies of a specific kind of music or individual musical piece, whether jazz, classical, rock, etc. You may spot them driving well built, practical cars that perform well, often in more conservative, understated, but less common colors.

Observable Characteristics of Cautious Thinkers

Verbal	Vocal	Visual
Fact and task-oriented	Little inflection	Few facial expressions
Limited sharing of feelings	Few pitch variations	Non-contact oriented
More formal and proper	Less variety in vocal quality	Few gestures
Focused conversation	Steady, mono-tone delivery	Slower moving
Less verbal, more written	Lower volume, slower speech	

communication

How Will You Know a Cautious Thinker by Phone?

"Good afternoon, Mr. Lomis. This is Jonathan Williams. You asked me to call back Monday morning." Formal greetings are one tip-off that you may be dealing with a Cautious Thinker. Time-conscious individuals of this type often get to a task just when they say they will. Monday morning it is! In this example, the Cautious Thinker also calls himself Jonathan, not Jon. We've noticed that many people in this category call themselves by their given names, not by nicknames. It's Elizabeth, Rebecca, Donald, and Peter, not Beth, Becka, Don, or Pete. Of course, there are exceptions. Actually, Jon may prove to be an effective and logical alternative for some Cautious Thinkers, but this type seems less likely to tolerate what they perceive as cute nicknames for themselves, such as Johnny, Ricky, Cindy, or Becky.

"May I speak with Mr. Holmes or Dr. Brothers?"

They prefer brief, to-the-point telephone calls. Although they may not tell you, call them Mister or Ms. or Doctor or whatever their titles happen to be. Cautious Thinkers sometimes view jumping into a first-name basis as invasion of privacy, so they deal with others on a more formal basis. If you think you're talking to Sherlock Holmes or Dr. Joyce Brothers, chances are you've contacted a Cautious Thinker. They typically retain their ground in stressful situations when they can maintain their position with concrete facts or reverse-control questions. They do this quietly and independently, by first avoiding others. Then they take on the problem in an orderly way which is aligned with their own plan.

"Need to know" basis

They're inclined to talk in rather structured, careful speech patterns, almost weighing their words as they say them. They tend to ask pertinent questions and talk in a quiet, observant, cautious way. Additionally, they may not volunteer much about their personal selves beyond the equivalent of name, rank, and serial number. "Yes, I'm married with two children. We live in New York." They prefer to keep the relationship formal, yet pleasant and business-like. Less can be more to a Cautious Thinker—less conversation, self-disclosure, and verbal communication equals more comfort zone. So we must learn to hear between the lines: Longer than average silences, especially when we ask them more private questions, may signal annoyance or reluctance. When this occurs, ask, "Am I getting too personal?" or "If I'm asking uncomfortable questions, how could you let me know so I don't make a problem for either of us?" They may relax more if they think they have an out.

Careful and correct

Like Steady Relaters, Cautious Thinkers tend to express themselves in a rather tentative manner. "I'll check on that and let you know tomorrow." Or they may want to provide you with information so you can form your own conclusions. "I have a copy of the Governor's report in my files. If I send it to you, perhaps you can find what you're looking for." Both these approaches satisfy Cautious Thinkers' need for caution and correctness. They simply may not want to get misquoted or, possibly, involved in the first place.

How Will You Know a Cautious Thinker by Letter?

Cautious Thinkers typically send letters to clarify or explain positions. Consequently, these letters may become rather long and filled with data. "I was struck by the similarities between the Noonan and Kilgary lawsuits." But they may also be somewhat reserved or vague. "I'm researching a company's file now that I literally can't talk about." Or the letter may be on the short side with enclosures, citings, or references to specific information. Whether they prefer the long or short form, they usually concentrate on processing data. They like to cover their bases so they are neither misinterpreted, incomplete, nor incorrect.

Like Dominant Directors, in the interest of time, they may sign personal cards with just their names or with individual mottos, like "In the spirit of growth, Jonathan Williams." Even if you know them well, this type may include their surnames so there's no mistaking who sent this card.

If the shoe fits

The dimensions that determine type—Direct/Indirect and Controlling/Supporting—have their own innate strengths and weaknesses. In fact, the strengths are closely allied to the weaknesses—the strengths taken to an extreme. The Direct-Controlling type can become overbearing when he pushes persistence too hard. Similarly, the Direct-Supporting type may turn manipulative; the Indirect-Supporting type, wishy-washy; or the Indirect-Controlling type, unreachable. These and other positive or negative characteristics shade the actions of all four types. Individuals representing all four may have the same assignment, but use different approaches. If a monthly report is due, one type may keep a day-by-day journal (Indirect-Controlling), another may delegate the work (Direct-Controlling), another may prefer completing it with a co-worker (Indirect-Supporting), and yet another may prefer to pull an *all nighter* to complete it at the last minute (Direct-Supporting). Take a look at two charts which further summarize many of the Distinguishing Characteristics and Daily Examples of these four basic types of individuals.

By now, you know how to recognize the four core types by observing environmental clues and external behaviors. The four combinations we've just discussed—Direct/Controlling, or Dominant Director; Direct/Supporting, or Interacting Socializer; Indirect/Supporting, or Steady Relater; and Indirect/Controlling, or Cautious Thinker—all behave differently from each other in various situations. Whether at home, work, a social activity, or in a romantic encounter, they all naturally act true to their own type. It's their attempts to fill their type's needs and expectations. By acting themselves, they show their true core behavioral colors.

In the next chapter, *Adaptability*, you'll read about getting along with all the behavioral types in their natural, and less natural, life environments. You'll learn how to have more productive relationships with people of all types. Thereafter, you'll read about applying People Smart concepts in the workplace (Chapter 5), leading and being led by each type (Chapter 6), and selling to and being sold by them (Chapter 7). Then you'll discover personal applications in Chapters 8 through 10 when you learn about the different types in social, family, and romance settings. So read on to discover more about your People Smart potential in different life environments.

DISTINGUISHING CHARACTERISTICS
OF THE FOUR STYLES

	STEADY RELATER	CAUTIOUS THINKER	DOMINANT DIRECTOR	INTERACTING SOCIALIZER
1) BEHAVIOR PATTERN	Indirect/Supporting	Indirect/Controlling	Direct/Controlling	Direct/Supporting
2) PACE	Slower/Relaxed	Slower/Systematic	Faster/Decisive	Faster/Spontaneous
3) PRIORITY	The Relationship/ Communication	The Task/ Process	The Task/ Results	The Relationship/ Interaction
4) FEARS	Sudden changes, Instability	Personal criticism of their work efforts	Being taken advantage of	Loss of Social recognition
5) GAINS SECURITY THROUGH	Friendship, Cooperation	Preparation, Thoroughness	Control, Leadership	Playfulness, Others' approval
6) MEASURES PERSONAL WORTH BY	Compatibility with others, Depth of contribution	Precision, Accuracy, Quality of results	Quality or impact or results, Track record & process	Acknowledgments, Applause, Compliments
7) INTERNAL MOTIVATOR	The "Participation"	The "Process"	The "Win"	The "Show"
8) APPEARANCE	Casual, Conforming	Formal, Conservative	Businesslike, Functional	Fashionable, Stylish
9) WORKPLACE	Friendly Functional Personal	Formal Functional Structured	Efficient Busy Structured	Interacting Busy Personal

DAILY EXAMPLES
OF THE FOUR STYLES

	STEADY RELATER	CAUTIOUS THINKER	DOMINANT DIRECTOR	INTERACTING SOCIALIZER
1) SEEKS	Acceptance	Accuracy	Control	Recognition
2) STRENGTHS	Listening Teamwork Follow-through	Planning Systematizing Orchestration	Administration Leadership Pioneering	Persuading Enthusiastic Entertaining
3) WEAKNESSES (GROWTH AREAS)	Oversensitive Slow to begin action Lacks global perspective	Perfectionists Critical Unresponsive	Impatient Insensitive to others Poor listener	Inattentive to detail Short attention span Low follow-through
4) IRRITATIONS	Insensitivity Impatience	Disorganization Impropriety	Inefficiency Indecision	Routines Complexity
5) UNDER STRESS	Submissive Indecisive	Withdrawn Headstrong	Dictatorial Critical	Sarcastic Superficial
6) DECISION MAKING PATTERN	Conferring	Deliberate	Decisive	Spontaneous
7) OCCUPATIONS	Family doctor Social services Teacher	Engineer Researcher Artist	Executive Military leader Newspaper editor	Sales Public relations Actor
8) CELEBRITIES	Kenny Rogers Edith Bunker Martina Navratalova	Mr. Spock Sgt. Joe Friday Katherine Hepburn	Mike Wallace McGarrett (Five O) Rambo	Carol Burnett Tony Danza Dom Deluise
9) SONG	"You've Got a Friend"	"Don't Rain On My Parade"	"My Way"	"Celebration"
10) VEHICLE	Station Wagon	"Best Rated Buy"	Full-Size Luxury Car	Sports Car
11) ANIMAL	Koala	Fox	Lion	Porpoise

People Smart Principle #4—The Adaptability Principle:
"Your willingness and ability to adapt your behavior is
a prerequisite for your personal effectiveness."

Chapter 4
Creating Personal Power Through Behavioral Adaptability

What is it?

Behavioral adaptability is the key to success with the different types. With adaptability, we can treat the other person the way he wants to be treated. We define it as the willingness and ability to engage in a range of behaviors not necessarily characteristic of your style in response to effectively dealing with the requirements of a situation or relationship. Behavioral adaptability is something applied more to yourself (to your patterns, attitudes, and habits) than to others. It involves making strategic adjustments to your methods of communicating and behaving, based on the particular needs of the relationship at a particular time. Adaptable people try to meet the expectations of others by practicing tact. They make the choice to go beyond their own comfort zone so others also feel more comfortable—especially with the derived results.

What adaptability isn't

Adaptability does not mean imitation of the other person's behavioral style. It does mean adjusting your Supportiveness, Controllingness, Directness, and Indirectness in line with the other person's preference. At the same time, it means maintaining your own identity and good sense. You modify your spots.

So does that mean that Cautious Thinkers prefer the company of Cautious Thinkers and that the other types prefer people who share their type? Yes and no. Two cliches apply. *Birds of a feather flock together*, and *Opposites attract*. Dominant Directors may personally admire other Dominant Directors like themselves for their accomplishments and success rates, but prefer to be more guarded with them at work in order to maintain their own power and authority.

Cautious Thinkers may appreciate Interacting Socializers for their joy of life, but steer clear of them at work because of their imprecision. Interacting Socializers may enjoy Cautious Thinkers for their command of matters of interest to them, but may stay aloof at work because of the Cautious Thinkers' desired perfectionism. Steady Relaters and Dominant Directors may also admire each others' qualities or feel alienated by them. So what's a person to do?

Remember, the willingness to try behaviors not necessarily characteristic of your type is called *behavioral adaptability*. It is not the same as your behavioral type. No members of any type corner the market on adaptability. No style is *naturally* more adaptable than another. In other words, Steady Relaters as a group are no more adaptable than Interacting Socializers, Dominant Directors, or Cautious Thinkers (and vice versa).

Your adaptability level affects the way other people perceive you. Raise your adaptability and you'll discover trust and credibility go up; lower it, and they go down. Behavioral adaptability means adjusting your behavior to allow others to be more at ease, encouraged, and successful in your relationship.

Which style is most adaptable?

No one style is naturally more adaptable than another. For a given situation, the strategic adjustments each behavioral style makes will vary. The decision to employ specific techniques of behavioral adaptability is made on a case by case basis. You can choose to be adaptable with one person and not with another. You can also choose to be quite adaptable with one person today and less with that same person tomorrow. Behavioral adaptability concerns the way you manage your own communication and behaviors. It also involves how you manage the requirements that exist for a task or situation—whether other people are involved, or not.

For example, when an Interacting Socializer works with a Cautious Thinker on a common task, one of the ways she can practice behavioral adaptability is by talking less, listening more, and focusing on the critical facts. Behavioral adaptability means adjusting your own behavior to make other people feel more at ease with you and the situation. You practice adaptability every time you slow down for a Cautious Thinker or Steady Relater—or when you move a bit faster for an Interacting Socializer or a Dominant Director. Adaptability occurs when the Dominant Director or the Cautious Thinker takes the time to listen to a human interest or family story told by an Interacting Socializer or a Steady Relater.

The Adaptability Recipe

Adaptability is a phenomenon which has many characteristics. In fact, formal research studies in which we have been involved have identified at least 10 such attributes of people who are highly adaptable and 10 characteristics of those who have lower adaptability—a total of 20 traits in all. Of course, no person is likely to be either totally adaptable or non-adaptable. Instead, each of us possesses:

- different general, overall levels of adaptability ranging from higher (more characteristic) to lower (less characteristic)

- personal differences in various situations regarding our level of the two basic ingredients of adaptability—flexibility and versatility
- specific key strengths and possible growth areas in the 20 behaviors which make up your overall level of development in adaptability potential

The 10 behaviors which define the person with high adaptability potential are different from behavioral type, so anybody can choose to enter the higher range characteristics of a more enlightened, functionally mature human being. Unfortunately, the 10 at the lower end represent the darker side more characteristic of lower order animals and species. But you (and every other individual) have the personal power to increase your level of adaptability if you are willing to learn the abilities to get there.

The high and low adaptors

The research conducted on flexibility has shown you view yourself as both more flexible and versatile than you actually are. In part, this is because you aspire toward who and what you want to be. As a result, your view of yourself includes both how you intend to act and how you actually do act. However, the reality of how you act is based only on the second element.

Another factor that explains this gap in our idealized versus actual level of adaptability is that it's not easy. If you're like most people, you may not be aware of all 10 behaviors which allow you to achieve your potential, let alone have already developed them as personal strengths. Similarly, you may not have thought about the 10 others which undermine your potential strengths. Here are all 20, broken down into 10 flexibility strengths and weaknesses and 10 versatility plus and minus points.

Higher flexibility is characterized by these personal attitudes:
- confidence—the attitude of belief in one's self, trusting your own judgment and resourcefulness

- tolerance—open-minded state of acceptance; willingness to defer judgment on the basis of limited time or information
- empathy—sensitivity to others point of view; caring approach towards others (without being overwhelmed or manipulated by people)
- positiveness—maintaining a state of positive expectations about people and situations, including a positive state of energy in your thoughts and emotional patterns
- respect for others—desire to understand, accept, and consider mutual and separate interests, choices, and commitments

Lower flexibility is characterized by these personal attitudes:
- rigidity
- competition against others
- discontent
- being unapproachable
- difficulty in dealing with ambiguity

Just think of the more successful individuals you have admired, both personally and from afar, and you'll probably notice your list is full of people with high flexibility strengths. Those with lower flexibility characteristics seldom seem to make the cut.

Now, for the other half of this adaptability formula—versatility. Our research indicates people have a more clear-cut understanding, and generally a higher developed level, of flexibility than versatility. Versatility, instead, involves a set of personal aptitudes which are distinctly different from merely being willing to adapt. Many people are willing to modify their behaviors, but simply lack the required set of abilities. Versatility is a complex set of mental and emotional abilities which we acquire over time through a variety of sources. These include formal education, daily life experiences, and observations of others who demonstrate these same behaviors.

The good news is that versatility can be learned. People aren't born either high or low in versatility. But more versatile people tend to approach every situation in each day of their lives as new opportunities for learning and growing. And, of course, others make a personal decision to opt for the lower road—getting the consequences that go along with the easier way of doing things in life.

Higher versatility is characterized by these personal aptitudes:
- resilience—learning how to cope, in spite of setbacks, barriers, or limited resources
- vision—foresight, creativity, and imagination
- attentiveness—being mindful and aware of stimuli in the environment; reality-focused
- competence—capability of managing required tasks and being knowledgeable about required subjects and people; including uses and updates of appropriate abilities
- self-correction—able to initiate and evaluate by oneself, seeking feedback as appropriate, characterized by a problem-solving mind set/approach to matters

Lower versatility is characterized by these personal aptitudes:
- subjectiveness
- bluntness
- resistance
- single-mindedness
- unreasonable risk-taking

Flexibility

The flexibility dimension of adaptability is the half that involves your personal attitudes toward yourself, others, and the situations you face. It indicates your degree of willingness to change your perspective and/or position, when appropriate. Examples follow of a lower and higher level of adaptability in a person, and the way each one is likely to respond.

Here's a brief summary of some of these key differences between such people:

Higher flexibility attitudes indicate . . .
- a higher level of security and sense of personal worth or well-being

- an open-minded, searching attitude in dealing with people and situations
- positive expectations about your own goals and desired results, and those of others

Lower flexibility attitudes indicate . . .
- a tendency to be reactive to people, conditions, or events—often responding out of fear or anxiety
- predetermined views, conclusions, or patterns of behavior which are non-negotiable
- a tendency to be negative about what may occur, especially if points of view or opinions change

As you review the following statements, you can see the differences in higher versus lower flexibility.

Lower personal flexibility

"What do you expect of me? That's just the way I am. It's me . . . my type of person or style I'm stuck with . . . so I can't do anything about it."

Higher personal flexibility

"Well, one thing I've learned is that each of us can be our own worst enemy in our own unique way. That's the real benefit I've gained from this *type* kind of behavioral style idea. Now, I realize my more natural strengths, preferences and short suits. As a result, I've made conscious efforts to monitor these to make sure they stay in the positive range while also learning how I can become better by modifying myself, at times."

Lower personal flexibility

"Look, each of us has our own cross to bear in terms of other people. I can't be expected to get along with everyone. There are such things as personality conflicts and that's all there is to it. So I try to seek out those people I get along with and stay away from all those other types that pose problems for me—and themselves, too."

Higher personal flexibility

"Obviously, since no two people are identical and there are few Prince Charming/Cinderella matches in the real world, each of us has to work at our relationships if we want them to be mutually satisfying. This means I have to be willing to accept every person as worthwhile, regardless of their style or values. The key is being willing to understand as well as accept them as people I want to get along with. When I do, I've found that things usually work out quite well; and when I don't, then it usually doesn't. The choice and the consequences belong to me."

Lower personal flexibility

"Look, I'm just your average, hard-working kind of person. I mean, I'm good at handling some types of situations, and not so successful with others. But I've learned to accept this fact. After all, nobody's perfect. So I just don't deal with those situations that pose problems for me. Instead, I either avoid them or try to get someone else to handle them. After all, why should I get all bent out of shape about these?"

Higher personal flexibility

"A few years ago I attended a public seminar on Situational Leadership. I found it really fascinating and since then have read some books and listened to tapes on the subject. Now, I consider myself a lot more effective as a person—both at work and in my personal life—because I've learned how to adjust my own preferred style of doing things when it gets in the way of the kinds of results I want to achieve. This has been a real breakthrough for me and has given me a much greater sense of confidence in my ability to deal with situations that arise. And it wasn't that I didn't have the ability to deal with them. It's just that this model helped me better process my own attitudes when I got stuck over how to handle different situations."

Versatility

By comparison with flexible individuals, highly versatile people demonstrate a set of distinctive abilities in realistically and productively managing a variety of situations. This includes the stresses that accompany this higher activity level. In addition, their actions are clearly goal-oriented, serving a meaningful purpose in their own personal aspirations, their relationships with others, and the desirable outcomes of situations. They also exhibit appropriate problem-solving actions which match the requirements that exist in dealing with a broad range of different situations.

Lower versatility is characterized by a tendency to be responsive only to one's personal preferences or expectations, discounting the reality of other factors that require consideration. As a result, these people tend to be more one-dimensional in their behavior. If they are Supporting and Direct, for instance, they have difficulty demonstrating other behaviors, even when different actions are more appropriate in a specific situation. Additionally, while they tend to be very adept at finding problems and passing them off to other people, they lack the same skillfulness when it comes to contributing to the solution of such problems.

Higher versatility individuals

Employee: "One of the things I really like about my job is that every day is different. I'm always learning something new and have the opportunity to respond to many types of situations where I can use my talents as well as develop other ones. In fact, our company gives us the chance to take a variety of training programs—both in-house and through continuing education programs—and they reimburse us for part of the cost. I'm always on the lookout for ones that fill in the gaps for my job and areas where I'd like to get better."

Homemaker: "I used to work before I had children, but now I really enjoy being at home. There are a wide variety of tasks and challenges I face in the job my husband calls chief executive officer of our home. We have three children, and as you might guess, each of them is quite different. My husband is, too. That significantly impacts the way I organize schedules, and respond to the many little stresses each one faces, from their own point of view. I also keep an eye on the bigger picture involving where we were, are, and want to go individually and as a family. That's sure a full-time job, requiring a lot of different skills to understand and manage the range of situations which arise."

Lower versatility individuals

Teenager: "I hate school. It's always the same old thing, day after day and year after year. About the only really good thing about it is I get a chance to meet a lot of people and get invited to a lot of great parties and things. In that way it's a lot better than just sitting around. But I don't really see how a lot of the stuff they try to teach us is really going to apply to what I do. After all, I have a part-time job at a local store and I don't really need hardly anything they teach me to get the things done that they expect of me. So, what's the point?"

Manager: "You know, one of the problems with people nowadays is that they expect a lot more than people did in the good old days. Back then, people just came to work and did what they were told. Even customers were satisfied with what they got as long as it worked and the price was fair. But now the whole world seems to have turned upside down. As a manager, I've got to also deal with a lot of other things that I didn't before. One of the most difficult is knowing how to deal with all of these different expectations which have dramatically changed the nature of the business we're in and how I have to do my job—handling all these people and their concerns. I just do the best I can at this point and try not to make too many waves, but it's confusing. I can't say I'm real clear as to what's expected of me nowadays, let alone how to do these things."

These comparisons indicate that you do not have to be a prisoner of your own behavioral tendencies and patterns. Instead, by increasing your personal flexibility and versatility, you can gain personal success and effectiveness by managing yourself, your relationships, and the situations you encounter. You are in charge of whether you choose to be a person with higher or lower flexibility and versatility.

The Road Map to Personal Adaptability

	How to Increase FLEXIBILITY	How to Increase VERSATILITY
IF you are a . . .	Lower your over-emphasis on . . .	Develop and demonstrate more . . .
DOMINANT DIRECTOR	control of other people and conditions	supportive skills and actions Examples: listening, open-ended questions, positive reinforcement of others
INTERACTING SOCIALIZER	approval from other people or groups as the primary determinant of appropriate choices for you	directive skills and actions Examples: self-assertion, conflict resolution, negotiations
STEADY RELATER	resistance to try or seek out new or different opportunities; limiting your options by undue demand for, dependence on, stability or risk-free choices	directive skills and actions Examples: negotiation, divergent thinking
CAUTIOUS THINKER	unnecessary perfectionism and the tendency to focus on weaknesses (rather than strengths) and on faults of self and others	supportive skills and actions Examples: empathic listening, positive reinforcement of others, involvement with others with complementary strengths

Everyone can become more adaptable

So the good news is you can, in fact, become more adaptable. The accompanying bad news is that it doesn't happen overnight, by wishing for it, or without occasional regressions back to the old behaviors you felt more comfortable with. Since adaptability involves learning techniques of mind over matter, you can speed up the process and increase your probability for success by focusing once again on the matter of who you are. Coming full circle, this means dealing with who you are. It also means personally committing to work toward overcoming these easier, more natural behaviors you will occasionally slip back into. After all, you've done them thousands of times more than these newer, competing behaviors.

Just as you consult a map when you swerve off course, you can remind yourself to stay on the road to adaptability when you fall back into your old habits. The *Road Map to Personal Adaptability* will help you increase your own flexibility and versatility. You can also use it to coach and assist your friends, family, co-workers, and others through the same learning process. Again, this process begins with who you are. From there, you can work on either those appropriate attitude changes or aptitude changes to develop the potentials related to your own unique behavioral tendencies.

Here's how to use your own road map. First identify your strongest behavioral tendency ("D", "I", "S", or "C"). Select just one goal—either flexibility or versatility—not both at once. Then look across the appropriate row and under the corresponding column to find what you can do to further develop yourself.

Since we don't behave in a vacuum, these general self-adaptations can obviously be further refined for greater success when used more selectively with some types of individuals, and less so with others. Here, then, is a brief *to do* list for ready reference use in deciding what specific types of adaptations are more appropriate when you are interacting with each of the four types of different individuals.

These four basic development action strategies for increasing flexibility and versatility are a good starting point for

Action Plan . . .

Steady Relaters

Cultivate a casual, easy going, personable, one-on-one relationship. Treat them with . . . warmth, feeling, and sensitivity

Cautious Thinkers

Use an orderly, logical, accurate approach which zeroes in on the process and procedures. Give them well thought-out, accurate documentation

Dominant Directors

Get right to the point quickly and decisively without getting bogged down in minute details. Operate with conviction, know what you're doing, and don't try to bluff

Interacting Socializers

Show your energy and liveliness while focusing on the give-and-take interaction. Make your encounter fun, upbeat and enjoyable!

increasing your own effectiveness. But based on the natural human condition, they tend to be ongoing challenges. Therefore, a second approach which complements this lifelong *road map* focuses on one of the many adaptability strengths noted above.

To see how this might work, picture some well-known characters who are generally agreed to be lower in either flexibility or versatility. The classic TV character Archie Bunker is a great example of low flexibility. As we review the prior list of higher flexibility strengths, notice how Archie could improve his relationships and his management of situations if he chose to work at developing four of the five strengths mentioned: tolerance, respect for others, empathy, and being more positive.

Another vintage TV character who is quite flexible—at times, too much so—but quite low in his versatility is Gilligan, the feature character of GILLIGAN'S ISLAND. He could be a more successful person if he develops the following key strengths of a versatile person: vision (the foresight to think ahead before letting himself get drawn into unfavorable situations); attentiveness (tuning in to what is going on around him); being realistic (about the motives and methods of other people); and competence (being both more self-initiating/evaluating and using a problem-solving approach). The benefit to Gilligan of his increased versatility would be reduced dependence on others to define both the problems he must deal with and the solutions he must put into action—without his consideration of whether their ideas will be in his best interests.

Creating Personal Power
Through Increased Adaptability

A wise person once commented, "A little knowledge can be a dangerous thing." In the field of formal education, this quote is sometimes called the sophomoric syndrome. That is, as people begin to learn about a new topic, they tend to jump to oversimplified and incomplete conclusions. When that happens, they are often less successful than is possible. But with continuing effort, thought, and increased study, they eventually graduate to a higher level of excellence. In terms of adaptability, this means it is essential for us to understand the following principles:

1. Adaptability is not a goal in and of itself, but a means to the end of increased personal effectiveness and success.
2. A key to effectiveness is to realize what level and type of adaptability component(s) are the critical factors in achieving a targeted goal.
   Examples:
   "The key to getting this sale is to be a lot more flexible than I am naturally with this type of strong-willed person."

   "If I don't lower my already high tendency to be overly flexible and accommodating, I'm likely to continue giving away the store. Conditions have changed and I can't afford to do that any longer because it conflicts with the results I'm looking for."
3. Being adaptable also means assessing the other available resources which can allow you to get your desired outcomes by acting smarter.
   Example:
   While you have developed the competencies required to successfully complete a known task, you work with three other people who also possess these same talents. But they don't have the same pressing, competing priorities facing them as you. So in this case, adaptability also includes having the vision and self-corrective aptitudes to seek out one or more available resources to help you appropriately manage your adaptabilities. Isn't that better than trying to be superhuman and doing it all yourself?

Adaptability, then, is important because it directly relates to your degree of achieved success in a wide variety of life's opportunities. These range from relationships to other people, to coping with changing conditions around you, to managing of different types of situations.

Extreme behavior can raise others' tensions

At times people may perceive extreme adaptability as acting wishy-washy, sashaying back and forth across the fence line, or acting two-faced. Former California Governor Jerry Brown had that problem when he ran for President. His flexibility disintegrated into vacillation on the issues to the degree that some reporters dubbed him the human windshield wiper.

Additionally, a person who maintains high adaptability in all situations may not be able to avoid personal stress and ultimate inefficiency. This was suggested previously by the superperson myth of doing it all yourself. There is also the danger of developing tension from the stress of behaving in a *foreign* manner with others. This is usually temporary and may in fact be worth it if you gain rapport with the other person.

The other extreme of the continuum is no behavioral adaptability. This causes people to view someone as rigid and uncompromising. He insists on behaving at his own pace and priority. An example is Stephanie Vander Kellan, the fish-out-of-water maid on THE BOB NEWHART SHOW.

Adaptability is important to successful relationships of all kinds. People often adopt at least a partially different role in their professional lives than they do in their social and personal lives. This is to successfully manage the professional requirements of their jobs. Interestingly, many people tend to be more adaptable at work with people they know less and less adaptable at home with people they know better. Why? People generally want to create a good impression at work, but at home may *relax and act themselves* to the point of unintentionally stepping on other family members' toes. Not an attractive family portrait, but often an accurate one.

We can gain a better understanding of how adaptability impacts the effective management of situations by looking at its application to a variety of professions and their related role or job requirements. This process is essentially the same one which is used by major selection, recruiting, and career development consulting firms around the world. To better acquaint you with this process, we'll examine a public service profession familiar to you—the Presidency of the United States. What does that job require from the perspective of the general voting public who have the power to select and replace this job holder?

To better understand this concept, compare the competing choices or finalists for this job in two of the elections. Incidentally, both elections included candidates with distinctly different types of behavioral styles. Picture Ronald Reagan (a Dominant Director with strong Interacting Socializer tendencies) versus Jimmy Carter (a Steady Relater); and George Bush (a Steady Relater) versus Michael Dukakis (a Cautious Thinker).

Ronald Reagan was a classic case of high flexibility who, as an actor in the White House, dazzled people with his different moves, about-faces, and social adeptness. Most critics, however, gave him low marks for his performance abilities or versatility: increased budget deficits, mass dismissal of staff for improper public performance, and lack of knowledge of specifics related to various critical tasks.

In contrast, Jimmy Carter was viewed as a highly qualified individual in terms of versatility, but he projected only a moderate level of flexibility regarding his willingness to play ball with other officials. Similarly, Michael Dukakis was perceived as having moderate-to-high versatility (the well-informed man who brought Massachusetts back from its legislature's well-documented mismanagement through its political *football games*), but he became known as "poker-faced Mike" in the Presidential campaign. In other words, he was seen as a highly inflexible individual who was not open to others' points or concerns.

Compare him with George Bush, a moderately flexible man. To capsulize the observations of many commentators, "There's not much choice between the two as the public views it—it seems to be which is the least undesirable of the two candidates." Whether or not these perceptions are true is questionable, but they reflect the reality of the desired characteristics of a Presidential jobholder requiring higher flexibility and a moderate to-higher level of versatility.

You can profile any role or job in the same way. That's

not to say a person's behavioral style isn't also important.
After all, there have been more people who exhibit aspects
of Dominant Director and Interacting Socializer types who
have been elected to that highest public office than individuals with the other two styles (more about mixed styles in
Chapter 11). However, once in office, their levels of flexibility
and versatility distinguish the higher performers from the
lower performers. Again, with the sophomoric syndrome in
mind, let's take a deeper look at this concept as it relates to
some other types of position requirements. A sales job which
involves a single, simple product line is most likely to require
high flexibility, but may not require much versatility. Another
sales job involving multiple products that are complex and
changing usually requires both high flexibility and high versatility. Contrast this with the position of nuclear researcher which
requires very high versatility, but much lower flexibility. This
lower flexibility actually protects this person and others from
being open to trying possibilities that may literally blow up in
their faces. Finally, picture the job requirements of a single
working parent of two teenagers. Here again, versatility is the
key ingredient in managing the myriad of competing expectations and demands. Of course, a moderate level of flexibility allows the lid to stay on so peace and order prevail and
the children don't end up parenting the adult!

Adaptability works

Effectively adaptable people meet the key expectations of
others in specific situations—whether it's in personal or
business relationships. Through attention and practice, you
can achieve a balance of strategically managing your adaptability by recognizing when a modest compromise is appropriate. You'll also understand when it's necessary to adapt
to the other person's behavioral style.
Practice managing relationships in a way that allows everyone to win. Be tactful, reasonable, understanding, non-judgmental, and comfortable to talk to. This results in a moderate
position between the two extremes. You're able to better meet
the needs of the other person as well as your own. Adapt
your pace and priority. Work at relationships so everybody

wins at work, with friends, on dates, and with family.

So self-knowledge of how Direct/Indirect and Supporting/Controlling you are provides help in better dealing with yourself and others. Just as you discovered your own unique behavioral type and the characteristics that go along with it, you'll learn to identify others' key strengths and weaknesses. Recognizing *sterling traits* and potential pitfalls of diverse people means you can better understand their behaviors and relate more effectively with them.

When you try to accommodate the other person's expectations and tendencies, you automatically decrease tension and increase trust. Adaptability enables you to interact more productively with difficult people, helps you in strained situations, and assists you in establishing rapport and credibility. It can make the difference between a productive or an ineffective interpersonal relationship. And your adaptability level also influences how others judge their relationships with you. Raise your adaptability level—trust and credibility soar; lower your adaptability level—trust and credibility plummet.

Another way of looking at this whole matter is from the perspective of maturity. Mature persons know who they are. They understand their basic behavioral type and freely express their core patterns. However, when problems or opportunities arise, they readily and deliberately make whatever adjustments are necessary in their core patterns to meet the need. Immature persons, on the other hand, lose effectiveness in dealing with the real world when they lock into their own style. By disregarding the needs of others, they end up causing conflict and tension which lead to less satisfaction and fulfillment in their life environments.

There are four key payoffs which make our efforts at becoming more mature and adaptable worth the effort. These benefits define the characteristics of people who are the higher performers in life. By reading, reflecting, and then taking the guided actions suggested in this book, you too can achieve this same level of excellence in your own life. The only questions are whether you wish to become more:

- successful
- effective

- satisfied
- fulfilled

If so, then today is your first opportunity to get started based on what you've already learned in these first four chapters. Now you can read the remaining chapters for even more powerful insights about how you can become all that you can truly be.

Part Two

Workplace Applications

People Smart Principle #5—The Principle of Complementarity: "People have the potential to complement other types of individuals at work tasks."

Chapter 5
On the Job

Problem-solving in the workplace

As you read this chapter, think of specific individuals you know at work who represent each of the four behavioral styles—Dominant Director, Interacting Socializer, Steady Relater, and Cautious Thinker. How can you apply what you learn about them to improve your working relationships with each one? What are some characteristics that work to the advantage of these people in their job performance? Which characteristics work against them?

It can be most helpful for your increased understanding of the connection between your behavioral type and your daily work performance to realize these four tendencies define the way you go about your work. In other words, they describe your *work style* or *how you actually perform your work duties*.

All jobs essentially involve different types of problem-solving tasks which have to be achieved to ensure satisfactory job performance. And, since such job requirements differ, so too does the degree of natural match or fit with your own preferred behavior pattern. As jobs become more complex, they call for increased adaptability to fulfill these job expectations which may be quite different from your own sources of natural inner motivation. Let's look further at how adaptability is critical in influencing these four behavior patterns. The graphic entitled "Our Problem-Solving Work Styles" provides you with a summary illustration of the four distinctly different types of problem-solving approaches to your daily work efforts.

Dominant Director Behavior in a Work Setting

Preferred jobs

Higher power positions and career areas where they can take charge
- President or CEO; i, e., the formally recognized leader
- Politician
- Policeman/woman
- Military officer
- Executive or manager
- Entrepreneur
- Owner of his or her own company
- General contractor

"I'll solve that problem"

A typical Dominant Director point of view consists of seeing himself as a problem-oriented manager who enjoys a challenge just because it's there. He likes the opportunity to complete tasks in a creative manner—which aligns with his way, of course! He's independent, strong-willed, restless, and goal-oriented. Other people tend to view him as having a high level of confidence, although this may not be the case. However, when he reads something he doesn't understand, he may instinctively react as if it must be a misprint. His self-image is high, and so is his output.

Because of their drive for specific and concrete results, Dominant Directors often put in extra hours at the office. At the extreme, their high results orientation can manifest in an overextended work pattern. When this happens, they pay a high price for their success—their personal and social lives may fall apart from neglect while their work-related attainments accumulate.

PROBLEM-SOLVING WORK STYLES

The Dominant Director (D) Style	The Interacting Socializer (I) Style
– Pragmatic – Reactive – Decisive – Competitive – Harsh	– Supporting – Trusting – Instinctive – Exploring – Appeasing
The Cautious Thinker (C) Style	**The Steady Relater (S) Style**
– Analyzing – Evaluating – Planning – Investigating – Critical	– Observing – Reflecting – Implementing – Applying – Avoiding

D's can juggle faster than the eye can see

When the Dominant Director perceives others' output as less than exemplary, he may react with a message to stimulate others to action: "Don't just stand there. Do something!" Dominant Directors typically show administrative and leadership qualities that reflect their ability to initiate and accomplish tasks, then juggle them.

They have the ability to pick up three balls (tasks) and keep them all in the air at the same time. They're multiphasic behavior specialists—able to simultaneously do many things well. After adapting to juggling three balls, they pick up another and another. They end up juggling all of them faster than the eye can see where one begins and the other ends. However, the pressure mounts as they try to maximize the quantity of tasks or the quality of results.

Logically, it makes sense to drop one ball to relieve some of the pressure. Not so with the Dominant Director. Admission that they can't do it all tarnishes their macho image. They like impressing other styles with their workloads until they get bored or tired of not-enough-hours-in-the-day balancing acts. Then they drop everything to take up a new direction or focus for their activities until they tire of the same pattern again. Dominant Directors typically refer to this as *reordering priorities*.

Efficiency is the name of the game

Adult Dominant Directors often like to accumulate items—especially ones they think will save time or money. Efficiency is the name of the game. One Dominant Director told us he's so impatient that he never buys green tomatoes. Another one is exhilarated by the fast-forward feature which lets her eliminate the time taken up by TV commercials as she plays her VCR. A third enjoys using her car phone so she doesn't have to waste time while driving, let alone stopping for pay phones; she can't wait to get others to implement her ideas. Yet another tells his secretary to *fax* his mail to him when he's away from the office.

Despite their *strongman* images, D's, too, have their own unique limitations. They're selective listeners who tend to tune out small talk. To increase their adaptability, their listening skills and awareness of others' needs require improvement. Instead of telling others what to do, hearing their thoughts and opinions can help them get things done more smoothly--for the good of everyone involved. Otherwise, people may interpret the Dominant Director's behavior as, "When I want your opinion, I'll give it to you."

Consequently, Dominant Directors tend to work more favorably with complementary types who contribute stability, predictability, and support towards their common objectives. Each of these other types can help the Dominant Director put tasks into perspective, recharge his or her batteries, or bolster a temporarily bruised ego. Other people's feedback can also help D's stay on track in terms of objectivity, accuracy, and responsiveness to others' needs.

D leaders

The Dominant Director is an outspoken, no-nonsense, take control type of individual. *Give 'Em Hell* Harry Truman summed up the Director's work-style attitude with his now famous statement: "If you can't stand the heat, get out of the kitchen." In fact, many Presidents of the United States have shared this same Dominant behavioral tendency with Harry. They include John F. Kennedy, Franklin D. Roosevelt, and Ronald Reagan. Each of them exhibited a personal need to decisively lead--including their willingness to use force to do it, if required. And each of them preferred the roads to the most direct action for fast results. When under stress, they lashed out and forcefully took charge in differing ways. All can be described as either strong, hard to budge, or both.

Generals George Patton and Napoleon Bonaparte, two Dominant Director military leaders, depict this "Go for the gusto!" "No guts, no glory!" perspective of their type. In battle, Dominant Director mottos translate to *Charge!* or *Follow me!* but not necessarily in that order. When taken to the extreme, Dominant Directors may, at times, seem to live by the watchwords, "Ready! Fire! Aim!" because they tend to naturally plunge in without a lot of risk-assessing forethought.

They may not be too busy for that, after all

Sometimes others may interpret the Dominant Director's hustle and impatience as, "Don't interrupt me. I'm busy." Ironically, when this happens, the Dominant Director may sabotage the very control which he desires. If co-workers and employees perceive him as swamped with too much work, they may hesitate to disturb or delay him. So the Dominant Director may know less about what's happening than he would if he had made himself more accessible.

Risk-taking excites D's.

Consider car manufacturer John DeLorean—a maverick who broke some written and unwritten rules in pursuit of his goals. Dominant Directors don't feel as bound by conventional practices as the other types. "That's for other people, not me." The higher authority they prefer to answer to is themselves; they sense a need to be their own boss so they can have control over the results they want. Opportunities for change are sought or created just to satisfy their need for results. They gravitate toward high-risk situations because the excitement of challenges fuels their actions.

They may combine pleasure with business

Dominant Director Dan decided to give his employees a special surprise for Christmas—a combined business/pleasure trip to Honolulu. From bus excursions to daily seminars and discussion groups, Dan arranged everyone's itinerary. He thought his staff would eagerly embrace his plans, but was extremely disappointed to overhear a few of them complaining about his fixed agenda:

"Who does he think he is? Giving us a supposed vacation and bouncing us around in workshops and seminars, not to mention spending every breathing minute with him!"

"Yes, I know what you mean. Just once, I wish he'd ask us what we want instead of doing what he wants."

"Here, here!"

Dan's first impulse was to rush in and tell those ingrates a thing or three, but he held himself back and decided to call his wife Jean to tell her what happened:

"I can understand their point, Dan. It sounds as though they just want to be part of the decision-making process instead of your telling them what to do," Jean observed.

"Hmmm. I guess the way I did it could seem a bit autocratic."

"I'm glad you see it that way, Dan," said Jean.

"Maybe I'll call an informal meeting so they can let me know just what they want," Dan decided.

So he did. The employees thanked him, but also told him they'd like a few days just to be with their families without having to check in with anyone but themselves.

"Is that all?" Dan asked. The group agreed. "This was a lot easier than I thought it would be," Dan observed.

Fortunately, Dan put himself in his employees' shoes and became willing to see their point of view—they wanted to help decide. For Dan, it seemed much easier to make the decisions and then tell everybody else to follow through. But what he wanted and what they wanted didn't necessarily match.

We know an elementary school principal who chose to manage her school in typical Dominant Director fashion—her way. She decided to arbitrarily rescind the privilege for parents to request teachers for their children because reading all those forms *wasted her secretary's time*. The parents had different ideas and became angry they hadn't been consulted. The resulting furor could have been prevented if she had only stopped to ask, "What do you think?" Actually, she didn't even have to do what the parents wanted, so long as she got their input. They resented her *dictatorial approach*.

The principal, following her Dominant Director instincts, focused on the result, not the steps leading to it. To accomplish that end, she tried to shape the environment by overcoming the opposition. Unfortunately for her, she discovered the parents didn't necessarily want their environment shaped, especially without their feedback. Even benevolent dictators collide with their subjects when they try to rule by themselves.

People, products, and profits

Lee Iacocca, another person with a Director work style, talks about how he learned to merge his temperament with other styles as he finally arrived at the following management philosophy, as described in his biography, *Iacocca*: "In the end, all business operations can be reduced to three words: people, products, profits. People come first. Unless you have a good team, you can't do much with the other two." Iacocca, a living Dominant Director legend, illustrates the fact that collaborative team playing pays off for Dominant people and others!

Hail to the chief!

Since he views himself as a chief, not just one of the tribe, the Dominant Director may resist deeper involvement in work teams. Stress, especially, brings out his natural apprehensiveness about people. When under duress, he may even seize control and make himself the leader—his natural *me first* tendency. Do you remember this happening when former general Alexander Haig tried to take charge when President Reagan was shot? Additional well-known Dominant Directors include IT'S ALL IN THE FAMILY's Archie Bunker, Margaret Thatcher, Dan Rather, FAMILY TIES' Alex P. Keaton, and Barbara Walters.

Consequently, the Dominant Director needs a co-worker who draws him into the group. Dominant Directors often take themselves too seriously and can benefit from gentle reminders to take life less seriously and laugh at themselves.

Competition motivates D's

Because he's so competitive, he may view himself as participating in perpetual contests with others. Other styles may see themselves as merely giving reports—period. Not so for the Dominant Director. His report jockeys for position against yours. He needs to have control, so one-upmanship can become one of his favorite games. In this extreme Dominant Director game, he fills the role of the all-seeing, all-knowing expert. Everyone else, by contrast, becomes a babbling idiot. Not a particularly appetizing thought for the rest of us.

D's can learn how to occasionally walk away

He can also help himself by learning when to walk away from a project and let others assume control. Otherwise, his tendency to hold on can frustrate the other types. People also tend to respond more favorably to the Dominant Director when he verbalizes the reasons for his conclusions and paces himself to project a more relaxed state. He can also soften his propensity for reprimanding others by tempering criticism with healthy doses of genuinely appreciative praise. Otherwise, about the only time you'll hear a Dominant Director say, "Well done!" is when he orders a steak.

Remember, people have feelings

As natural doers, they may need some help channeling their energies. Why? Because they may have trouble distinguishing the realistic from the awe-inspiring. Of all the types, this one is the most likely to try even harder if told, "That's impossible."

When Dominant Directors learn to become aware of other people's feelings, they become more successful in developing satisfying relationships with them. Since this type has a natural inclination toward authoritarianism, he can work on recognizing when it's appropriate to consciously back off, slow down his fast pace, and listen more to other people's opinions, ideas, and concerns. Besides bolstering his people skills, he can also attend to analyzing tasks more thoroughly. He instinctively wants to hurry on to the next challenge, but he can ward off many problems that result from his typical hastiness by learning more details about projects than he would otherwise seek out.

Other behavioral types may not share the Dominant Director's preferences for quick results and blunt straightforwardness. Becoming less rigid in his direct approach with others, he can better learn to manage the differences between people and modify his own.

Remember . . .

DOMINANT DIRECTOR
BUSINESS CHARACTERISTICS

- Prefer time frames
- Seek personal control
- Get to the point
- Strive to feel important and be noteworthy in their jobs
- Demonstrate persistence and single-mindedness to reach a goal
- Express high ego strength
- Prefer to downplay feelings and relationships
- Focus on task actions that lead to achieving tangible outcomes
- Implement changes in the workplace
- Tend to freely delegate duties, enabling them to take on more projects

DOMINANT DIRECTOR:
PREFERRED BUSINESS SITUATIONS

- Like to call the shots and tell others what to do
- Like challenging workloads which fuel their energy levels
- Tend to personally oversee, or at least know about, their employees' or co-workers' business activities
- Like to say what's on their minds without being concerned about hurting anybody's feelings
- Enjoy taking risks and being involved in changes
- Prefer to interpret the *rules* and answer to themselves alone
- Interested in the answers to *what* questions, not *how* ones
- Like to see a logical road toward increasing and ongoing advancement, since *bigger is better* to them

At Work with the Interacting Socializer

Preferred job positions
Careers that maximize influence with people where they can socialize, mingle, and gain positive feedback

- Public relations
- Entertainment—acting, singing, reporting, public speaking —being on stage or in the public eye
- Professional host or hostess (talk show, party, restaurant, airline, etc.)
- Recreation director
- Politician
- Personnel interviewer
- Salesperson

People are their business

The Interacting Socializer likes to be treated with warmth, friendliness, and approval. Because he favors interacting with people on more than just a business level, he wants to be your friend before he does business with you. If a client suggests meeting for lunch, a social drink, or dinner and asks things like, "What exciting things are happening with you?" you're probably dealing with an Interacting Socializer.

Like the Dominant Director, the Interacting Socializer shares a quick pace. While the Dominant Director busies himself with tasks, the Interacting Socializer tends to move about the office in a flurry of activity. He even walks in a way that reflects his optimism and quick pace . . . lively and energetically. He observes and "sight-sees" as he goes, avoiding obstacles and potential problems.

I's like to bounce ideas off others

Interacting Socializers think out loud. Desks confine them, so they typically stroll around the office talking to nearly everyone, from the custodian to the boss along the way, calling them by their first names. All the while they seek others' reactions to almost anything and everything, but they visibly warm up to comments about themselves.

Non-Interacting styles may view Interacting Irv's behavior

as goofing off. "That Irv spends more time gabbing at the soda machine than he does working. What does he get paid for, anyway?" But, appearances may fool us. While Irv weaves his way toward a drink, he bounces ideas off the people along the way. "John, if you got a coupon in the mail for free dessert at Cafe Eduardo's with any dinner for two, would you go? I'm working on new advertising possibilities for them. What would motivate you to try a new restaurant?"

Irv often doesn't merely talk—he actually brainstorms out loud with virtually anyone he encounters. It's important for him to find out how other people feel about his ideas. He likes the feedback and the occasional pats on the back which his conversations provide. He enjoys a casual, relaxed environment where he can allow his impulses free rein. Desk-hopping also satisfies his need for companionship. Like other Interacting Socializers, he seeks out people to first share the present, with one eye on future additional experiences with them. Talking with co-workers happily mixes business with pleasure for this type. They like to play and mingle as they learn, earn, and do practically everything else.

I's seek "people power" positions

Since the Interacting Socializer is naturally talkative and people-oriented, these positions of people power meet his needs for inclusion by others, popularity, social recognition, and (probably) freedom from a lot of detail. They utilize his natural strengths. As with the other types, jobs do not equal behavioral type; but many Interacting Socializers tend to gravitate toward people-oriented, high visibility professions to fill their innate needs.

Take Disneyland employees, for example. Disneyland seems to hire vast numbers of Interacting Socializers who act as peppy and people-oriented at 10 p.m. as they did at 10 a.m. Tour guides usually still smile and carry on verbal repartees with guests at the end of their shifts. This characteristic cannot be taught; employees either become energized by mingling with people, or they don't. Interacting Socializers do. Disneyland even provides people-free *decompression* areas for their employees during breaks so they can maintain their positive energy levels with guests.

They're smooth-talking dreamers

At heart, the Interacting Socializer is a dreamer who is good at getting others caught up in his ideas. His persuasive powers may simultaneously amaze his admirers and frustrate his detractors. The Interacting Socializer shows smooth-talking tendencies which, at the extreme, can be interpreted as either silver-tongued oration or evasive double-talk. Or he can appear to be a verbal Pied Piper with a seemingly unending gift of gab or a wheeling and dealing chatterbox.

Chin up!

As a leader, the Interacting Socializer likes spontaneous, expressive actions for noticeable results. "Chin up! Think positively," he may say, to encourage his employees, peers, or superiors to function smoothly. Statements like "Follow that dream," and "Climb every mountain," sum up Interacting Socializer feelings. Though typically somewhat less motivated by change than Dominant Directors, Interacting Socializers become more susceptible to risk-taking when pressured by others to take the chance. If they haven't fully considered the ramifications, they may regret their impulsiveness after it's too late.

A classic Interacting Socializer who sought the U. S. Presidency was Hubert Horatio Humphrey, the charismatic Minnesota Senator. When he died, he received a stately funeral with more attention and sympathy than many who had won the Presidency. Without such triumph, he moved the hearts of the entire nation.

What do I's want at work?

Interacting Socializers want companionship and social recognition, so their contributions to group morale often satisfy these needs. At work, they like to know everybody's first name and something about everyone. They can benefit from feedback from their co-workers, especially those who represent other behavioral types. Just as Steady Relaters contribute stability, Cautious Thinkers seek accuracy, and

Dominant Directors add decisiveness, Interacting Socializers give their enthusiasm and energy. Tactfully reminding and assisting them so they will prioritize and organize can help the entire office function more smoothly. Since Interacting Socializers tend to be *open books*, the other types can detect when they are having an off day and give them a boost with a compliment or two.

As true extroverts, Interacting Socializers typically look outside themselves to renew their energies. They enjoy motivating books, tapes, and speeches—pick-me-ups that recharge their batteries to help them overcome obstacles. These are viewed as practical growth opportunities. They even prefer the terms *opportunity* or *challenge* instead of *problem*. A problem is too mired in negativism to comfortably fit with an Interacting Socializer's optimistic nature.

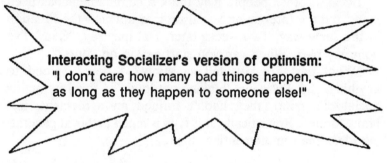

Interacting Socializer's version of optimism:
"I don't care how many bad things happen, as long as they happen to someone else!"

They prefer the "big picture"

As inductive thinkers, Interacting Socializers naturally think first about the big picture, then of supporting details. After seeing the broad overview, they prefer not to personally dwell on specifics. "Collins can work out the details." Interacting Socializers are intuitive and may naturally come up with assorted ideas—some practical, some not—but if they *feel right* to them, they *talk up* those ideas to others to elicit their feedback and enthusiasm. This can also serve the purpose of pulling Interacting Socializers back to reality if they venture too far out into *La-La Land* (one Dominant Director's description of this behavior at its most extreme). "Earth to Fred, earth to Fred!" may get an Interacting Socializer who's become too carried away back on course by using one of his own techniques—humor.

I's think out loud

Since Interacting Socializers like to talk more than average —to others and to themselves—they're likely to say inappropriate things more often than most of the other types. When talkativeness and emotionality mix, then hoof-in-mouth problems may set in with this behavioral type. Learning when to stop talking and start listening can help Interacting Socializers grow. Sometimes their naturally impulsive behaviors energize us; at other times their spontaneity requires more restraint.

They're idea people who throw ideas out. "Hal, we could do this (and this, or this, etc.)." This impulsive habit can get them in trouble. Why?

Because other people may think a commitment has been made, but the Interacting Socializer may not view the situation in the same way. Two weeks later, Hal may say, "Okay, I've done my part. When can you start action on yours?"

"What part are you talking about? I never agreed to anything, Hal. I was just thinking out loud." In this Interacting Socializer's mind, they hadn't formed an agreement, just brainstormed. Realistically, this type is much better at generating ideas than implementing them.

Fire! Fire! Fire!

Interacting Socializers can pump up their flexibility by better controlling their time and emotions and by developing a more objective mind set. They can benefit by spending more time checking, verifying, specifying, and organizing, or getting someone else to do it for them. Otherwise, Interacting Socializers may succumb to their excitable *Fire! Fire! Fire!* tendencies. If they concentrate on the task and take a more logical approach, then they can improve their follow-through.

For instance, Interacting Socializers may have so many things going that they may forget to finish tasks by a deadline; or they procrastinate until the last minute because of their multiple priorities. Writing things down and prioritizing can help the Interacting Socializer remember when to do what

Remember . . .

INTERACTING SOCIALIZER
BUSINESS CHARACTERISTICS

- Like to brainstorm and interact with colleagues and others
- Want freedom from control, details, or complexity
- Like to have the chance to influence or motivate others
- Like the feeling of being a key part of an exciting team
- Want to be included by others in important projects, activities, or events
- Get easily bored by routine and repetition
- May trust others without reservation—take others at their word and don't check for themselves
- Typically have short attention spans, so they do well with many short breaks

INTERACTING SOCIALIZER PREFERRED
BUSINESS SITUATIONS

- Like to work participatively with others
- Need immediate feedback to get, or stay, on course
- Like to mingle with all levels of associates and call them by their first names
- Enjoy compliments about themselves and their accomplishments
- Seek stimulating environments that are friendly and favorable
- Motivated to work toward known, specific, quickly attainable incentives or external motivators (dislike pursuits which drag out over long time periods)
- Open to verbal or demonstrated guidance for transferring ideas into action
- Like to start projects and let others finish them

with whom. They can benefit from handy pocket calendars that go everywhere with them. If you fit the M. O. of this type, you can forget about using some little corner of an envelope to write on— you're probably too impatient to riffle through piles of paperwork to find it later.

Steady Relater Behavior at Work

Preferred job situations

Secure positions and careers where they can specialize in some areas and be part of a team
- Financial services
- Social worker
- Family doctor/nurse
- Residential or community services
- Teacher
- Personal assistant/secretary
- Insurance agent
- Librarian
- Customer service representative

Stability motivates them

In business and in their personal lives, Steady Relaters take one day at a time and may consciously avoid gambles and uncertainties. They tend to respect traditions and often demonstrate loyalty to everyone else while they trek along. Because stability in the workplace motivates them, Steady Relaters are apt to have the most compatible of all working relationships with each of the four types. Steady Relaters have patience, staying power, and stick-to-it-ivity, so they commit themselves to making relationships work.

They are extremely uncomfortable with conflict. In the workplace, this type may notice how others complete their tasks, but typically say nothing negative about their observations (with the possible exception of a close friend or family member). Why? They don't want to make waves and they don't want to appear to be know-it-alls. Silently, Steady

Relaters may think they're shouldering the lion's share of duties, but they generally won't tell the boss or fellow employees. They'll just continue performing their own work and make the best of it.

"Be prepared"

If they need to make a presentation, Steady Relaters will probably thoroughly prepare and organize their material in advance. Since they feel comfortable with proven methods, they like to carefully acquaint themselves with each step of a procedure so they can duplicate it later. When taken to an extreme, this adherence to following instructions and maintaining the status quo can limit their actions.

Since Steady Relaters wear well and favor step-by-step procedures, they're natural choices for assisting/tutoring others, maintaining existing performance levels, and organizing systems. They often enjoy helping set up or implement guidelines that allow others to be more organized. Remember, Steady Relaters are the ones who assemble all their equipment first, set up their tools, and begin to work only when everything is in place.

For instance, when she's ready to collate, Steady Relater Paula places all the pages in descending order on a table. Next, she places *Tacky Finger* on one side of the desk, then a stapler on the other, extra staples close to that, and finally a large enough opening near page one for the completed stacks. When everything is ready, she begins to work on the completion of this task. Many a Dominant Director and Interacting Socializer who initially rolled their eyeballs at what they viewed as a laborious preparation stage have later found themselves marvelling at such assembly line efficiency. At this point, a sincere compliment on her work procedure might be both appropriate and welcome. "Paula, your collating technique is more efficient than I could have imagined, let alone be likely to do myself."

The typical Dominant Director may want to delegate and oversee such a procedure: "Paula, you can start without assembling all that paraphernalia, can't you?" But for Steady Relaters, that's not a comfortable approach because they're advocates of the *Be Prepared* and *Plan Ahead* schools of thought. An Interacting Socializer may tend to haphazardly set up such a collating area, possibly on the floor, and omit key items like extra staples or adequate copies of page 13. "Darn, I need to go to the closet again," or, "Oh, no! I'll have to run to the store for more paper." Both of these individuals can waste more time than they thought they'd save because they didn't prepare as well as the Steady Relater.

Both the personalized people factor and going along with established practices rate high with this type. So when problems bombard Steady Relaters, they try to solve them by helping or working with others, following tried and true procedures, or a combination of the two. If these tactics fail, they may quietly do nothing. Doing nothing may include higher absenteeism—when conflict and stress increase, Steady Relater tolerance may decrease.

"Are we ready yet?"

As with any trait, the Steady Relater's propensity for studying procedures and doing repetitious tasks can sometimes be taken to an extreme. For instance, the following anecdote about the Steady Relater type illustrates this point. After completing the frescoes on the ceilings of the Sistine Chapel, the Pope asked Michelangelo (a Cautious Thinker, our next type) to draw up architectural plans for St. Peter's Cathedral. Since Michelangelo had passed his 80th birthday, he drew up the massive and complex plans in less than two years and then turned them over to his most promising apprentice—a Steady Relater. This slower moving cohort's approach to implementing these plans was to study them step by step, day after day, year after year, time and again. Finally—after 23 years—he was ready to direct his efforts to the actual building of this world famous cathedral.

Service is their business

Steady Relaters tend to gravitate toward relationships which provide them with security, stability, and large doses of routine; these positions satisfy some of their rather maternal or paternal needs. While we know that not all elementary school teachers are Steady Relaters. Yet this personality type is inclined to pursue careers that fit their natural desire for repeated group and one-to-one people contact, preference for sameness, and the opportunity to help or support others. Personally, we've observed many Steady Relater pre-school, elementary, and middle school teachers—especially among those employees reporting higher levels of job satisfaction.

Service is Tony Gwynn's business

If the job doesn't necessarily fit a Steady Relater's requirements, then, like the other styles, he too may shape it accordingly to fit with his personal performance style. For instance, even when Tony Gwynn, the three-time champion National League batter, seemingly single-handedly wins a baseball game, he has been quoted as saying things like, "I couldn't have done it without a lot of help from my other teammates. Today's game was a real group effort." On the other hand, a typical Dominant Director may respond: "Well, it's because I've been practicing so hard that I had this outstanding performance that resulted in our winning today's game." He may toss in a salute to his teammates as an afterthought, but the primary focus of his remarks is clear—he did it. Similarly, an Interacting Socializer may bask in the adoration of his fans. "Moments like this make it all worthwhile." He may include his team in the spotlight, too, but not as easily, as often, or as naturally as the Steady Relater does.

In a community service role, Steady Tony Gwynn volunteered to emcee at an award ceremony for an elementary school Jog-a-thon, casually dressed in a sweat suit and old baseball cap. Shortly after he congratulated all the runners for their hard work, he commented, "Kids, I'm so nervous standing up here in front of you that my knees are knocking together. Playing baseball is one thing; but talking to all of you is another." Although Tony Gwynn was apparently not as at home in the speaking arena, he still couldn't refuse doing a good deed by servicing the kids of his community.

Actions speak louder than words

Inherently modest and accommodating, Steady Relaters usually think their actions speak for themselves. While Dominant Directors and Interacting Socializers pat themselves on the backs, Steady Relaters tend to simply nod and listen. Inwardly, they may want to divulge a personal triumph, but they won't volunteer it. If someone asks them about it, fine. Or, better yet, an ally may pipe up about the Steady Relater's coup. Steady Relaters tend to adopt a *Me last, if there's time*, attitude. At work, this type may think he should get a promotion, but is likely to just wait for the boss to notice what a good job he's doing, rather than bring it to his supervisor's attention.

S leaders

Politically, Steady Relaters act approachable and down-to-earth. Consider President Dwight D. Eisenhower, who also served as NATO's Supreme Allied Commander during World War II. His Presidential campaign button said simply, "I like Ike!" a Relater-like understatement if there ever was one. The man was probably one of our most popular Presidents ever. Voters warmed to his down-to-earth, *Aw, shucks* mannerisms and easygoing smile. But despite their likability, Steady Relaters naturally have difficulty taking tough stands. Both President Gerald Ford and Vice President "Fritz" Mondale have shared this problem, as did U.S. Vietnam military leader General George Abrams.

Steady Relater military leaders go by the book—a manifestation of their deductive, convergent, left brain orientations. They are driven by a basic need to use predictable, steady actions to yield known, proven results. At the most extreme, their battle cry is *Ready! Ready! Ready!* In fact, they might still be getting ready when the enemy fires. Then they may react by saying to others in their group, "Hold the fort!" Or "Toe the line!" Or "What's the SOP (standard operating procedure) for us to follow in this kind of situation?"

S's want to be part of the group

Since Steady Relaters seek security and inclusion with the group, they can contribute to the workplace with their natural planning skills, consistent pace, and their desire to fit in. Like Interacting Socializers, they favor work relationships on a casual, first-name basis; but Steady Relaters generally prefer developing special, more in depth friendships with selected co-workers than do their social butterfly, Interacting Socializer counterparts. So while Interacting Socializers may talk to anyone who will listen, Steady Relaters prefer involvement with a closer group of confidants.

Steady Relaters also want stability, steadiness, and a calm atmosphere in the workplace. They contribute to harmony in the office, so they usually fit comfortably into the work environment, but they also often become overly dependent on using the same old methods over and over again. Sometimes these procedures include unnecessary steps needed when they learned the procedure, but which can now be discarded. They may improve their work productivity by using shortcuts that eliminate extra labor. Dominant Directors and Interacting Socializers can often help them with this. And, when asked, Cautious Thinkers can generally demonstrate new ways to get things done through other processes.

Why change?

The Steady Relater is the optimistic realist among the four types. A pragmatist, he likes to do routine things with familiar people to maintain the same situation. He performs regularly and deliberately toward this end of holding onto or striving for continuity, peace, and orderliness. Changes and surprises make him uncomfortable because they alter the current formula. Instead, he prefers to refine existing practices.

"Modesty is the best policy"

Just as they may think their own job performance needs no self-promotion, they may think (not say) the same about others' work. "I wish John would stop boasting about what a wonderful job he does. He seems to spend half the day promoting himself, rather than doing the work that's already

Remember . . .

**STEADY RELATER
BUSINESS CHARACTERISTICS**

- Need to know the order of procedures
- Operate well as members of a work group
- Motivated by usual, known, and proven practices
- Oriented toward more concrete, repeatable actions
- Want order and ability in the workplace
- Focus on how and when to do things
- Work in a steady and predictable manner
- Like a long-term relationship with their business place and their fellow employees

**STEADY RELATER:
PREFERRED BUSINESS SITUATIONS**

- Like to perform the same kinds of duties day by day (no matter what the importance of the type of work involved)
- Prefer to work cooperatively with others to achieve common results
- Dislike taking risks
- Enjoy working in a stable, steady, low-key environment which has a minimum of changes
- Like to know each step toward completing their duties
- Prefer to make decisions by group consensus or other accepted practices rather than by themselves
- Enjoy feeling like valued members of the work group

on his desk." They often figure that if the boss (or anyone else) doesn't see what's going on, they don't want to have to be the ones to confront others about this unpleasant reality.

How do they know, unless they see it themselves?

Steady Relaters operate predominantly from a deductive perspective. Instead of naturally sensing (Dominant Director), or feeling (Interacting Socializer), Steady Relaters think about things: "I think that something is really troubling John. His eyes are bloodshot, he's short-tempered and edgy, and he's been getting to work about an hour late for two days in a row." Even their feelings about others seem to be based on their thoughts about them. This ties in with the Steady Relater's more concrete or literal orientation. He often needs to see something with his own eyes before he's sure about it.

S's take the indirect route

As naturally interested listeners, Steady Relaters appreciate this same behavior from others. They like others who genuinely share a common interest in exchanging thoughts, feelings, and experiences. This sometimes takes some extra effort, however, because Steady Relaters tend to speak indirectly. They seldom come right out and say what's on their minds, especially if they think something may be amiss. For example, a Steady Relater may know that everyone thinks a certain employee isn't pulling his own weight or has brown-nosed his way to the executive suite. Yet when pressed on this situation, he's likely to respond, "I don't want to say anything. I'd rather you observe things for awhile and come to your own conclusions."

At Work with the Cautious Thinker

Preferred jobs

Careers in which they can strive for perfection, creativity, and completeness
- Forecasters (political, weather, etc.)
- Critics (film, history, literary, etc.)
- Engineers
- Research scientists
- Data analysts
- Accountants/auditors

- Artists/sculptors/architects
- Inventors

Process and perfection

They see themselves as problem-solvers who like structure, concentrate on key details, and ask specific questions about identified factors. They're masters at following important, established directions and standards, while still meeting the need to control the process by their own actions. Process-oriented, Cautious Thinkers want to know why something works, since such insight allows them to determine for themselves the most logical way to achieve the expected results—from themselves and others.

In business, Cautious Thinkers are practical and realistic. They seek neither utopias nor quick fixes. Because of their low risk-taking tendencies, they may over plan when change becomes inevitable. They like working in those existing circumstances which promote quality in products or services. When possible, they prepare ahead of time for their projects and then work diligently to perfect them to the nth degree. Their thorough preparation is designed to minimize the probability of errors. They prefer finishing tasks before or on schedule without mistakes caused by last minute rushing and inadequate check-out or review.

Cautious Thinkers rank second only to Steady Relaters in their pursuit of logic. They rely on reasoning to avoid mistakes, so they tend to check, recheck, and check again. But they may become mired down with data collection. Amassing facts and specifics, they are uncomfortable with giving opinions or partial information until they've exhausted all their resources. This can frustrate people who want to know what's going on now, the types with faster paces. Additionally, all that checking can result in a disruption of the work flow.

They can benefit from checking only the critical things, not everything. This procedure allows them to sort out and control the important details, and still get things done well. They can hold onto their high standards without becoming bogged down in relatively trivial business details. Cautious Thinkers need to learn to accept that perfection is an impossible quest worth the effort in some instances, but not in others.

C's prefer the "right" way

When airline pilots prepare to fly a commercial plane, they have a checklist of safety points before take-off. Cautious Thinker pilots have been found to focus far more on the most critical factors, using the remaining time to review the less crucial ones. In their typical Cautious Thinker style, they complete the checklist the *right* way, by checking known factors against unknown variables. By contrast, Dominant Director pilots have been known to delegate this duty to someone else. With this, they then see to it that the task gets done their way. Interacting Socializer pilots have been observed getting *off task* by talking to co-workers they see during this process. Then they may wait till the last minute, due to their difficulty in assessing the amount of time needed to complete such detailed tasks. Steady Relaters go through each point, in the listed order, completing it in a step-by-step way, but without the same rigorous attention paid to those most critical items that the Cautious Thinker pilot scrutinizes. Although all four types finish the checklist, they have completed this task quite differently—according to their different work styles—and with the possibility of different outcomes as a result of their different approaches to the same task.

Old questions, new answers

Whether or not this type opts for a scientific or artistic career, they often follow a scientific method or intuitive, logical progression to achieve their objectives. Because of their natural inclination to validate and improve upon accepted processes, Cautious Thinkers tend to generate the most native creativity of the four types. Consequently, they often find new ways of viewing old questions, concerns, and opportunities.

Many artists and inventors fall into the Cautious Thinker category, many leaning toward experimentation and the possibility of coming up with new answers. Just as Michelangelo's creative mind envisioned completed sculptures entrapped in a solid piece of marble, Leonardo da Vinci perfected the Mona Lisa's expression in such a manner that its meaning still evades contemporary experts. Similarly, Galileo's creativity formulated precisely detailed plans of "impossible" futuristic inventions. These three Renaissance men left lasting memorials as evidence of the quality-consciousness often associated with Cautious Thinker tendencies.

C leaders

Political Thinkers range from Thomas Jefferson to Henry Cabot Lodge and Adlai Stevenson. Each was a private person who exhibited calm, cool, objective behaviors which detractors at times viewed as aloofness and insensitivity. President Woodrow Wilson, often dubbed by scholars as the most intellectual 20th century President, also predictably fits this Cautious temperament. A former university professor, Wilson established far-reaching policies and practices, some of which still exist today. An intense, though private and contemplative individual, he was known as a man who was far ahead of his time in his Think(er)ing. The press had a heyday with *Silent Cal*(vin) Coolidge and his typical one or two word comments which often amounted to a clipped yes or no.

Cautious Thinker military leaders may use planned, careful actions to achieve their desired results. They may instruct their troops, "Don't ever let your guard down," or, "CYA (Cover your anatomy)!" If under extreme pressure, Cautious Thinker leaders may tend toward the *Aim! Aim! Aim!* mind set. They just keep aiming until they think they'll make a perfect shot.

People may complicate things

Like Steady Relaters, Cautious Thinkers are basically more introverted individuals who seek solace and answers by turning inward. Cautious Thinkers' natural orientation is toward objects and away from people. From their perspective, people are unpredictable and complicate things. The more people added to the formula, the more chance of getting unpredictable results.

Cautious Thinkers often choose to work with colleagues who promote calmness and thoroughness in the office—often either other Cautious Thinkers or Steady Relaters. Since Cautious Thinkers seek perfection, the other two types may help them modify that quest into a more time-efficient procedure. Dominant Directors can contribute by helping to explain realistic deadlines and parameters, so Cautious Thinkers can build those time frames into his procedures. Interacting Socializers, too, can help them *lighten up* more at work and teach them that there is more to the workplace than working alone eight hours a day.

When encouraged to do so, Cautious Thinkers can share their rich supplies of information with small groups of co-workers who can benefit from their wealth of experience and knowledge. This can (1) enhance the Cautious Thinker's status with colleagues and (2) become a bridge toward building teamwork and mutual understanding. (3) Sharing with others can also serve to lessen Cautious Thinkers' reservations and suspicions about associates; or, (4) even encourage C's to stand up for themselves against those very people they may prefer to avoid.

They can also participate in more coffee machine conversation that may just give them a better understanding of co-workers, and possibly, some work problems. Carrying on a dialogue with associates may even provide them with insights into themselves. For instance, someone may observe, "Harold, you're furrowing your brow again."

Cautious Thinker Harold replies, "I am? I wasn't aware that I was."

"Yes, you do that a lot. That's why I've never said more than 'hello' to you. I thought you were either deep in thought or worried about something."

"Thank you for bringing that to my attention," Harold says. "I'll monitor that from now on."

Since Cautious Thinkers want clarity and order, they can contribute a natural sense of thoroughness to their company. They usually don't care about knowing everyone's name in their department, but they may make it a point to find out who they think exhibits the same thoroughness and precision they themselves have: "What's the name of the artist who drew up the graphics for the Robinson account?"

When the going gets loud

Cautious Thinkers (prefer to) get going. When discussions and tempers become hot and heavy, "I want to get out of this place," may represent the Cautious Thinker viewpoint. Because they want peace and tranquility, they avoid and reject hostility and outward expressions of aggression. At the extreme, they can numb themselves to conflict to such an extent that they may have difficulty tapping into their feelings . . . not only anger and hatred, but caring and love.

By learning to accept others' expressions of emotions, Cautious Thinkers can also learn to accept their own feelings. Ideally, if the Cautious Thinker can consciously raise his tolerance for aggression, he can then begin to increase his ability to successfully deal with it in a more open manner through mutual exchanges.

C's take themselves seriously

Since Cautious Thinkers often detect many of life's complexities which escape the other types, they can become perfectionistic and worrisome, with both themselves and others. While this quality control aspect can be very positive, when taken to an extreme, associates may dismiss the Cautious Thinker's caution as *crying wolf*. When willing to bend their standards on small matters, co-workers are more likely to listen to them for the bigger issues.

In the NASA space shuttle disaster, for instance, engineers repeatedly emphasized the need for more research. But after a few delays, the public pressure became so great that the Challenger was launched prematurely. That time, pushing the researchers harder and faster resulted in tragedy. The message: Listen to Cautious Thinkers about the big things. At the least, both positive and negative sides will come to light; at the extreme, the bleakest results will be projected. In either case, unknown factors become more clearly defined. At the same time, the obstacles and resources required for success are identified. The C's exploratory process results in moving closer to the more desired goal or state shared by all parties.

Remember . . .

CAUTIOUS THINKER
BUSINESS CHARACTERISTICS

- Concerned with process; want to know *how* something works
- Intuitive and original; once they know the expected structure, they may invent their own structure, method, or model
- More interested in quality than quantity; prefer lower output to inferior results
- Want to be right, so they employ logical thinking process to avoid mistakes
- Over-attend to details, sometimes impeding progress with regular checking and rechecking
- Dislike changes and surprises
- Reject aggression

CAUTIOUS THINKER:
PREFERRED BUSINESS SITUATIONS

- Colleagues and superiors do not criticize their work or ideas
- Can set the quality control standards and check to see if they're properly implemented
- Work with complete data systems, or can formulate some themselves
- Superiors value correctness and let them know they are key workers in the organization
- Workplaces are organized and process-oriented, with a minimum of socializing

People Smart Principle # 6—The Principle of Personal Leadership: "To know and accept who you are—including strengths, weaknesses, and growth potentials—is essential for effective leadership behavior."

Chapter 6
Leadership Styles

Making this chapter meaningful to you

Picture a Dominant Director, Interacting Socializer, Steady Relater, and Cautious Thinker who manage you or whom you manage. As you read, bear in mind each of these particular people and specify what you can do to improve your relationship with them. Focus on each one's more productive traits as well as each one's less productive characteristics.

To begin answering these questions, we have found a common *universal leadership language* which exists around the world in management circles. Whether you are a corporate president, chairman of the board, head of a small company, a board member, director of a non-profit organization, an independent consultant, or senior pastor of a church, you can greatly increase your effectiveness as a leader by learning to speak this language. It involves the most widely known leadership concept in continued practice today—the managerial grid—which reveals a person's leadership influencing approach.

The essence of this concept is that all people have their own natural, and thus preferred way, of doing things, including exerting influence over people and/or managing tasks or organizations. In this respect, Dominant Directors are the most observably directive in their style of leadership. On the other hand, Interacting Socializers are the most naturally supportive in the way they go about their efforts to influence others and manage situations.

By contrast, the remaining two behavioral types are more introverted by nature and less easily identifiable in their leadership practices. You can still see, however, that *liking-motivated* Steady Relaters are more like supportive Interacting Socializers. But Steady Relaters are secondarily concerned with being supportive to provide the expected service or accomplish the identified result. And finally Cautious Thinkers are more similar to *self-determined* Dominant Directors. The difference is that Cautious Thinkers are concerned with achieving their own desired standards in a way that does not cause further problems by rubbing other people the wrong way.

The graphic entitled "Our Primary Natural Leadership Styles" will help you better understand the differing natures of these four leadership styles as well as those among the people you work with/for. You may want to note your own *strong suit* and *least developed approach* (as well as those of significant individuals in your work environment) before moving on to gain additional insights about both, which are provided in this chapter.

Unfortunately, when commonplace stresses and pressures accompany particular situations in the workplace, leaders often revert to their own instinctive state. If this happens, a less effective response is illustrated by "The Ineffective Expression of Our Natural Leadership Styles" graphic.

The Dominant Director Leaders

Move over and let them do their thing

They're like wild horses who don't like to run in rigid formation. But why hobble them if they're able to get blue ribbons in their own way? Or even start and develop their own herd? If you confine them, Dominant Directors may become harsh and stubborn; let them do their own thing and they may very well impress you. Agree on the goal and specify

YOUR PRIMARY
NATURAL LEADERSHIP STYLES

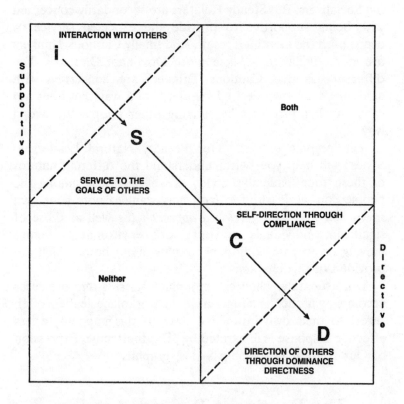

THE INEFFECTIVE EXPRESSION OF OUR
NATURAL LEADERSHIP STYLES

the boundaries of the playing field. Then get out of their way.

This requires other people to ignore some of the Dominant Director's natural competitive spirit and, instead, focus this energy on a common goal for bettering the organization. Dominant Directors seek this sort of encouragement and feedback to function most effectively within the general framework of shared expectations. But don't expect them to follow every procedure to the letter.

How to develop D's

When coaching a Dominant Director, he likes to learn the basic steps to quickly sift out what he wants. "I don't really plan to read this 200 page computer manual just to learn how to set up pages in three columns. Just teach me what I have to know so I can do that." In the interest of saving time, D's may try to find shortcuts, so show them the simplest, fastest route to get them to their stated destination.

The thought of reassuring someone or explaining something more than once smacks of frittering away precious moments that he'd rather spend on action and results. So he doesn't bother with details. Focus on the high points, please, like what is to be done by when. He wants to know only those details required to get a contraption to function so he can then turn to other important new opportunities—like making money, for instance. Instead of covering steps one through 24, he prefers hearing about key steps 1, 6, 12, and 24. Forcing him to sit through all 24 points seems like torture to a D. This lack of attention to details can result in his searching for new ways to streamline his routine jobs in getting his desired effects more readily.

Toward appropriate management

When Don Cipriano, the number one, all-time salesperson worldwide for Performax International, conducted a session on Motivational Management in London, he said, "We manage people the way they need to be managed, not the way we want to manage." One manager, John, commented that concept really hit home because his high D (Dominant

Director) behavior was creating some problems with his S (Steady Relater) and C (Cautious Thinker) staff. For four months, John ran his office according to the way his staff needed to be managed, but when a new employee began working in his department, John didn't have the same success he had with the others. One day, she made an appointment with John and told him, "If you'd stop wasting time providing all those details, I could get my work done." John had made the common mistake of being so used to managing just S and C behaviors that he failed to recognize the high D behavior of his new employee. John later said to Don Cipriano, "I fell into the same trap, managing everyone the same way."

What's this company's philosophy?

Similarly, when Dr. John Lee, a renowned time management expert, conducts workshops, he often asks, " What is the operating philosophy of your company?" He says presidents of organizations seem floored when they notice the diversity of answers mentioned by their staff members. If a CEO doesn't verbalize, clarify, and gather input about what everyone is working toward, how can the company function smoothly? Like Dan's misguided idea of a dream company vacation, employees can benefit by a common, agreed-upon vision. Dan still made the ultimate decision, but with a little help from the group.

Who's managing whom?

Managing Dominant Directors is no easy task because they want to manage you! You can squelch them or you can encourage them to take control of certain arenas. Why not work with the D's strengths by allowing him to take the reins, where qualified, on particular projects? His preference for change and innovation makes him the natural choice for *new frontier* programs where he can implement his own ideas. Make sure the Dominant Director understands he needs to check with you at specific intervals, or he may demonstrate the renegade syndrome—doing his own thing, without answering to anyone but himself.

Getting D's to decide

Dominant Directors tend to make autonomous, no-nonsense decisions. If the decision will help them meet their goals, they go for it; if not, they'll typically say no. One of the few times this type will procrastinate in reaching a conclusion is when it will take too much time or effort to do the homework to determine the best alternative. You can prevent this procrastination by simply providing a brief analysis for each option you present to a D.

Motivating D's

Provide them with options and clearly describe the probabilities of success in achieving goals. "Ross, here are four possibilities for developing the Evans Estate. I've highlighted the key points for each suggestion, and included costs and time projections on the bottom of each one. The choice is yours."

Compared to the other types, Dominant Directors are more likely to thrive in pressure cooker situations. They naturally gravitate toward those power positions and career areas where they can take charge: executives, politicians, military officers, stock brokers, and newspaper reporters. Think of win-at-any-cost tennis pro John McEnroe. When in doubt, he questions the decisions made by the referee. For better or worse, he deals directly with the source. It's not how you play the game—it's winning! And winning, more than anything else, motivates this type. Just think of Donald Trump, author of *The Art of the Deal* and *The Trump Game*, as one example of this leadership style.

Complimenting D's

Mention their achievements, upward mobility, and leadership potential. Omit personal comments and focus on their track record. "Jones, you've exceeded our company goals every month for the past year and have put in more hours than anybody but the top officials here. The CEO has his eye on you for an upcoming Vice Presidential slot."

Counseling D's

Stick to the facts. Draw them out by talking about the desired results. Then discuss their concerns. Focus on tasks more than feelings. Ask them how they would solve the problem. "Anne, we've heard a few comments that need to be addressed. It seems that some of your employees don't feel appreciated for the extra hours they've been putting in for you on the Evans project. They say they've given up social engagements and worked 14-hour days to beat your deadline. How do you think we can bolster their morale?"

Correcting D's

Describe what results are desired. Show them the gap between actual and desired. Suggest clearly the improvement that is needed and establish a time when they will get back to you. "We need to streamline communication around here so that one hand knows what the other is doing. Last month, we had two separate divisions calling on the same CEO for corporate donations. I want you to work up a plan to keep everybody informed of who's working on what so we don't duplicate our efforts. Get back to me by the end of the week."

Communicating with D's

Be prepared to listen to their suggestions, the course of action they have in mind, and/or the general results they are considering. This enables you to begin on a positive note by indicating the areas in which you already agree. Then you can work backwards toward gaining agreement on the results you both want—and are willing to either mutually or independently allow the other to achieve. "Sarah, this format will give you the freedom to develop your branch your way and still allow Vern and Ellen to structure theirs another way . . . without sacrificing time or morale."

Making decisions and problem solving with D's

They will want to provide their own initial view of the decision to be made or problem to be solved and the process they prefer to follow in reaching a clear-cut, preferably quickly chosen solution. "As I see it, you have the most experience in organizing seminars like this, Charles, so why don't you throw out a few ideas!" You can anticipate, where possible, and be open to summarizing the achievements you've made (or, possibly in a case like this, your lack of achievements in this area). "Hal, you flatter me, but I've never undertaken an international convention like this before. As for ideas, why don't we decide who wants to perform which function and then we can all do what we feel comfortable doing!" With this approach, you're more likely to reach mutual agreement with the least hassle for everyone concerned . . . yourself included.

When suggesting a different idea, opinion, or action to them, be sure to point out you are trying to work in ways that are acceptable to them—and also yourself. Focus on your desire to identify solutions which will also meet their expectations. Stress that you don't want to cause difficulties for either them or you. "Phil, instead of writing this report as it occurs to you and me, I'd rather write an outline first and then the report. I know it takes longer initially, but it saves time in the long run because the writing will be better organized and make more sense to the readers."

When acknowledging D's

When it's appropriate to reward or reinforce their behaviors, focus on how pleased you are. Assume they are also pleased with achieving the desired outcome in that situation. Also mention how glad you are to be a part of that process working with them to make things better for both of you through cooperation. The bottom line? Each of you get better results by combining your energies on a common targeted goal: "Phil, this report turned out much better with your wonderful anecdotes and asides. Now we have something that's interesting, clear, and well-organized!"

Delegating with D's

Give them the bottom line and then let them do their thing. So that they can be more efficient, give them parameters, guidelines, and deadlines. "We need to get that mall built a month sooner or we'll lose our shirts. Fourteen tenants are threatening to bail out of their contracts if we don't open in

Action Plan . . .

WHEN *YOU* ARE
THE DOMINANT DIRECTOR

- Allow others to do things without excessive or untimely interference
- Participate in the group without expecting always to be in command
- Modify the tendency to give orders to others
- Enlist others' input and support through participative, collaborative actions
- Give others credit when they deserve it
- Praise people for jobs well done
- Let colleagues and employees know that you realize it's only natural that you and others will make mistakes
- When delegating, give some authority along with the responsibility

WHEN OTHERS ARE DOMINANT DIRECTORS,
HELP THEM LEARN TO:

- More realistically gauge risks
- Exercise more caution and deliberation before making decisions and coming to conclusions
- Follow pertinent rules, regulations, and expectations
- Recognize and solicit others' contributions, both as individuals and within a group
- Tell others the reasons for decisions
- Cultivate more attention/responsiveness to emotions

time for the holidays. Don't spend more than another $30,000, keep everything legal and out of the newspapers, and get back to me by Monday morning."

We know one Dominant Director who became visibly, though not consciously, agitated if anyone stayed in her office beyond 10 minutes. Her staff knew this, but anyone outside the office had no inkling until she began fidgeting and examining her stacks of paperwork, hoping the person would leave. One day, it dawned on her to delegate an *alarm clock* duty to her secretary. Then, whenever anyone stayed more than ten minutes, Mrs. Myers knocked on the door or buzzed her on the phone reminding her of the *next appointment*.

Catch people doing something right

If you happen to be a Dominant Director manager, use what you now know about behavioral types to make the workplace more productive. Try mentoring, training, or consulting as appropriate development practices, instead of criticizing or leaving them alone without guidance. Catch your employees doing things right and tell them about it. Ask employees for their feedback about policies, deadlines, and programs. Bouncing ideas off your co-workers can give you insights into how you can better motivate people to help you achieve your goals.

The Interacting Socializer Leader

Help them focus their abilities

With their energy and enthusiasm, Interacting Socializers can get so involved with so many different activities that they may accomplish goals with a flourish. Or, they may show flurries of activity, but not actually accomplish things in the most efficient way. Managers and co-workers can help channel that energy and enthusiasm with tactful reminders and hands-on assistance to help them prioritize and organize. Then, the entire office may function more smoothly. Since Interacting Socializers tend to be open books, the other types often can detect when Interacting Socializers are having off days and give them verbal boosts with a compliment and personal attention.

How to develop I's

When coaching Interacting Socializers, don't give them too much at once or they'll become overwhelmed. Skip as much of the detailed, boring stuff as possible. Get them involved. Interacting Socializers are typically kinesthetic, hands on learners, so let them try by first getting a feel for what's involved, and then showing you what they understood so you can give them structured feedback. Frequently, this type wants to jump in and try before they're ready, or before they fully understand everything. Allow them to save face when they do something wrong, and heap on those compliments when they get it right!

Prioritizing with I's

Many Interacting Socializers find that sorting out priorities and solutions becomes very difficult when too many opportunities bombard them. When this happens, they may become uncharacteristically mute and immobilized . . . temporarily, of course. Other people can help by prioritizing items for Interacting Socializers to tackle. "This account needs attention sometime today, but I need your input on the Chase report in less than an hour." This approach enables him to separate his feelings from the facts at hand as well as other people's expectations. Ironically, when the Interacting Socializer's tasks become more organized, his anxiety level lessens—despite the fact that he bristles at the thought of organization. More importantly, since he can't be all things to all people, focusing and refocusing on what's most important, second-most, etc., is essential to his well-being.

Support I's dreams

Interacting Socializers operate predominantly from a multiple-focus, right brain perspective. They see mental pictures first, then convert those pictures to words. Preferring main ideas and generalities, not details, they base decisions on their impulses, gut feelings, and others' recommendations and testimonials. For this behavioral type, emotions rule. "Something tells me that I should buy this stock." This doesn't mean that they never use logic or facts, but that feelings and emotions come first, thinking processes being factors that are the servants to their feeling state.

Get ready to act more enthusiastic with an Interacting Socializer. Show you're interested in him by letting him talk and by using more animation in your own gestures and voice. Illustrate your ideas with stories or mental pictures that relate to him and his goals. He likes to interact with people, so try not to hurry your discussion. Include opportunities for small talk and getting personally acquainted.

Socializers like to envision the big picture. Generally less motivated by many facts and details, they respond better to short overviews or capsule summaries of what you plan to cover. Attempt to develop some stimulating, enjoyable ideas together while focusing on supporting their opinions and dreams. Interacting Socializers turn off to people who douse their dreams. Then support their ideas while showing them how they can transfer their talk into actions.

If you disagree, try not to argue because they dislike conflict. You might not win an argument with them anyway because their strong suit is feelings and intuition. If trapped, they can twist people around through very clever manipulation of feelings with their usage of words and emotions. Try to explore alternate solutions, instead. When you reach an agreement, iron out the specific details concerning what, when, who, and how. Then document the agreement with them, since they tend to naturally forget such details.

Motivating I's

They like special packages and a little something extra to inspire them to go the whole nine yards. "Hawkins, if you can clinch the Babbitt account, I'll give you an extra week's vacation and take you and Sharon to the fanciest restaurant in town." Or, show them how they can look good in the eyes of others. "When you close your next order, that will be your tenth major success story this year. You can all but clinch the President's Productivity Award with your name engraved on a plaque next to the big boss himself."

Many businesses use yearly contests to motivate their employees. Interacting Socializers tend to sprint toward a quick win—for the first week or two. Then they may say to themselves, "Hey, I have a whole year to win this contest. Why am I working so hard now?" They may further get sidetracked by other things and do nothing more about it until a week before the contest ends. If they can get excited enough, they may win anyway, but the truth is they haven't worked toward the goal for 11 months. How can these types keep up their motivation? Since Interacting Socializers like constant rewards along the way, they may favor shorter contests with smaller payoffs, perhaps culminating in the *big one* when the year ends. One person even jokingly suggests, "How about an employee of the hour award?" Or, they may enlist other colleagues' assistance who are better at implementation than they are.

Complimenting I's

Pay direct personal compliments to them, as individuals when legitimately deserved. "You are a terrific person and a wonderful employee." Mention their charm, friendliness, creative ideas, persuasiveness, and/or appearance (or better yet, all of the above). While other types respond to more specific job-related comments, Interacting Socializers can mentally relive more global generalizations for weeks to come. "We are so lucky to have you with us, Dee. You're a real gem."

Counseling I's

Give them ample opportunity to talk about whatever may be bothering them. Pay attention to both facts and feelings, but put your primary emphasis on their feelings. Ask probing questions and involve them by asking how they could solve the challenge or difficulty. Sometimes, just airing their feelings and thoughts relieves tension for these individuals. Talking allows them to get something off their chests and can even become an end in itself, since their energy is largely influenced by the quality of their relationship with a person.

Correcting I's

When stress hits I's, they prefer looking the other way and searching for more positive, upbeat experiences. They avoid problems as long as they can. If the pressure persists, they tend to literally walk away from the problem. When this tactic fails, they may become emotionally candid in attempts to meet their needs. "I can't believe I let this happen, but I brought it all on myself." Sometimes stress manifests itself in animated panic. "I can't talk now, Hal. It's really hit the fan this time!"

Let these individuals know specifically what the challenge happens to be. Define the behavior that can eliminate it and confirm the mutually agreeable action plan in writing to prevent future misunderstandings. Since they prefer keeping the conversation light, avoid what they view as negative or distasteful approaches. Rather than, "Why did your sales drop off 50% last month?" use more optimistically stated questions like, "How'd you like to bolster your sales up to your normal range and beyond it?" They'd simply rather deal with things going right.

Communicating with them

Be prepared to listen to their personal feelings and experiences, since they have a need to be both expressive and able to share their emotions with others. Their style requires open and responsive interaction with others, preferably in a manner of congenial and unhurried conversation. It's much like that between long-time friends. "Just between you and me, Chris, I feel very uneasy about Jill and Howard handling this account by themselves."

Making decisions/solving problems with I's

They'll want to avoid a discussion of more complex, negative-sounding or otherwise messy problem situations. It's difficult for them to feel positive or agreeable with you or anyone else under these circumstances. In making decisions with them, they will be open to your suggestions—as long as these ideas will allow them to look and feel good—and not require a lot of difficult, follow-up, detail work or long term commitments. "You know just about everybody who is anybody, George. Since we need to get $350 in pledges for the Y by the end of February, why not go ahead and wrap up all your calls by Friday. Then you can relax a lot more next week." When suggesting a different idea, opinion, or action to them, be sure to point out you are doing it that way if it's acceptable to them. Focus on your desire to identify solutions which will also meet their expectations. Stress that you don't want to cause difficulties for either them or you.

Above all, offer your suggestions as gifts which can make this situation (task or relationship) easier and more beneficial to them—as well as to other people who you feel are also likely to find this very acceptable and desirable. "You're lucky I'm on the Nominating Committee, Marilyn. So many people wanted the Hospitality position that I couldn't manage it for you this year, but I think I've got one that's even better than that—How about Junior High Dances?"

When acknowledging I's

When it's appropriate to reward or reinforce their behaviors, focus on how glad you are they have succeeded in finding a pleasant solution to their concern or objective. In addition, let them know how much you appreciate them for their openness and willingness to be responsive to you in a way that allows everyone to end up feeling good about the results afterwards. "George, I'm so glad we could reach a solution that both you and I feel good about. I appreciate your openness about only being able to call prospective donors on Friday night. That's fine with me. We'll work this out so that everyone is happy."

Delegating with I's

Again, make sure to receive clear agreement. Set up check points/times to avoid long stretches with no progress reports. Otherwise, I's may lapse into their natural way of doing things—spontaneously completing particulars which feel best while postponing less stimulating tasks, especially those that involve follow-up and checking.

By now, you realize that Interacting Socializers exhibit a natural talkativeness and ease with people. This makes them good choices for maintaining group morale and motivation. They think out loud and enjoy participating in brainstorming sessions anyway, so why not get their opinions and assistance on recognition awards, entertainment, or fund-raising activities? They want to fill their natural need by striving for recognition, so activities which draw attention to themselves appeal to them.

I's are often concept people who come up with plenty of ideas, but not necessarily the means of carrying them out, so steer them toward ways of assuring the implementation of those ideas. "Olivia, this proposal for the King Company looks good so far, but how about including more direct benefits for each employee. Marian has surveys filled out by each employee. Get together with her, bounce some ideas around, and then include more essential information about the eight or so key people in your proposal. Add some extra *plus points* on the others . . . 12 pages in all. In this manner, you should do the job very well. And, Olivia, thanks for making the extra effort on this project. It's really important to all of us."

In this example, the manager praises the work done so far, tells Olivia where to go for more facts, encourages a participative exchange between Olivia and Marian, spells out the parameters (12 pages), and shows her the path for staying on track. He's utilizing this Interacting Socializer's natural strengths and allowing for her potential weaknesses. Instead of delegating someone to perform large tasks that are naturally stressful for them, why not structure the tasks to fit the natural work style of that person? As one bumper sticker we spotted on a passing car advised, "Never teach a duck to sing. It's a waste of time and it annoys the duck."

The Steady Relater Leader

Encourage them to update their methods

Steady Relaters contribute stability and perseverance to their workplace. Since they work toward harmony in the office, they usually fit comfortably into the work environment, but they may become used to using the same old methods again and again. Sometimes their procedures include unnecessary steps that may have been needed when they learned the procedure, but can now be discarded. They may improve their work practices by utilizing short-cuts that eliminate extra steps. Dominant Directors and Interacting Socializers can often help them with this. And, when asked, Cautious Thinkers can generally demonstrate new ways to get things done.

How to develop S's

When he's in training for a job, he favors one-on-one, hands-on instruction with a real live human being, starting at the beginning and ending at the end. By learning each step, he generally is more comfortable with his functions. During training and in other newer situations, the S tends to observe others for a longer than average time. When he feels he can do a task, then and only then will he comfortably begin. This slower pace can frustrate Dominant Directors and Interacting Socializers, both of whom like to plunge right in with, "Oh, sure! I can do that," whether they've done it before or not! So understanding that Steady Relaters need to do things slowly can reassure the faster-paced types that the job will get done.

Get ready to be ready with the S. Have a step-by-step list of procedures or a working timetable/schedule at your disposal. Steady Relaters need to feel secure in their mastery of procedures until their actions become *second nature* and more routine. At the same time, they prefer a pleasant and patient approach while they learn what's expected of them.

Motivating S's

Besides thinking they can learn to master a series of procedures, S's like to also feel that their relationships with others can benefit from their follow-through. "If you can learn to use this computer by next week, you can send the whole Christmas mailing for Mr. Hawkins on Monday. Then he can go to Texas for his family reunion." Or show Steady Relaters how to strengthen their relationships with others. "When this office makes its 1000th sale, it can win the Outstanding Division Award for the year. And you, Arthur, can help that

Action Plan . . .

**WHEN *YOU* ARE
THE INTERACTING SOCIALIZER**

- Attend to key details, when appropriate
- Improve your follow-through efforts
- Monitor socializing to keep it in balance with other aspects of life
- Write things down and work from a list, so you'll know what to do when
- Prioritize activities and focus on tasks in order of importance
- Become more organized and orderly in the way you do things
- Get the less appealing tasks of the day over with
- Pay more attention to time management of activities
- Check to make sure you're on course with known tasks or goals

**WHEN OTHERS ARE INTERACTING
SOCIALIZERS, HELP THEM LEARN TO:**

- Prioritize and organize
- See tasks through to completion
- View people and tasks more objectively
- Avoid overuse of giving and taking advice (or can result in lack of focus on task)
- Write things down
- Do the unpleasant, as well as the *fun things*
- Focus on what's important now
- Avoid procrastination and/or hoping others will do things for them
- Practice and perfect, when appropriate

happen by getting Mr. Arens to look at this new demographic data."

Complimenting S's

Mention their teamwork and dependability. "Pam, besides plugging along on this project for two years, I really appreciate the fact you've encouraged everyone else to do their part. We couldn't have done it without you." Or remark about how others regard them, how well they get along with co-workers, and how important their relationship-building efforts have been to the company. "Limbrecht, you've been the glue holding this place together for the last 20 years." Effusiveness can arouse the suspicions of Steady Relaters, so stick to praising what they've done rather than more abstract, personal attributes. Otherwise, their modesty and your vagueness may cause them to dismiss your comments.

Counseling S's

Allow plenty of time to explore their thoughts and feelings so you can understand the emotional side of the situation. Steady Relaters usually express their feelings less directly, so draw them out through questioning and listening responses. Bear in mind this type tends to balk at sudden change, whether the change is good or bad. The key point is that their stability-motivated state is disrupted by the unknown. You can help reduce their fears by showing how specific changes will benefit them and their company. "Barbara, moving to Dallas will be an adjustment for all of us at first, but 80% of our staff has agreed to go. The company will move you and your family, sell your house, add more medical and dental benefits to your health plan, and give you a 10% bonus for loyal service. We like to take care of our own, and you are a valuable, trusted employee. And besides, you'll still be with many of the same friends, co-workers, and the company you've always been with day in and day out."

Correcting S's

Reassure them that you only want to correct a specific behavior. S's tend to take things personally, so remove the *something is wrong with you* barrier as quickly as possible. Don't blame or judge the person; keep the conversation focused on the behavior and its appropriateness. If the problem involves a procedure, help them learn how to improve it. Point out in a non-threatening way both what they're already doing right while also emphasizing what needs changing. "Norma, I admire your persistence on this proposal, but we have to add more details to The Idea section before we send it out. For example,"

Communicating with S's

Be ready to do more talking than listening with them, since they don't naturally feel comfortable when the limelight is focused on them. You will want to clarify any key agenda item with them, working to stay organized and moving forward steadily but slowly as you check to make sure they both understand and accept what is being said: "Did you want me to stick around the office at a particular time each day in case you need to telephone me for emergency questions on this account, or do you want me to call you?"

Making decisions and solving problems with S's

In dealing with problems and decisions with this type, make sure to deal with only one subject or situation at a time, one step at a time. To gain clarity, before moving on to other items, make sure they are ready, willing, and able to do so. Recalling that they need stability, deal with matters calmly and in a more relaxed manner. Encourage them to share their suggestions as to how the decision might be made in a way that is likely to add even more stability to the current conditions than already, or previously, exist. "Would you mind writing down a schedule of your office's activities so I can get my proposal written up without missing anything? "

When suggesting a different possibility to S's, point out how you are trying to identify ways that you can help continue to make things pleasant for them. You simply have an idea or opinion in this respect which will also help stabilize your own relationship expectations with them and which is important to you, too. "I know that we initially agreed on 10 phone calls per day, but some of our volunteers are unable to make that commitment. Would you be comfortable making 15 calls a day if those calls included your personal friends and family?"

When acknowledging S's

When it's appropriate to reward or reinforce their behaviors, focus on how you genuinely and sincerely appreciate their willingness to work to make things good for you and others. Approach matters in a more systematic, low-keyed, and understandable manner. Also, point out how you have noticed they make important contributions when they take the initiative to share their own ideas, interests, and insights in helping make sure these results are achieved. "Just say anything about the impending merger that you want to share. We certainly don't want to use any high pressure tactics which is precisely why you meet our own expectations so well. John, thank you very much for your willingness to provide us with this desired input."

Delegating with S's

Steady Relaters may be reluctant to ask others to do their own share of the work. So you could make a personal appeal to their loyalty and sense of sportsmanship. "Al, you're an example for this company of genuine cooperative spirit. Your staff wants to please you, so by giving everyone in your department just 10 of those names to call, you can all reach the goal together by noon tomorrow. Otherwise, you'll probably have a lot more difficulty reaching all those people by the target date." Give them the task, state the deadlines that need to be met, and explain why it's important to do it that way. "I'll need 500 copies of these summaries typed and collated by 5 p.m. today. Mr. Jeffries is getting back from New York two days early and he wants them by tomorrow morning."

Action Plan ...

**WHEN *YOU* ARE
THE STEADY RELATER**

- Stretch by taking on a bit more (or different) duties beyond your comfort level
- Increase verbalization of your thoughts and feelings
- Speed up your actions by getting into some projects more quickly
- Desensitize yourselves somewhat, so that you aren't negatively affected by your colleagues' feelings to the point of affecting your own performance
- Learn to adapt more quickly to either changes or refinements of existing practices
- Bolster your assertiveness techniques

**WHEN OTHERS ARE STEADY RELATERS,
HELP THEM:**

- Utilize shortcuts and discard unnecessary steps
- Track their growth
- Avoid doing things the same way
- Focus on the goal without attending to other thoughts or feelings
- Realize there is more than one approach to tasks
- Become more open to some risks and changes
- To feel sincerely appreciated
- Speak up and voice their thoughts and feelings
- Modify the tendency to do what others tell them
- Get and accept credit and praise, when appropriate

The Cautious Thinker Leader

Help them substitute quality for perfection

Since this type is characterized by the most complex thinking pattern, they base their decisions on proven information and track records. They want to make rational choices based on facts, not on other people's opinions or testimonials —unless those people are those Cautious Thinkers' personal heroes. Even then, they'll probably want to see it in writing. When a C says, "I need to think about it," she usually means it. You can help her make a decision by supplying the materials she requests and by allowing her the time to make the right decision for her. Focus on emphasizing deadlines and parameters, so the Cautious Thinker can build those time frames into her procedures.

How to develop C's

When coaching a C, point out the most important things to remember first. Then demonstrate the procedure in an efficient, logical manner, stressing the purpose of each step. Proceed at a relatively slower pace, stopping at each key place in the process to check for his or her understanding. Ask for possible input, especially regarding desired refinements which may be appropriate. This approach ensures success with the task and minimization of stress for the Cautious Thinker.

Motivating C's

Appeal to their need for accuracy and logic. This type doesn't respond well to fancy verbal antics, so keep your approach clear, clean, and documentable. Better yet, provide illustration and documentation. Avoid exaggeration and vagueness. Show them how this is the best available current option. "Ms. Alberts, our office cleaning service should meet almost all your cleanliness needs. I think that a neat and sanitary environment is a key standard for more productivity. Do you agree or see it differently?"

If they decide to take part in a competitive situation, they'll probably do it as they do other tasks—bit by bit—until they do it right. Unlike their colleagues who may show enthusiasm at the beginning, C's often show the patience and follow-through to ultimately win—if they perceive the contest as worthwhile and don't become too preoccupied with details along the way. Whereas some people focus on winning shorter term battles, the Cautious Thinker is motivated by the ultimate sense of lasting personal glory derived from triumphing in the overall war.

Complimenting C's

Mention their efficiency, thought processes, organization, persistence, and accuracy. Don't mix personal and professional comments unless you know them very well. Even then, they prefer more privately communicated, plausible praise. "Jeffries, you were so thorough on this project that we had every shred of information we needed—and then some just in case we required a safety net. Thanks again for another good job!"

One C told us, "Compliments don't mean much to me. I really don't think about them. But I do like genuine, heartfelt appreciation once in awhile, like, "You did a fine job," or, "I've really benefited from your work and so have others who have told me about your contributions." In other words, keep praise simple and concise for a Cautious Thinker. He went on to say that what he thinks about some accomplishment is much more important to him. "I'm hard on myself."

Counseling C's

Elicit their thoughts about processes, procedures or problems, perhaps by asking something like, "If it were in your power, how would you change this to make things even better?" Like Steady Relaters, they often express their thoughts and opinions indirectly, so persist in your attempts to get them to talk. This type dislikes change because they typically view changes and the future as unknown variables where unforeseen mistakes might happen. They need to plan for change ahead of time so they can identify and bring under control any key considerations that have to be addressed in the process. When possible, allow them to investigate possible repercussions, especially at the beginning stages. That way they'll know more about the future and may be more comfortable with possible changes.

Correcting C's

Show C's the way to get a job done and they'll typically master the format, then modify it to suit their individual needs. They tend to start with what they have to work with, then personalize it, almost from the beginning, so that it works better as they see it. So they may avoid people whom they perceive might tell them to do things differently. This is one way Cautious Thinkers maintain control of their work. They tend to side-step authorities who they think are endeavoring to correct them. At the extreme, this behavior can appear sneaky to other types, especially if the C gets caught.

Specify the exact behavior that is indicated and outline how you would like to see it changed. Establish agreed-upon checkpoints and times. Allow them to save face, as they fear being wrong. "Nelson, your work here is typically done neat, on time, and right on the money. Now that we're switching the office to computers, you'll be able to turn out the same quality of work, only faster. I'd like you to take this computer class . . ."

Communicating with them

Be well-organized and clear in your communications, since they are likely to ask lots of questions about a situation or subject in their search for a logical conclusion. You may want to have them clarify what their more pressing key concerns are. Ask your questions in a more discreet, non-judgmental manner to elicit the points, objectives, or assurances Cautious Thinkers want. "Lenny, I'm not trying to pressure you, but are you just not interested in only the auditor's position, or in any other different position?"

Making decisions and solving problems with C's

Set the stage by making sure they are open to discussing the problem or decision being considered at this time. If they aren't ready, either set a definite time that's better for both of you or explore their concern in even pursuing this subject.

When the situation is being explored, review your impression of the entire process. "My understanding is this—you'd like to think it over for a week or so and figure out what kind of time commitment you'd be able to make to the group. When may I call you about your decision?" Decide on a logical approach for gaining common agreement about both the nature of the problem or decision involved and the most reasonable way of finding how to resolve it. Do so in a way that is likely to be most satisfactory to them, you, and any other key individuals involved.

When suggesting a different possibility to C's, point out how you would like to be able to identify those ideas, perspectives, or actions likely to allow you, them, and others to reach a more perfected solution or situation. Stress how less difficulties or confusion are likely to result. Ask them what insights and suggestions they, or individuals they know and value, could bring to this situation. "Carol, if we leave at 10 o'clock Friday morning and get to Palm Springs around 11:00, we could meet with Mr. Conkill and his V.P.'s for lunch to present our ideas for organizing their grand opening party. Do you know any wholesalers we can contact there so we can come up with a realistic estimate for making their party a bona fide hit?"

When acknowledging C's

Focus on your realization of how difficult it can be at times for them to attempt to meet the high personal standards they set for themselves. Also focus on how much you appreciate this personal characteristic for what it's done to make things better for you in your relationship with them. Cite a specific and appropriate example which proves this point. "Robert, you're a very good chef. That salmon was cooked perfectly; juicy and flavorful without a hint of dryness. I don't want to embarrass you, but I feel obliged to share with you how truly impressed I am. Thank you for your efforts." Then, notice his reaction. If it's discomfort, share with him that you did not mean to embarrass him, but just to let him know how much you value him. If his reaction is more positive, ask him to tell you more about the sense of satisfaction and enjoyment he derives from similar things. "I'll bet you like creating other recipes, too. Is that correct?"

Delegating with C's

Take time to answer their most critical questions about structure and/or guidance they require in a specific situation. The more they understand the details, the more likely they will be to complete the task properly. Be sure to establish deadlines. "Angela, the court date on the Mortimer case has been moved up to Monday, so we have to respond by speeding things up a bit. It will proceed almost as efficiently as if you researched everything by yourself if we enlist two associates to help you work, under your direction, on tasks you delegate to them and then review. Before getting started, do you have any preferences on the *who's* or *how to's* of this process that you think are essential to check with me at this time?"

The "best" leadership style

Remember, there is no such thing as one best, all-purpose leadership style. Instead, the best leaders are those who realize what a job, role, or specific situation requires for successful performance and then ensures those outcomes. At times, this may involve a clear-cut match between your own strengths and the required actions. At other times, behavior requirements may vary. The effective leader may adapt his own natural style by using new behavior methods he has learned. Or he might call upon other qualified individuals whose talents and energies can more productively handle the immediate problem. Or a good leader may take action to modify the environment. This could include shifting the work priorities to ensure the successful completion of the necessary task without sacrificing the well-being of other people. Productivity will be maximized by using these breakthrough leadership techniques and options.

Action Plan ...

WHEN *YOU* ARE THE CAUTIOUS THINKER

- Modify criticism (whether spoken or unspoken) of others' work
- Check less often, or only check the critical things (as opposed to everything), allowing the flow of the process to continue
- Ease up on controlling emotions;engage in more *water cooler interaction*
- Accept the fact that you can have high standards without expecting perfection
- Occasionally confront a colleague (or boss) with whom you disagree, instead of avoiding or ignoring them (and doing what you want to do, anyway)
- Tone down the tendency to OVER prepare

WHEN OTHERS ARE CAUTIOUS THINKERS, GENTLY REMIND THEM TO:

- Share their knowledge and expertise with others
- Stand up for themselves with the people they prefer to avoid
- Shoot for realistic deadlines and parameters
- View people and tasks less seriously and critically
- Balance their lives with both interaction and tasks
- Keep on course with tasks, with less checking
- Maintain high expectations for high priority items, not necessarily everything

People Smart Principle #7—The Magic Principle of Sales and Service: "Successful sales and service happen when you get what you expect, or more."

Chapter 7
Selling and Servicing With Style!

Every sales or service call has certain similarities; however, the techniques differentiate the professional salesperson from other salespeople. Professionals focus more on helping than selling, more on listening than talking, more on problem-solving than persuading, more on creating long-term customers than one-shot sales.

The techniques used by professionals are simple, yet powerful. Salespeople who use this approach concentrate on a consultative process that allows both the customer and the salesperson to feel good about the sales/service exchange and each other. Professional sales and service staff go through five specific steps, though the approach may vary, depending on the personality style of their prospects.

You can apply the tips in this chapter to help you maximize your sales and service encounters, whether you fill the role of buyer or seller. Think of someone you know in a sales or service situation who sounds like the Dominant Director, Interacting Socializer, Steady Relater, and Cautious Thinker. How can you benefit with each one of them in a business relationship?

Step #1—making contact

The purpose of talking with your prospect is to begin building a business relationship by opening up lines of communication. Professional salespeople know that a solid business association goes beyond the immediate product or service being offered. The relationship, and therefore, the sale, require the establishment of trust and the building of credibility. When prospects know you sincerely have their best interests in mind, the rest of the process can continue. Today's buyers are appreciative of professionals who show an interest in them, their businesses, and their lives.

Step #2—studying needs

Professional sales and service people spend a great deal of time studying their prospects' needs. They look not only for needs but for opportunities. Searching just for needs implies customers just have problems that must be solved. Looking for or creating opportunities puts the salesperson in the position of a consultant who can take someone's current conditions and improve upon them. They can encourage the prospect to become involved in this exploratory process. By asking well-structured questions, offering thought-provoking possibilities, and studying the many facets of the prospect's situation, you build cooperation—and a foundation for shared commitment.

Step #3— proposing solutions

After meeting with the potential customer and studying his or her situation, the next step is to propose a solution to the problem. The professional approach is one in which the presentation is custom tailored to the prospect's needs. Because of the comprehensive discussions the service or salesperson has had with the prospect, benefits naturally emerge as they relate to specific problems.

Step #4—gaining commitment

This is a logical conclusion to the ongoing communication and agreement that has been taking place with the prospect. Since the salesperson and prospect have worked together on a common goal since the beginning, there are few reasons why objections would be voiced at this point. There may be details to work out, but they won't get in the way. For professional sales and service people, the confirmation becomes a question of when, not if. If resistance occurs, it simply indicates there is a need for gathering more information or clarifying some details. Gaps in communication are not a problem because experienced salespeople are willing to spend time with the prospect until everything is understood and acceptable.

Step #5—assuring satisfaction

Professional sales and service people thrive on satisfied customers and see them for what they are—assets! These veterans begin assuring customer satisfaction after the sale by changing hats from salespeople to quality service providers. They make sure the customer receives the proper order on the right delivery date. They also help the customer track the results and analyze the effectiveness of the product or service for the specific problem(s) addressed. By assuring the satisfaction of each customer, professionals build a clientele guaranteeing future business that will become annuities for life.

How to Sell Your Product or Service to Dominant Directors

Dominant Directors want to know the bottom line. "What will this do for me?" and "By when?" Just give them enough information to satisfy their need to know about overall performance. They don't want you wasting their time reconstructing your product bolt by bolt, giving a laundry list of testimonials about your other satisfied clients, or getting too chummy with them. Even if you don't consider yourself a salesperson, remember that everyone sells something every day—whether ideas, integrity, credentials, image, or a less than palatable looking picnic lunch. Regardless of your work, you can probably apply to your everyday life a few sales tips that typically work with Dominant Directors.

#1—making contact with the D

When you write, call, or meet a Dominant Director, do it in a formal, businesslike manner. Get right to the point. Focus quickly on the task. Refer to bottom line results, increased efficiency, saved time, return on investment, profits, and so on. In other words, tell him what's in it for him.

If you plan to sell something or present a proposal to a Dominant Director, take care to be well-organized, time-conscious, efficient, and businesslike. As impatient as they are with a slower pace, Dominant Directors become especially wary if they question a person's competence. Make sure they don't question yours. Remember, Dominant Directors don't want to make friends with you; they want to get something out of you if they think you have something to offer. And they're usually willing to pay for it.

As a sales or service person, it is your job to provide both sufficient information and enough incentive for the Dominant Director to meet with you. When you call, you might say, "Some of the ways I thought we would be able to work together are X, Y, and Z. Could we discuss those when I call you at a time of your choice?" By planting a seed, you may raise his interest level and the priority of your next call, unless, of course, he just isn't interested. Since individuals who fit this type pride themselves in being busy, they dislike granting several meetings. But if they think that time spent now will save time later, they're likely to initially explore matters with you now, rather than later.

#2—studying D's needs

To head off the Dominant Director's impatience before it surfaces, keep your queries interesting by alternately asking questions and giving additional information. Do this in a practical manner. Dominant Directors need to view the meeting as purposeful, so they want to understand where your questions ultimately lead. When asking a Dominant Director questions, it is essential to fine-tune and make them as practical and logical as possible. Aim questions at the heart of the issue and ask them in a straightforward manner. Only request information which is unavailable elsewhere.

When information gathering, ask questions showing you have done your homework about their desired results and current efforts. Know the Dominant Director's industry and company. Be sure to make queries that allow him to talk about his business goals. "Since your leadership has brought your company from 27th to 3rd in the country, what happens now?" Gear your studying toward saving the Dominant Director time.

#3 — proposing solutions for D's

Your presentation, whether it is combined with studying or given on its own, must be geared toward the Dominant Director's priorities. He is concerned with saving time, generating money, and making life easier and more efficient. If you gear your presentation toward how he can become more successful, you'll no doubt get his attention. Zero in on the bottom line with quick benefit statements.

Because of their lack of time, Dominant Directors do not focus as much energy on contemplating and evaluating ideas. They want you to do the analysis and lay it out for them to approve or disapprove. Dominant Directors like rapid, concise analyses of their needs and your solutions.

So how can a salesperson get into a better business relationship with a Dominant Director? Act like a Boy Scout and *Be prepared*. In addition, demonstrate your competence and show him how your product will help him achieve his goals. Focus on results and highlight important specifics. Cut out intermediate steps when you make your presentation, eliminate the small talk, and stick to business. Professionalism counts with the Dominant Director.

During those times when it's appropriate to give historical data about your company or a more detailed presentation, write it out before you call. This allows you to highlight key points with a marking pen before you see him. Otherwise you're liable to bury him in a mass of paperwork. Skip over less important facts and show him the bottom line basics. Then leave a copy of the printout with him so he can refresh his memory later. Or he may want to delegate the fact checking to someone who really enjoys it—a Cautious Thinker or Steady Relater.

There's another good reason for reviewing your material, printing it out, and highlighting it. A Dominant Director may fire off questions at what seems to be a faster-than-the-speed-of-mouth rate. When he wants to hear about how your product ties into the bottom line, he wants to know now. Determine if he really needs the information immediately to make his decision or if he just wants to challenge you. In many cases, if he gets the information an hour from now, you can still meet his needs.

#4—gaining commitment with the D

With Dominant Directors, you can come right out and ask whether they're interested. You might say, "Based on what we've just discussed, are you interested in starting our service or carrying our product?" A Dominant Director will often tell you yes or no in no uncertain terms. At times, though, this type can put you off as if they can't make a decision, when, in fact, they aren't even thinking about it. They can become so preoccupied with other business that they literally do not have the time to evaluate your ideas, especially if they don't have enough information.

When you draw up a commitment letter, pay attention to how much time you spend on points the Dominant Director may not care about. Explain your commitment to attain both his bottom line results and your goals for a mutually acceptable agreement.

Consequently, the best way to deal with a Dominant Director is to give him options and probable outcomes. Bear in mind that the Dominant Director likes to balance quality with cost considerations, so include this information when you want him to make a decision. Then offer options with supporting evidence and leave the final decision to him. "The way I see it, you can go with Option A (tell pros and cons), Option B (more pros and cons), or Option C (still more pros and cons). I've outlined these three plans, costs of implementation, and approximate completion dates. Which one sounds best to you?" Dominant Directors seek control, so let them make the

> ### SALES AND SERVICE STRATEGIES FOR DEALING WITH DOMINANT DIRECTORS:
>
> - Plan to be prepared, organized, fast-paced, and always to the point
> - Meet them in a professional and businesslike manner
> - Learn and study their goals and objectives—what they want to accomplish, how they currently are motivated to do things, and what they'd like to change
> - Suggest solutions with clearly defined and agreed upon consequences as well as rewards that relate specifically to their goals
> - Get to the point
> - Provide options and let them make the decision, when possible
> - Let them know that you don't intend to waste their time

final decision. Brief and to the point, like the Dominant Director himself, this approach automatically fills his need to have the final word.

#5—assuring D satisfaction

Since Dominant Directors usually don't emphasize a personal relationship in business, if you sell to one, don't rely on past sales to ensure future purchases. Follow-up with the Dominant Director to find if he has any complaints or problems with your product. If he does, fix them or his impatience may motivate him to seek help elsewhere, probably with another company. As Willy Loman found out in *Death of a Salesman*, contacts meant nothing in an age that emphasized change and product performance.

Impress upon your prospect that you intend to stand behind your product or service. Further stress that you will follow-up without taking a lot of his time. "You're buying this to save effort and time. I want to make sure it continues to work for you. I'll periodically check back to make sure everything is running smoothly, but I don't want to waste your time with unnecessary calls. When I telephone, if everything is fine, just say so and that will be it. If anything is less than what you expect, I want you to call me right away and I'll see to it the problem is fixed immediately." You may also want to offer a money back guarantee "If you aren't satisfied that you got your money's worth, I will personally take back the merchandise and write you a check."

How to Sell Your Product or Service to Interacting Socializers

As with the other types, apply your active listening skills, but be an especially empathic listener with Interacting Socializers. Give positive feedback to let them know that you understand and can relate to what they're feeling. When you talk about yourself, remember to use feeling words instead of thinking words. To paraphrase this concept, share your vision of the world in terms of your emotions, opinions, and intuitions. Tell stories about yourself, especially humorous or unusual ones, to win the heart (and sale) of an Interacting Socializer. Allow them to feel comfortable by also listening to their stories, even to the point of talking about topics that may stray from the subject.

#1—making contact with the I

When you write to or personally meet an Interacting Socializer, give the letter or meeting an upbeat, friendly feeling and faster pace. Don't talk about features, specifics, or performance data. In your initial benefits statement, stress those aspects of your product or service that will give them what they want—status, recognition, excitement, and being the first one on their block to have the newest, most dynamic product or service you can offer.

The first time you call an Interacting Socializer, use a more open-ended, friendly approach. Tell him who you are and say something like, "I'd like to come by and show you an exciting new product that will analyze and organize your accounts and help you become even more of a top performing salesperson."

When you meet an Interacting Socializer, think (or more specifically feel) in terms of someone running for election. Shake hands firmly, introduce yourself with confidence, and immediately show interest in him personally. Let him set the pace and direction of the conversation. Since Interacting Socializers typically enjoy talking about themselves, ask questions about them. "How did you got into this business?" Prepare for lengthy answers, though. Plan to have as many meetings with an Interacting Socializer as necessary to build the relationship and gather information. After your first visit, you may want to meet for breakfast or lunch. Placing a time limit on those two meals is easier than putting a cap on dinner.

#2—studying I's needs

Interacting Socializers get bored quickly when they're not talking about themselves. That's why so much information gathering needs to revolve around them. But remember to strike a balance between listening to their life's stories and gathering the information you need to be an effective sales consultant. When asking business questions, keep them brief. If you can, work these exploratory questions in with the social questions."You mentioned people as one of the keys to your success. How do you find (recruit) the people you work with? What kind of training do you give them?" The better your relationship with an Interacting Socializer, the more willing he'll be to cooperate and talk about the task at hand.

Interacting Socializers can be so open they may tell you their fondest hopes and aspirations. If you can demonstrate how your product or service can get them closer to their dreams, they may become so excited about your product—and you—that they're likely to sell themselves to you.

#3—*proposing solutions for I's*

Style is as important as substance, so sell the sizzle as well as the steak. The presentation should show an Interacting Socializer how your product or service will increase his prestige, image, or recognition. Talk about the favorable impact or consequences your suggestions will have in making their working relationships more enjoyable. Give them incentives for completing tasks by stressing how their contribution will benefit others and evoke positive responses from them. Presentations need impact for this type, so involve as many senses as possible. Interacting Socializers want both the presentation and the product to feel great. They also want to be reminded of who else has it; but spare them the details of other people's successes. Show them how you can save them effort and still make them look good.

Back up your claims with testimonials from well-known people or corporations. Interacting Socializers respond well to other people's positive experiences with your product or service—so tell them who else uses it. If one of their heroes tries something, they're likely to try it, too. Better yet, name some satisfied acquaintances that the Interacting Socializer knows and admires. He may even respond with, "Go no further. If it's good enough for Frederick Mullens, it's good enough for me. He probably spent weeks researching, comparing, and contrasting. He really knows what he's doing. You should put that guy on your payroll."

#4—*gaining commitment with the I*

Be open and ask, "Where do we go from here?" or, "What's our next step?" If your inventory is low, tell them. "I see you really are excited about this. I only have three left. Do you want one now?" Interacting Socializers are very spontaneous and respond well to the bandwagon approach— "Everybody's doing it." If they like something, they buy it (all other things being equal). You may have to hold them back because they also tend to overbuy, a behavior that both you and your customer may live to regret.

Interacting Socializers don't like paperwork and details, so they're likely to hesitate, and even procrastinate, when it comes to spending the time required to create a commitment letter specifying who does what by when. "Do you really think I won't live up to my word?" While a handshake is usually good enough for them, you'd be wise to have a written understanding. Both of you may hear the same words, but Interacting Socializers tend to interpret those words in a positive light—and often to their advantage. For this reason, it may help to draw up a summary in advance and go over it with this type of prospect. Make absolutely sure that you agree on the specifics or, later on, you can almost bet on some degree of misunderstanding and disappointment.

When the Interacting Socializer tells you a written agreement isn't necessary, simply say that you need such a clear summary for your own benefit so as to help yourself and others remember what is expected. Also mention that you appreciate their show of faith in you. You might say something like, "I just want to make sure that we're in 100% agreement, Mark. I'll feel better about this if I keep a record for us to have if we ever need to refer to it in the future." When you put your concerns in terms of such desired positive feelings, how can the Interacting Socializer object?

"Okay, if it will make you feel better about it, but I"m already 100% sure," he may respond. Next, if required, change whatever details require changing and the job will be done, quickly and painlessly. Finally, go ahead and write up this agreement as a means of verification and send or, better yet, give him a copy in person. Then you'll have a much better shot at a more long-standing, productive business relationship.

#5—assuring I satisfaction

In business, as in love, Interacting Socializers frequently buy before they're sold. When they jump in too quickly, the probability that they may suffer buyers' remorse is higher than for the other personality types. Interacting Socializers need ongoing reminders that they've made the right purchase decision because they get bored quickly, even with new things. So make sure you reinforce their decision by giving them plenty of service and/or assistance immediately after the sale. Be certain they actually do use your product, or this type may

get frustrated from incorrect usage and either put it away—
never to be used again—or return it for a refund.

Think of yourself as an organizer for a basically less
organized type to allow them to get the most out of your
product. As a bonus for the extra effort, remember that they
tend to *talk up* or *talk down* whatever pops into their minds.
Since they mingle with so many people, you can even ask
them if they would be willing to share with others their
glowing testimonials about you and your product or service.

**SALES and SERVICE STRATEGIES FOR
DEALING WITH INTERACTING SOCIALIZERS**

- Show that you're interested in them, let them talk,
  and allow your animation and enthusiasm to
  emerge
- Take the initiative by introducing yourself in a
  friendly and informal manner and be open to new
  topics which seem to interest them
- Support their dreams and goals
- Illustrate your ideas with stories and emotional
  descriptions that they can relate to their goals or
  interests
- Clearly summarize details and direct these
  towards mutually agreeable objectives and
  action steps
- Provide incentives to encourage
  quicker decisions
- Give them testimonials

How to Sell Your Product or Service to Steady Relaters

Steady Relaters, concerned with maintaining stability for
themselves, want to know step-by-step procedures that are
likely to meet their need for details and logical follow-through

action. Organize your presentation—list specifics, show sequences, and provide data. If possible, outline your proposals or materials. Satisfy their need to know the facts, but also elicit their personal feelings and emotions by asking for their input on how to aspects.

Listen patiently to Steady Relaters, projecting your true interest in them as individuals in their own right. Express your appreciation for their steadiness, dependability, and cooperative teamwork. Get to know Steady Relaters personally. Flex yourself to be non-threatening, pleasant, friendly, but still professional. Develop trust, credibility, and friendship at a relatively slow, informal pace. Then communicate with them in a consistent manner on as regular a basis as is required.

#1—making contact with the S

Letters to Steady Relaters are best when soft, pleasant, and specific. Include the human element as well as references to things. Mention the name of the person who referred you and relate everything about your product or service to its impact on calls. "Hello, Mr. Newhouse, I'm Sheldon Doolittle with the Pinpoint Acupuncture Clinic. Mary Walsh said you would appreciate knowing about me and my clinic. Oh, she did call you? Good. If you'd like, I could come by, we could get to know each other, and I can tell you about the ways other people have relieved their allergies with our treatments." Remember, you may have the best product or service in the world, but if the Steady Relater doesn't like you, she'll settle for second, or even fourth-best, from a salesperson she likes.

#2—studying S needs

Steady Relaters can be excellent interviewees. Talk warmly and informally and ask gentle, open questions that draw them out, especially around more sensitive areas. Show tact and sincerity in probing about their needs. "Mr. Harmon, I noticed that you've been here for 30 years. You must have seen a lot. Hypothetically speaking, how would you go about refining a few of the things that aren't working around here in the Information Systems Department?"

If they do not have a good feeling about your product, company, or even you, they will not take the chance of hurting your feelings by telling you so. They want to avoid confrontations, even minor ones. So Steady Relaters may tell you what they think you like to hear, rather than what they really think. This same reticence may apply to telling you about their dissatisfaction with your competitors. Even though this is exactly what you want to hear, the Steady Relater may think, "I know it hasn't been working well, but they're such nice people. I don't want to say anything negative about them."

#3—proposing solutions for S's

Show how your product/service will stabilize, simplify, or support their procedures and relationships. Clearly define their roles and goals in your suggestions, and include specific expectations of them in your plan. Present new ideas or variations from their current routines in a non-threatening way. Provide them with the time and opportunities to adjust to changes in operating procedures and relationships. When change becomes necessary, tell them why. Explain how long the changes will take and any interim alterations of the current conditions. Design your message to impart a sense of stability and security. "This plan will enable you to continue doing things the same basic way, with a few updates here and there. Don't worry about the updates because I'll be here to walk you through them each step of the way. And the real benefit, in the final analysis, is that this refinement will result in more stability than we now have."

Concentrate on security, harmony, steadiness, and concrete benefits. "This pension plan could help your entire staff save for their retirement with a minimum amount of worry. Even though Social Security may be tapped out by the time they retire, they'll be able to depend on this safety net." Answer their concerns about how and what as well as you can. Reassure them that you'll find out about the information they want to know; then do it. Stress that this isn't a big change, just a way to help them do what they already do . . . only better.

Steady Relaters like to be shown the appropriate steps to follow, so share those with them. "After you turn the equipment on, push the blue button to activate the computer. When you hear the motor, begin." Involve them by asking their opinions. "Is this an important concern for you, or are you looking for some other specific benefit, instead?"

#4—gaining commitment with the S

Steady Relaters are slow, deductive decision-makers. They listen to the opinions of others and take the time to solicit those opinions before making up their minds. So make a specific action plan. Provide personal guidance, direction, or assurance as required for pursuing the safest, most logical course to follow. When you reach agreement, try to explore any potential areas of misunderstanding or dissatisfaction. Steady Relaters like guarantees that new actions will involve a minimum risk to their desired stable state, so offer assurances of support.

Try not to rush them, but do provide gentle, helpful nudges to help them decide, when needed. Otherwise, they may postpone their decisions. Involve them by personalizing the plan and showing how it will directly impact them and their co-workers. "Our system will identify which employees deserve immediate raises at a faster rate than our old method." When asking for a commitment, guide them toward a choice if they seem indecisive. "We've gone over all the possibilities for improving customer service, Seymour. I think this option is the best because it will generate the most customer interest. Why don't we go ahead and implement it now?"

Another approach is to lead Steady Relaters. Once you have determined which action is in their best interest, lead them to the confirmation with your recommendation. "Jean, we've talked about a lot of things and I firmly believe this is the best solution for you. I would not recommend it if I wasn't 100% convinced it will work for you." When you've gained agreement, you can gently lead the Steady Relater to the next step. "If you agree with everything we've just discussed, our next typical step with a customer is to fill out the agreement and then begin the process with a deposit."

SALES AND SERVICE STRATEGIES FOR DEALING WITH STEADY RELATERS:

- Get to know them more personally and approach them in a non-threatening, pleasant, and friendly . . . but professional. . .way
- Develop trust, friendship, and credibility at a relatively slow pace
- Ask them to identify their own emotional needs as well as their task or business expectations
- Get them involved by focusing on the *human element*. . .that is, how something affects them and their relationships with others
- Avoid rushing them and give them personal, concrete assurances, when appropriate
- Communicate with them in a consistent manner on a regular basis

There is nothing pushy or manipulative about this if you have studied your prospect's needs and are now recommending a solution that you honestly believe best satisfies their needs. Then it's a win-win situation. Anything less is actually a losing proposition for this prospect.

#5—assuring S's satisfaction

Practice consistent and predictable follow-up. Give them your personal guarantee that you will remain in touch, keep things running smoothly, and be available on an *as needed* basis. Steady Relaters like to think they have a special relationship with you, that you are more than just another business acquaintance. Remember they dislike one-shot deals, so follow-up to maintain your relationship. Of all the types, they most prefer a continuing, predictable relationship. Impersonal, computerized follow-through is not as appealing to this type, so continue building your business relationship with your low-keyed attention and offers of assistance. "I'll call on you once each month to make sure you're satisfied with our product. If you have any problems or concerns at all, just phone me at my office and I'll get back to you as soon as I can. In fact, here's my home number."

How to Sell a Product or Service to Cautious Thinkers

Cautious Thinkers are precision people, efficiency experts who want to do their jobs as they want to do nearly everything else: the correct way. They also seek confirmation that they're right, but won't typically volunteer that need. Going about tasks slowly so they have enough time to check things out, they dislike rushing or being rushed. They operate on a level that prefers *thinking* words, not *feeling* ones, so build your credibility by remembering to think with your head, not with your emotions. Focus on their level of understanding about the *what's* and *why's* of your proposal.

#1—*making contact with the C*

Before meeting, tell them briefly what you'll cover so they know what to expect. This can be done when you make the appointment. Show them logical proof from reliable sources that accurately documents your quality, track record, and value. Once you've verified your credentials, preferably in writing or with tangible examples (make copies of a few), you can establish your product's or service's credentials, too.

Speak slowly. Economize on words. Explain why you are contacting them. This type doesn't care as much about social interaction, beyond courtesy and pleasantness, so get to the point. Avoid making small talk and speaking about yourself, except to initially establish your credibility. Cautious Thinkers tend to be somewhat humble and are naturally suspicious of those who *talk themselves up.*

#2—studying C needs

Cautious Thinkers often like to answer questions that reveal their expertise, so they can be very good interviewees. As long as you ask logical, fact-oriented, relevant questions, they tend to enjoy talking to you. Phrase your questions to help them give you the right information. "How many pages of completed copy do you typically write per week?" Ask open and closed questions that investigate their knowledge, systems, objectives, and objections. "When do you foresee finishing this project?" or "What possible problems do you think you might encounter?" Let them show you how much they know.

Make your own answers short and crisp. If you don't know the answer to something, don't fake it. Tell them you'll get the answer for them by a certain time, then do it.

#3—proposing solutions for C's

Emphasize logic, accuracy, value, quality, and reliability. Present obvious disadvantages. Make your points, then ask if they want further clarification. They dislike talk that isn't backed up with both supporting evidence and achievement-focused action. Describe the process that you plan to follow. Then outline how that process will produce the results they seek. Elicit specific feedback. "So far, what are your reactions? Do you have any reservations that you'd like to clear up?" (They probably do, so encourage communication). "Specifically, how do you view the practicality of applying this computer program to satisfy your current requirements?"

Of all the types, this one is the most likely to see the drawbacks, so point out the negatives before they do. Such honesty will only enhance your credibility. If you don't draw attention to the disadvantages, this type may view your failure to do so as a cover-up. Instead, let them assess the relative costs versus benefits which are typical trade offs when making realistic choices between available, competing, yet imperfect, products or services.

#4—gaining commitment with the C

Provide logical options with documentation. Give them enough time and data to analyze their options. Unlike Dominant Directors and Interacting Socializers, this type is uncomfortable with snap decisions. When they say they'll think about it, they're probably serious. On the other hand, when a Steady Relater says, "I'll think about it," he may be stalling, or may, in fact, not want your product.

Unless Cautious Thinkers have already researched the field and determined that your product is the best, they probably have your competitors calling on them. Know your competition so you can point out your advantages relative to what

---

SALES AND SERVICE STRATEGIES FOR DEALING WITH CAUTIOUS THINKERS:

- Prepare, so that you can answer as many of their questions as soon as possible
- Greet them cordially, but proceed quickly to the task; don't start with personal or social talk
- Hone your skills in practicality and logic
- Ask questions that reveal a clear direction and that fit into the overall scheme of things
- Document how and why something applies
- Give them time to think, so avoid pushing them into a hasty decision
- Tell them both the pros and cons as well as the complete story
- Follow through and deliver what you promise

---

they offer. This type is the most likely to do their own comparative shopping, so mention your company's strengths as you suggest questions they may want to ask your competitors.

"Ask them if they have an unconditional money-back guarantee," or, "How long have you been in business?" or, "Will they also train new employees at no additional cost?" In short, point out the things your company does as well or better than your competition. Do this in a factual, professional way that is based on allowing them to do a comparative *cost-benefit* analysis of the options.

#5—assuring C customer satisfaction

Set a specific timetable for when you'll measure success. Continue proving your reliability, quality, and value. Make yourself available for follow-up on customer satisfaction. "Mr. Quimby, I'll check back with you on Tuesday morning, if that's all right, to make sure that your new phone system is functioning correctly. Here's my card with the numbers of my office, home, and emergency 24-hour hot line if you experience any problems."

Part Three

Personal Applications

Chapter 8
The Social Scene

Accentuate the positive

Again, to get the most out of this material, picture real people you know who fit each of the basic four descriptions in a social setting. What are each one's more effective traits in a social encounter? The less effective ones? As you read, visualize how you can maximize your communication with each of them by appealing to their natural strengths.

Dominant Director Social Behaviors

A time and place for everything

By their nature, Dominant Directors are motivated to manage, lead, organize and rule. At times, however, this may be inappropriate; for instance, at someone's wedding, funeral or social lunch. For many Dominant Directors, respecting people's rights and opinions, allowing others to take charge, and just plain *letting go* are learned, acquired behaviors. Yet these are precisely the behaviors that can enable Dominant Directors to experience enhanced emotional satisfaction in their personal and social relationships.

The point must be clear

"Why are we doing this?" a Dominant Director might ask, especially if she has something better in mind. She doesn't like to participate in fun for fun's sake, but for a specific purpose. Regardless of how friendly the atmosphere or close her relationship to others involved, this type generally tries her hardest to be the best—and win—whether in the boardroom promoting an idea or the living room playing a party game. She tends to give 100% effort. She's not interested in a lot of details or in postponing her quest for victory with conversation, jokes, or other digressions.

Business and friendships often overlap for Dominant Directors. They like to mix their own business interests with pleasure, so they often pick friends from their work pool. When they find time for making friends, they do it by experimentation. If the experiment works, and it often hinges on how much potential friends agree with them and help them get desired results, great! If not, goodbye! Also they don't like doing anything they don't want to do. For instance, they may very well bring their own cars to escape early, disappear to make a phone call, start reading the newspaper, or otherwise do something they enjoy.

The joke is often on you!

Dominant Directors favor humor that's to the point and pulls no punches, often with more than a bit of self-importance thrown in! They have been known to enjoy making fun of others. Don Rickles, Joan Rivers, and Roseanne Barr have all built careers from this type of perspective. Generally speaking, though, in many settings, Dominant Directors tend to take themselves too seriously. A well-placed joke can often help them and others benefit from laughing more and enjoying the humorous side of their own and others' actions.

Do You Really Want to Know?

If the Dominant Director just wants to kick back, that, too, is his decision. But he may prefer running an activity or pulling strings to get things done. Just ask and he'll generally tell you. As one astute observer noticed, "If you can't handle

the answer, don't ask the question." Naturally blunt, Directors
tend to tell it like it is—at least from their perspective.

For party planners everywhere: Give
Dominant Directors something to do...from a
set of options, of course. That way, they
have control of the final decision and will be
more comfortable.

It's whether you win

Dominant Directors may engage in what they view as
healthy competition with their more assertive friends. This can
accelerate to a battlefield of keeping up with the Joneses, if
not monitored by all concerned. Who has the biggest, most
expensive house? Who gives the best parties? Who has the
most charming personality? And on and on. Dominant Director friends may even compete in catching each other in
inconsistencies. "No one was supposed to start yet, Dom. I'm
just repeating what you said, remember? Penalty, here! "
Often Directors need to learn to cultivate tact and diplomacy,
instead of telling others how they feel so bluntly that it yields
counterproductive results for their social relationships.

Social niceties aside, Dominant Directors usually do not
want to be saddled with the worst player(s) when they're
working hard at winning. Knowing that Howard has virtually
no know-how in *Trivial Pursuit* and that the hostess favors
man versus woman teams, Dominant Director Marv may
suggest, "Why don't we play with four teams instead of two?
Carol, you and I can be partners." If he can avoid almost
certain defeat with Howard, he'll do it.

Similarly, when this type works on an activity and strives
to win, they keep score. "The men have beaten the women at
Trivial Pursuit the last four times we've played. This time
won't be any different." Then they may naturally immerse
themselves in the game, sometimes provoking hurt feelings,
and even heckling, along the way. "I can't believe you don't

know the answer to that question. And you were an English major?" Down playing their verbalizations of superiority can result in everyone having a better time. It is only a game!

They love taking the credit

One Dominant Director trait that can drive people up the proverbial wall is when they hear or read about a good idea and come to believe the concept really originated with themselves. "When the doctor told Rob to eat less and exercise more, I suggested that he join the Beach and Tennis Club and offered to sponsor him. Now he's claiming that the whole thing was his idea!" Maybe Rob actually believes it himself. Remember, Directors need to be in charge. When they think they're firmly in the driver's seat, their fear of relinquishing the controls to anyone else lessens. So creating ideas (or thinking they do) fits into that pattern of maintaining control. If you can live with that, fine. If not, jostle their memories in private in a joking way.

Lost without a task

For many Dominant Directors, learning what to do in situations that don't require 'giving it their all' can be a difficult lesson. Director Melody says that when she was at a Super Bowl party, where everyone sat around and watched TV, she had no idea what to do. She usually tries to avoid situations like that because she literally doesn't know how to act. "When I'm not focused on a task, I'm very uncomfortable." Melody could benefit from letting go occasionally and allowing events and conversations to just happen, instead of looking for some heavy, underlying purpose.

Dealing with Dominant Directors

Remember they have a basic need to feel and be in personal control. They don't like thinking that you may be considering competing with, exploiting, or otherwise using them. As a result, try to convey your openness and acceptance of them as individuals through both your non-verbal and verbal responses. "Harry, you're still an unbelievable go-getter whether you win at this game of Monopoly, or not."

Remember . . .

DOMINANT DIRECTOR
TYPICAL SOCIAL BEHAVIOR

- Actively compete
- Play games to win
- Want to know the purpose of a function
- Like playing with toys and hobbies
- Play parallel to, but not necessarily with, others
- Prone to talk shop at gatherings
- Choose friends by experimentation

DOMINANT DIRECTOR
PREFERRED SOCIAL SITUATIONS

- Want options between which to choose: Example: either swimming, dining out, or playing bridge
- Pay more attention to concrete things; less to emotions
- Resistant to doing anything they don't want to
- Favor direct humor with a touch of superiority
- Prefer groups subject to their control
- Like being in charge of something at social events and activities--score-keeping, judging, giving directions, cooking, chairing a fund-raiser

Action Plan . . .

WHEN YOU ARE THE DOMINANT DIRECTOR

- Consciously concentrate on listening to others
- Respond positively to others feelings
- Apologize or admit mistakes, when appropriate
- Slow down and take time to smell the roses
- Cultivate a less serious outlook
- Admit and then laugh at personal limitations
- View a game as a game and not life or death!
- Give sincere compliments
- Cultivate tact and diplomacy

WHEN OTHERS ARE DOMINANT DIRECTORS

- Convey openness and acceptance of them
- Listen to their suggestions
- Summarize your achievements/accomplishments
- Give them your time and undivided attention
- Appreciate and acknowledge them when possible
- Ensure all activities will be acceptable to them
- Meet their expectations when possible
- Focus on how pleased you are with their results
- Thank them for their contribution

Socializing with D's

They have a need to be considered important by others. Therefore, give them your time, undivided attention, and genuine appreciative acknowledgment when possible and appropriate. By watching their response, you'll probably know whether your actions are satisfying an important unfulfilled need for them. You'll also learn if some other need—in communication or decision-making, for example—requires filling. "Hal, you're a take charge kind of guy. Why not see that we get these jobs done so we can hasten this party along."

Interacting Socializer Social Behavior

"People who love people"

Interacting Socializers specialize in just that—socializing. Most aspects of their lives are open books. They're likely to tolerate most subjects, no matter how close or remote your relationship. Showing and sharing their feelings come naturally to this personality type. Of the four groups, Interacting Socializers feel most comfortable talking about personal topics—marriage, finances, politics, aspirations, and problems— in the first 15 minutes of conversation, or, in more intense Interacting Socializers, even in the first five minutes. They also jump from one activity or topic to another. After a conversation with one, you may think, "Wow-ee! Uh, what did we just talk about?" Or "Their thoughts are like gumballs. They just fall to their tongues and roll out."

Did you hear the one about

Events that may strike terror in the hearts of the other types often become positive experiences for Interacting Socializers. And, as adults, their hair-raising personal anecdotes make exciting, entertaining conversation pieces. So they delight in recreating their near-crash-en-route-to-London saga or their love at first sight stories. The more unique the situation, the better. And of course, Interacting Socializers may embellish a story so it sounds better than what literally took place. They view this tendency toward stretching the truth as *spicing things up* for interested listeners. Since they love to talk, telling a story better and funnier than it happened comes naturally to them. Upon occasion, the more talkative Interacting Socializers have been known not to let facts get in the way of a good yarn.

Oh. Was that confidential?

This tendency may cause problems when friends tell secrets to Interacting Socializers. Unless they're expressly told not to tell anyone about confidential information, Interacting Socializers are not likely to realize the importance of remaining silent out of respect for others.

When you divulge your innermost fears to an Interacting Socializer, he's likely to encourage you with a pep talk. "I know you can do it, Harry! Whatever you decide, I know that decision will work out okay for you. Good luck, Buddy!" Interacting Socializers praise and support others en route to creating a positive environment where they can satisfy their own needs for social approval. They hate isolation, so they sometimes support others to prolong social interaction. Plus, compliments and encouragement make Interacting Socializers feel good, even when they're meant for somebody else. If no one praises him, he's likely to turn his attention to someone else's upbeat comments.

Life of the party!

This type also likes to wax poetic and exaggerate. We know one who, when attending her son's baseball games, cheered the batters on with personalized nicknames—Robert the Rocket, Slugger Seth, Go Johnny Go, Handy Andy, and so on. The other parents called her the resident poet laureate. They either enjoyed or tolerated her enthusiasm. Fortunately for her, no one told her to stop. Interacting Socializers seem to invite controversy, but the best approach in dealing with them is to behave non-judgmentally. If you express your disagreement, they love a good debate, as long as nobody else dominates it; they don't like too much head-to-head competition where they may lose face.

At parties, Interacting Socializers typically meet more people in the room than do the other types. They may stand with their arms around each other, hug, or show some other outward expression of their support for others. After all, it's a perfect setting for them to gain socially-acceptable approval from many people in the same place and in a short period of time. They tend to be life of the party types who can make the transition to party animals relatively easily. We know one who makes extra money hiring himself out as a professional mingler and conversation starter at social functions.

For party planners everywhere: At a sit down function, avoid placing Interacting Socializers together at one end of the table. Sprinkle them amongst the other types or the noise level on one side may well drown out the conversations on the other.

They love the dynamics of relationships and talking; they despise feeling bored. People rally around them because they know how to create fun and find the action. The Interacting Socializers are the most like playful porpoises among the four types who need to feel that many others enjoy their companionship.

That's the general idea

Interacting Socializers typically speak more vaguely when using facts and logic than do the other types. "I read about a case like this last year—in England, I think." Or, they may exaggerate and generalize facts and details they don't know. For example, they tend to round up: "Yeah, Andy made around $100,000 last year." (Actually, Andy only made $75,345.17.) Interacting Socializers feel more comfortable using "best guesstimates" than do the other types. Saki (H. H. Munro), a short story writer, succinctly described this Interacting Socializer tendency when he wrote: "A little inaccuracy sometimes saves tons of explanation." At the extreme, exaggerators like the ad character Joe Isuzu fit this description.

Interacting Socializers may even adopt quotes that strike a fond chord and then conveniently forget the source. As Buckaroo Banzai said, "Wherever you go, there you are." Next, it may change to, As someone once said, "Wherever you go . . ." Finally, extreme Interacting Socializers may say, "As I've always said, Wherever . . ." After a few usages, they may figure that it becomes theirs.

I's are sensitive

Of the four types, Interacting Socializers tend to exhibit the most emotionally sensitive qualities. They naturally scan people's body language, vocal inflections, and eye contact to determine how real the person's feelings seem to be. Their natural, emotional radar system leads them to quickly formulate their impulsive feelings about people. Besides feeling sensitivity for others, they also take perceived slights to heart, so their feelings get hurt rather easily. In fact, at the extreme, they can act so sensitive when it comes to their favorite subject—themselves—that others may perceive them as caring only about *me, me, me!* This habit of bringing their own names, achievements, experiences, and stories into conversations can give others the impression that they're less serious or concerned than they really are. As with any behavior, too much of a good thing can result in overkill.

Slapstick humor and belly laughs

When it comes to humor, Interacting Socializers prefer poking fun at themselves and others. They delight in slapstick humor and belly laughs that smack of high emotion. They look at the lighter side of serious subjects and our own idiosyncrasies and limitations. Rodney Dangerfield, Buddy Hackett, George Carlin, Norm Crosby, Carol Burnett, Gallagher, Dom Deluise, Goldie Hawn, Tracy Ullman, and Jackie Mason all deliver their lines along this self-deprecating (and sometimes other-deprecating), physical vein. These Interacting Socializer comedians involve their audience in characteristic *let loose* ways, leaving them with a lasting impression far beyond the influence of their non-stop talking act.

Lovers of gadgets, bells and whistles

Adult Interacting Socializers love gadgets, but they tend to prefer them most with the works—bells, whistles, and gongs! They also like to be the first ones on their block to own the new whatchamacallit nobody else has even heard of yet. This type may become captivated by calculators that double as video games or watches with alarms, radios, and TV screens. This gadget mentality reflects the need to seek out fun, as well as ways to simplify or lessen unavoidable types of work. Flurries of activity coupled with an opportunity for seeing and being seen constitute a nearly resistance-proof formula for attracting an Interacting Socializer.

I's enjoy making a grand entrance!

Showing up fashionably late is a technique appealing to many individuals of this type. The grander the entrance into a roomful of people, the greater the impact for Interacting Socializers. But sometimes they legitimately forget the details of their social obligations and then tend to fly by the seats of their pants. They may amble in an hour late to a dinner party, then feel embarrassed and say, "Gosh, I thought I was supposed to arrive any time between 7:00 and 9:00!" This type can avoid some of these minor tragedies by reading invitations thoroughly, putting them in a prominent, visible spot, and highlighting key points—such as when and where.

We know one Interacting Socializer who missed her best friend Amy's surprise bridal shower, given by Amy's law firm, because she misplaced the invitation. Ordinarily, Interacting Sheila would have relied on Amy as an optional strategy to keep the details straight. But Sheila didn't call the office to find out more because she didn't want to arouse Amy's suspicions. Two days after the shower, Sheila found the invitation and ended up apologizing profusely for unintentionally, yet somewhat predictably, standing up her friend.

Flight before fight

When stressful situations prevail, Interacting Socializers may say something like, "Boy, you could cut the tension in this room with a chain saw." They typically diffuse conflict with a joke or funny observation. Or they down play the tension by trying to smooth things over. "C'mon, this isn't worth fighting over, is it?" They prefer to minimize stress by ignoring it. Under extreme pressure, Interacting Socializers bail out; to avoid a fight, they take flight. If stress continues to build, they tend to lead with their hearts, sacrificing logic to gut feelings. When they finally do fight, they do so emotionally. At their worst, they may name call or insult their adversary, sometimes saying things in anger which they regret later.

You can't please all the people all the time

It's difficult for the Interacting Socializer to accept that there are some folks out there who will not be charmed by his exciting personality and warmth. Some more controlled, precise behavioral types may even view more extreme Interacting Socializer behavior as flakiness or *form over substance*. The Interacting Socializer may worry about the disapproving person and attempt to win him over with his customary show of intimacy, perhaps divulging a deep personal secret which he feels may bond the two of them. But this may only widen the rift; depending on the other person's behavioral type, he may expect the Interacting Socializer to behave more formally and seriously, with more facts and thoroughness.

Socializing with them

They want to be considered important and need recognition from others, both privately and publicly. You can demonstrate you like and enjoy being with them by giving your attention, time, and physical presence in sharing common activities with them. "Let's share a position on the PTA Board next year so we can do more things together. We'll have a great time!"

Remember that they need to feel accepted and worry-free regarding others' approval of them. Therefore, focus on a positive, upbeat, and warm approach which conveys this

Remember . . .

INTERACTING SOCIALIZER: TYPICAL SOCIAL BEHAVIOR

- Want to be liked and admired
- Fear public humiliation
- Will discuss most subjects, regardless of how distant or casual your relationship
- Are naturally warm, expressive and enthusiastic
- Enjoy bouncing ideas off others
- Are reluctant to fight or confront stressful people or situations
- Perceive life according to feelings
- Naturally discuss emotions with others
- Choose associates and friends by trial and error

INTERACTING SOCIALIZER: PREFERRED SOCIAL SITUATIONS

- Prefer physical contact
- Like hosting or attending impromptu gatherings
- Prefer fun people with different interests
- Seek more positive people and settings
- Find it easy to laugh, joke and play games
- Seek higher visibility positions: host, emcee, etc.
- Prefer humor that pokes fun at their own and others' foibles
- Try to diffuse mild tension with jokes or funny observations
- Prefer to ignore stressors
- Like to share the moment with others

Action Plan . . .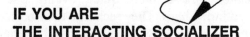

IF YOU ARE
THE INTERACTING SOCIALIZER

- Speak less and listen more
- Focus on facts as well as feelings
- Stick to the subject!
- Realize you can't please everyone
- Fulfill social obligations responsibly and on time
- Work at following through to completion
- Balance socializing with tasks
- Avoid procrastination
- Focus more on substance, less on form

IF OTHERS ARE INTERACTING SOCIALIZERS

- Focus on a positive, upbeat, warm approach
- Listen to their personal feelings and experiences
- Respond openly and congenially
- Avoid negative or messy problem discussions
- Make suggestions that allow them to look good
- Do not require a lot of difficult, follow-up, detail work or longer term commitments from them
- Give them your attention, time and presence
- Publicly and privately acknowledge them
- Suggest different opinions, ideas, and actions by offering them as desirable gifts
- Focus on how glad you are when they succeed

attitude towards them. "Simon, we've been eagerly awaiting your arrival. Now the party has officially started!"

Steady Relater Social Behaviors

To find the answer, look within

Steady Relaters are actually quiet, evenly paced, and inwardly focused individuals. They recharge their batteries and renew their energy by looking for answers within themselves and a relatively small group of friends, family, and associates. As warm and open as they may appear, they have private thoughts they're unwilling to divulge to almost anyone. Their energy drains when called upon to tell all.

They're optimistic realists

Steady Relaters distrust the intangible. They dislike deviating from the established order and dealing with abstractions, preferring instead to follow a predetermined, sensible format. Like Sancho Panza in Don Quixote, their feet stay firmly planted on the ground in concrete reality.

They like routine, predictability, and stability. Consequently, they tend to anchor the other types with their patience, cooperation, and follow-through. They need a firm grip on the facts before feeling ready to proceed, so provide them with step-by-step information whenever possible. They enjoy team efforts and work willingly to bolster comfortable, efficient working conditions.

A pleasant time is the name of the game

People of this type often like to support and encourage everyone concerned, not just the kids on their own child's sports teams, for example. Priscilla usually roots for everyone on both soccer teams. "Nancy, your Cindy is such a conscientious goalie, she's caught every ball so far. Oh, my Laurie has the ball now. O-o-o-oh! Too bad, Laurie. Next time. But good catch, Cindy." We know one Steady Relater dad who had to leave a game early. As he walked away, he actually called out, "I hope the team that plays the best and acts the nicest wins. And, remember, Carrie, enjoy yourself playing no matter what!"

Party time for S's

At parties, Steady Relaters like to seek out people they know quite well, or make advance arrangements to go to the event with someone else they know has been invited. Then they may end up conversing with that same person all night unless they remind themselves to mingle. They prefer having others approach them. In fact, they may project such a calm, accepting attitude that others often do seek them out. Sometimes, their peaceful demeanor can elicit unexpected responses. "Paul, this is only the second time I've talked with you, but I feel as though I could talk to you about almost anything." Paul may involuntarily blush, but after the fact, he may feel satisfied and appreciated by the compliment.

For party planners everywhere: Seat Steady Relaters with others who have the potential to become close friends with them. However, in a pinch, since Steady Relaters tend to tolerate diverse behaviors from others, this type is the best bet for placement near *less agreeable* guests. Be sure to prepare them beforehand, though, and express your appreciation in advance.

Low-keyed cheerleaders

Steady Relaters often spur on their group's effort in team board games: Pictionary, Scruples, or Trivial Pursuit, for instance. When it's their turn, though, they may inwardly cringe at the thought of all eyes being on them. They usually prefer to work behind the scenes and let others (often Dominant Directors and Interacting Socializers) accept the starring roles. They naturally tend to spread the credit around. "Joel is the one who came up with the answer. I just helped him a little."

Safe, stable relationships

They often choose friends by the test of time method. That is, if the relationships last, then they're the genuine article, safe and dependable. Like Interacting Socializers, they operate somewhat on a feeling level. However, for them, steady thinking comes first. They depend on ways of keeping their lives stable and secure. General conformity is one means used to satisfy their need to feel included by others. Steady Relaters like sincere attention from people and enjoy feeling well liked. They find it easy to listen and have a natural preference for participative communications. In fact, they can almost act so nice dogs seem to want to walk up and pet them!

Extreme niceness can equal gullibility

At times, the flip side of this niceness is that it can present real problems. For instance, they may respond overcarefully to people so as not to hurt their feelings. Consequently, they find it hard to muster up an occasional no, often allowing more assertive types to take advantage of them. Steady Relater Michelle fits this modus operandi to a T. She's just a girl who can't say no. While driving from a San Diego shopping mall one drizzly afternoon, she stopped for a red light. After a second or two, she noticed a clicking sound on the passenger side of her car. Michelle turned to see a middle-aged woman with an arm load of packages opening her door. Instinctively, Michelle moved her own bags from the passenger seat so the woman could sit down.

"Can you drive me to my mother's?" the stranger asked.

Michelle says she heard herself reply, "Sure. Do you need to make any other stops on the way?"

Luckily, the woman answered, "I just want to get there before it rains any harder."

So Michelle dutifully went out of her way to drive her new acquaintance to her mother's, without a hint anything about their encounter seemed out of the ordinary. In fact, she says

she drove all the way home before actually realizing that
something unusual had happened.

Patient people may finish first

Steady Relaters are often naturals at eliciting others'
feelings. When it comes to venting, they can be virtual shock
absorbers. If a hotel or airplane becomes overbooked, for
example, a Steady Relater may typically patiently wait his turn
in line to confirm his reservation—despite the fact that a
disgruntled person ahead of him has announced there is no
more space available. Having listened to a barrage of complaints from the people ahead of him, the Steady Relater
finally reaches the harried desk clerk. "It looks like you've
been having a bad day." When the clerk nods her ascent, the
Steady Relater says, "What happened? Would you like to tell
me about it?"

The poor woman tells him her frustration about the bad
weather and the overbooked conditions, then heaves a sigh
of relief. Poof! Her burden is gone! (We call this the poof
phenomenon.) She looks gratefully at this patient *sounding
board*, now more calmly stating, "Even though all of our
regular space is booked, we still have the Presidential Suite
(or first class seating) open. Would you like to have it, at no
extra charge?"

Lesson: Humble and patient people may inherit a hotel room
(or other perks) just for displaying genuine concern and
thinking of others first, rather than themselves.

An even keel

In the best of all Steady Relater social worlds, everyone
would act friendly, pleasant, and cooperative. No one would
strongly disagree, yell, participate in rowdy scenes, or talk
anyone into anything against their will. Realistically, though—
and this type does operate in a realistic mode—they generally
prefer that people they associate with function without making
a ruckus out of trivial matters. But they often accept others
at face value. "Carl is really a nice guy. He's just rattled about
a few things today." They tend to judge people by how they
act with them, not according to other people's experiences

with them. "I feel sad for Steve when I hear Jack and Bonnie tell those stories about how obnoxious he can be, but he hasn't done anything like that to me. Until he does, I still want to be friendly with him."

The present may be good, but the past is better

"Make new friends, but keep the old; one is silver and the other gold," lines from an old Girl Scout song, apply to Steady Relater types. Chances are they still keep in contact with childhood friends, or even teachers or now-retired doctors. Because familiarity feels so comfortable to them, they may prefer to live in the same neighborhood or area as they did during childhood. Their memorabilia tends to mean more to Steady Relaters than to the other types. It makes them feel more connected to the present, more secure. In this respect, they are possessive about things they own. Similarly, if something has worked in the past, they'll probably try it again. In most aspects of their lives, new or different things don't appeal to them as much as the *good ole* tried and true.

The same activities other types may perceive as monotonous often appeal to a Steady Relater's desire for repetition. Lunch at Leon's on Mondays from 12:00 to 1:00, Tuesday night movies with their best friends, and Friday night aerobics classes with the exercise gang from 6:00 to 7:00 at the Y perpetuate Steady Relaters' fondness for regularity. For them, familiarity doesn't breed contempt, but contentment!

Similarly, Steady Relaters exhibit a rather dry, straightforward, seemingly uncomplicated sense of humor. Henny Youngman's one liners or the perennial George Burns's wit and wisdom often employ just one humor technique, namely the use of reverse logic. They look at life from a slightly skewed, off-center perspective with predictable results in the punch line. Often, the listener can guess the outcome of the joke before it's ever completed.

They keep on keepin' on

Steady Relaters find it difficult to reach beyond their comfort zone and to take chances, so they may need a push to help them grow. They don't give up easily and can persevere for years. But this single-minded resolve has another darker side, too—stubbornness! Although they might remain quiet about resisting change, they may secretly decide to passively revolt. They naturally let little annoyances slide, overlooking things that bother the other types more.

They may bail out

Although Steady Relaters exhibit more patience and long-suffering behaviors than many of their counterparts, they sometimes allow certain irritations to build up so long that the burden becomes overbearing. Because they don't like to rock the boat, they may give in rather than take issue with something. Steady Relaters also bruise easily. You may hurt their feelings without realizing it. When this happens, their attitude tends to be, "What did I do now to upset him that way? They have difficulty separating out others being upset as separate and distinct from their own actions. As a result, they sometimes are rather easily confused or hurt by others and try even harder to improve matters.

What makes them seem so nice?

Steady types may appear almost saintly, simply because they usually don't say anything when something bothers them. They don't want anyone to dislike them. When the chips are down, they're likely to clam up, going into their own protective shell. They often think if they say what's on their minds, they're less likely to remain friends. So they'll avoid confrontation—their biggest fear—at almost any cost. When confrontation becomes unavoidable, they'll typically submit so the relationship can get back to normal, ASAP.

So this desire for peace and stability can motivate Steady Relaters to succumb to compromise just to maintain favorable conditions or to avoid conflict. Ironically, instead of jeopardizing their position with others, speaking up and taking a stand can sometimes enhance their position—especially with people who may view Steady Relaters' tendency to give in as a weakness. Additionally, voicing their thoughts and feelings before they reach the end of their tolerance level can actually help Steady Relaters salvage some relationships before it's too late.

Dealing with Steady Relaters

Remember their primary need is to maintain stability in their own setting. On the other hand, they also fear and resist those changes which they feel are likely to result in more instability than presently exists. Your best approach is one that focuses on how you want to continue to make things as good as always for them, if not better—but on their terms, as they see it. To demonstrate your friendship, you might say, "Angela, I know your best friend's illness may mean you'll go back to Oklahoma for awhile, but you can count on me to keep an eye on things. I'll make sure Molly gets to school every day and that everything else goes along almost as though you were here."

Socializing with S's

They don't like being in a crowd. Instead, they're more comfortable in smaller groups, with people they've known for a longer time and had pleasant relationships with. They like to do things which are planned or at least known in advance. This provides them with a more predictable social experience with known dimensions—such as when things start and finish, when they will take place, who will be there, and how things will be done. To help them get mentally prepared, spell out the parameters and elicit their input. "John, your role in making telephone calls to organize our community Dance-a-Thon will begin about May 14 and end on the day of the event, October 31. If you make 10 phone calls a day, you'll more than meet our goal of 200 attendees; and, of course, you can invite anyone you choose, too. Are you comfortable with this plan, or would you like to modify it in some specific way?"

Remember . . .

STEADY RELATER:
TYPICAL SOCIAL BEHAVIOR

- Like to build ongoing relationships with a small group of people
- Want to be involved in and identified with their group
- Relate to others on a one-to-one basis . . . preferably with predictable role behavior by each person
- Prefer more casual, calming relationships
- Give and expect sincere attention
- Seek stability in their lives by practices like conformity to ensure inclusion by others

STEADY RELATER:
PREFERRED SOCIAL SITUATIONS

- Like to participate in the group's communication and activities
- Enjoy performing regular activities at the same time, same place and same way
- Prefer to communicate in a conflict-free gathering of associates or friends
- Want to know how to play games or complete activities through well-defined, step-by-step procedures
- Like to feel appreciated and well-liked by others, just for who they are and what they contribute

Action Plan . . .

IF YOU ARE THE STEADY RELATER

- Stand up for yourself when others become in-sistent, or even belligerent
- Respond more favorably to required changes
- Occasionally vary your schedule and try new things
- Expand your circle of acquaintances by partici-pating in activities with new people more frequently
- Respond somewhat less sensitively to others
- Occasionally confront others
- Consciously allow occasional disruption of your peace and stability

IF OTHERS ARE STEADY RELATERS

- Focus on a slower-paced, steady approach
- Avoid arguments and conflict
- Respond sensitively and sensibly
- Privately acknowledge them with specific, believable compliments
- Allow them to follow through on concrete tasks
- Show them step-by-step procedures
- Behave pleasantly and optimistically
- Give them stability and a minimum of change

Cautious Thinker Social Behaviors

Cautious Thinkers ponder

This type has the tendency to contemplate things until the opportunity may well slip away. They like to examine the pros and cons of a given situation, so they want to take everything into account. This need to weigh the possibilities and ramifications can create stress in the more impetuous behavioral types: Dominant Directors and Interacting Socializers. But conversely, Cautious Thinkers' innate caution can serve to modify the more impetuous tendencies of other types so that a workable solution may be reached.

C's are sensitized

If we were to say that Interacting Socializers show the most sensitive' behavior, then Cautious Thinkers exhibit the most sensitized behaviors. Their internal antennae are primed to absorb virtually everything around them. As highly intuitive, astute observers of their surroundings, they are like electronic sponges, taking in and processing information about people and things. In fact, Cautious Thinker types often report having difficulty falling asleep and then getting back to sleep if they wake up during the night, saying, "I just can't turn off everything that keeps running through my mind." Additionally, since they are naturally comfortable accessing both the left and right sides of their brains, Cautious Thinkers tend to process many of the complexities of life that escape the other types.

Computerized thinking

Comparatively speaking, Cautious Thinkers operate much like the creator of a computerized program. Initially, they scan the occurrences transpiring through the course of a year. This includes special events or experiences that might require action on their part. An example would be sending cards or gifts to those who've done the same for them—based on their understanding of another's efforts in sending such items. And by the way, if they view such a relationship as lop-sided, you may never hear from them again. Above all, they value privacy, individual space, and discretion in their relationships with others.

They act reserved and distant until they feel they know and can trust you well enough to let down their guard. They plan and select their relationships with others strategically and cautiously. Because they're such private people, they sometimes seem mysterious. Like the elusive Greta Garbo, the fabled film star of the '30's, they may want to be alone. Yet in pursuit of their need for privacy, Cautious Thinkers are tactful, serious, and organized.

Non-verbal clues

When Cautious Thinker Raymond went to a beach party, the party-goers left their garbage wherever it happened to fall. Raymond's facial muscles tightened and he gritted his teeth. Without saying a word, he picked up everyone's litter and threw it in a trash can. But sometimes this precise behavior can embarrass others who may interpret it as, "He's so holier-than-thou." If the partiers had been given a chance to save face, maybe the outcome could have been different. Perhaps Raymond could have used humor instead of apparent disgust to motivate the others to action. For instance, (talking through a bullhorn made from a plastic cup), "This is the Shore Patrol speaking. Pick up your junk or proceed directly to jail. Do not pass GO, do not collect $200." Humor can be a great equalizer.

Since Cautious Thinkers do not readily discuss their feelings, or often even their thoughts, their initial responses can speak volumes about how they really think or feel. That first little smirk or quick, one-syllable laugh can tell you that they're pleased. Or the involuntary clenched fist or pursed lips may indicate disagreement. Watch Cautious Thinkers to detect these automatic, and often accurate, indicators of how they really react to someone or something.

In this respect, when they are upset, don't wait around for them to engage in a verbal boxing match. Instead, their attitude is most likely to be: "I'm not going to get angry; I'm going to get even." They retain a little black book in their minds and keep score. With memories akin to the size of an elephant, they seldom forget, especially when they think they've been wronged. So when you offend them, they mentally turn to the page with your name on it and put down another check mark. When the page fills up, which may take several years, watch out! Then, pow! The curtain descends on your relationship and they're gone, figuratively, and sometimes even literally.

For party planners everywhere: Introduce Cautious Thinkers to others who may have common interests. Be sure to specify what those interests are. Additionally, place them near conversationalists who can draw them out without intimidating them.

Long on results

Cautious Thinkers aren't comfortable with stories or anecdotes about themselves or with sharing their feelings. When asked how they feel about an issue, they may respond with comments like, "I haven't made a final decision yet," or, "I like to keep my opinions to myself." If they really feel pressured by someone, they may tersely say, "That's my business." American cowboy movies often capture the essence of the Cautious Thinker. The Lone Ranger perhaps best symbolizes their short-on-words, no-nonsense, emphasis-on-results approach.

Unique, witty humor

Cautious Thinker humor typically shows a down-home, witty perspective, often from an unexpected third angle. It frequently seems to include a reactive, straight-man element, such as the Will Rogers *last sane man on the face of the earth*, ironic technique. Jack Benny, too, represents the Cautious Thinker comedian par excellence.

And what about Mark Twain or Dick Cavett? Like Woody Allen, their unique brand of humor typically emerges from thinking hard about human feelings and experiences. Then they capture them in timeless stories with penetrating insights of human nature—stories which have been clearly, simply, yet powerfully, communicated.

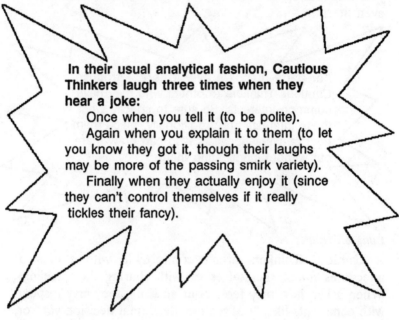

In their usual analytical fashion, Cautious Thinkers laugh three times when they hear a joke:

Once when you tell it (to be polite).

Again when you explain it to them (to let you know they got it, though their laughs may be more of the passing smirk variety).

Finally when they actually enjoy it (since they can't control themselves if it really tickles their fancy).

Who's on first?

Bob, a successful financial planner who enjoys coaching youth baseball, exhibits classic Cautious Thinker behaviors worth noting. He notices the details of the games and whether or not each player performs correctly. He naturally picks up on body positioning—how the boys swing the bats, anticipate catching balls, run and slide to the bases, and play according to specific patterns and rules.

Whereas people of other types may not quite put their fingers on what's amiss, Bob seems to see the problem with little effort. He enjoys discovering their latent talents, especially when he can point out that he was *right about Jeremy's pitching arm* to the other coaches. He even keeps charts to trace the height and weight patterns of the baseball playing adolescents in his neighborhood. From these, he projects each boy's anticipated growth spurts and eventual size.

At ease, but that takes time

Socially, Cautious Thinkers usually opt for small numbers of people with whom they are comfortable. It takes awhile for this type to reach a true comfort zone with others, allowing them to be at ease. In stressful situations, Cautious Thinkers may ask a single question, often confiding in a trusted colleague or friend they can count on for feedback. This confidante may even act as a spokesperson for them. Cautious Thinkers may not speak directly to the source, but instead prefer to work through a known, proven channel. This channel may be another person, a medium of communication, or a productive procedure or process.

Dealing with C's

Remember that they have a basic need for accuracy. Therefore, they are more fearful of mistakes or criticisms resulting from the natural state of human imperfection, which they find difficult to accept. So focus on your appreciation and realization of how hard they work to try to do things correctly and on how you, too, feel this is important, whether you have this same motivation or not. Let them know you value this attribute in them and the accurate results derived from it. "Lenny, when I want something done right, I know you're the one to ask. If you'll agree to fill the auditor's slot for our club, I will be very grateful to you, since we'll be able to rest easy that we won't have lots of problems with our books."

Socializing with C's

They are the most private of the four basic behavioral patterns, so they require more time and space in their dealings with people. They often think others complicate matters, so they prefer to keep involvement down to a few people. The more individuals, the more potential problems and the less independence and efficiency. "If we go away for the weekend with the Bergsons, that means their three children will come, too. That's not my idea of a relaxing weekend."

Remember . . .

CAUTIOUS THINKER:
TYPICAL SOCIAL BEHAVIOR

- Quiet and observant; like to collect information before they enter relationships
- Socially cool and distant--wait for others to take the social initiative
- Discreet and tactful; usually won't tell secrets or the naked truth
- Serious--Naturally suspicious of others unless they've proven themselves in the past
- Guarded--Prefer small group of friends with whom they can let down their shield

CAUTIOUS THINKER:
PREFERRED SOCIAL SITUATIONS

- Attend a small gathering of close friends who have proven their value in the past
- Participate in organized activities where they can be right
- Converse logically about complete bodies of knowledge, adding key details to the conversation
- Can talk facts, not feelings
- Favor conflict-free environments

Action Plan . . .

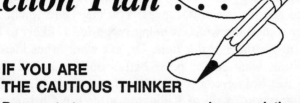

IF YOU ARE
THE CAUTIOUS THINKER

- Demonstrate more concern and appreciation to others with shared feedback: "I really appreciate your thoughtfulness."
- Deal more directly with difficult people and situations
- Adjust quicker to changes, disorganization, and errors
- Avoid dwelling on someone else's mistakes
- Take more initiative by talking to someone else first
- Act somewhat less formal and more casual
- Accept and laugh at personal limitations
- Elaborate on a response instead of replying just yes or no

IF OTHERS ARE CAUTIOUS THINKERS

- Use a logical approach
- Listen to their concerns, reasoning, and suggestions
- Respond rather formally and politely
- Negative discussions are OK, so long as they aren't personally directed
- Privately acknowledge them about their thinkings
- Focus on how pleased you are with their procedures
- Solicit their insights and suggestions
- Show them by what you do, not what you say

This type can be extremely diplomatic and accommodating to others (at least, on the surface) because they often mask their own inner thoughts and feelings. For a truer indication of where they stand, tune into their initial non-verbal reactions to situations, especially those which may require them to make a choice about their preferences. You may want to check out whether something which is being suggested is likely to be *the right thing for them at this time.* Or, ask what other ideas they have about what might be a better option, based on past experiences or interests you've shared with each other. "Gregg, your suggestion to ski at Killington after the Christmas rush was inspired. We skied all day on uncrowded slopes. What do you think about vacation spots this next year?"

People Smart Principle #9—The Principle of Togetherness: "People who stay together communicate and reciprocate with each other."

Chapter 9
It's All in the Family

Try something extra

Someone once said, "You can pick your friends, but you can't pick your relatives." Families are a given entity, so it's inevitable that you may find somebody in yours who is more difficult for you to deal with than in those other groups where you have the luxury of self-selection. Think of someone in your family who typifies each behavioral style and envision how you can better communicate with him or her. What are their more compatible qualities with you? What behaviors do they exhibit which make the two of you less compatible? How can you modify your own behavior to make all four types of people more compatible with you?

Dominant Directors and Their Family Interactions

Options . . . with concise supporting analysis

A variation on the theme of providing options for the Dominant Director still applies in a family setting. "Howard, I've narrowed down our vacation choices to four: Maui, St. Thomas, San Juan, or Acapulco, all warm places with modern conveniences, just what you said you wanted (reference to quality). Here are the costs and travel times for each one. Let me know your preference and I'll make arrangements with the travel agent."

Done that, been there

Dominant Directors specialize in taking charge and getting things done. They are masters and mistresses of delegation and like overseeing the final results. Even on vacations, they enjoy the bustle of performing many activities. For example, when the Brodericks visited Paris, Brian, the husband and father, wanted to see everything. He made sure they were all up by 6:30 a.m. so they could squeeze everything into five days. "Otherwise, what's the point of going to Paris if you don't see all the famous places?" And see the sights they did, whether they wanted to or not.

On the second day, they finally reached the Louvre at 4:00 p.m. That gave them exactly one hour to see the Mona Lisa, Venus de Milo, and thousands of other priceless treasures housed there. Unlike the other three, Brian was happy with literally seeing the sights, however quickly and haphazardly. "Done that, been there!" summed up his perspective on touring Paris. Brian, like other Dominant Directors, has a tendency to look over his family's shoulders to make sure they're conforming to his own expectations. He naturally expects the same breakneck pace from them that he does from himself.

What else can they find to manage?

He even orchestrated his own wedding—set a date (the day after his comprehensive exams from graduate school), secured a hall, planned the buffet menu, found a photographer, and generally managed the entire affair. "Don't worry about a thing," he told his fiancee. "I'll take care of it." And he came through.

Similarly, he planned a budget tour of Europe a year after their marriage. It was another *Hurry up, we've got another place to see* experience. Having visited eight countries in 28 days in their whirlwind travels, they literally fell into bed by 8 o'clock, too exhausted to walk another step.

Another Dominant Director we know assembled his son's crib in the living room. His wife observed, "How are you going to get it through the doorway? The crib is wider than the door."

"No, it isn't," he protested.

She came back with a measuring tape: "It's one inch wider than the door jamb. Start taking it apart and I'll help you haul the parts into Danny's room."

"Don't worry, I'll get it through," he said.

"This is ridiculous. Just admit it won't get through and start over."

"No way. It's going to fit, and that's that." And somehow he crammed that crib through the doorway. He won; but the door lost!

Work can become an obsession

Art, one Dominant Director we know, liked to work so much his career literally took over his life. When he and his wife Jean were invited to play bridge, he'd ask, "How long do we have to stay there? I want to be home by 9 o'clock so I can finish the Steinberg prospectus."

He thought he had to attend occasional formal dances for the business contacts and for the *ring kissing ceremonies*, as Jean described them. Since he disliked dancing, Jean learned to negotiate four dances per event. Finally, she said, "I'm sick and tired of your putting a ceiling on fun! Lighten up or I'll either be a rich widow in 10 years or a rich divorcee in six months." This, and subsequent marriage counseling, woke Art up to the realities of working on more things than his job. Working continued to be his greatest source of pleasure and pride, but he learned to add his wife, children, and friends to his list of priorities.

About D children

Dominant Director children typically busy themselves with things—puzzles, blocks, game shows, or sports—that keep them occupied for hours. They delight in showing Mom and Dad the fruits of their labors. Dominant Director toddlers exhibit tell-tale traits early in life. Dominant Director Justin seldom responded to strangers' overtures. In fact, his mother says, he usually ignored them or looked at them as though he was thinking, "Who is this person and what does she want?" He seemed to focus on his own preferred results soon after infancy. By age four, he demanded flash cards at bath time to the point where his parents contemplated burning them in protest!

If this Dominant Director child temporarily loses his parent in a public setting, his eyes may begin to brim with tears, but he'll usually hold his feelings inside instead of crying, as he actively searches for the missing person. Once taught to do so, you'll easily recognize older Dominant Director youngsters by the way they quickly seek out clerks, security guards, or police if they want help locating an *errant parent*, other person, or things that interest them.

Dominant Director Child: "Did I ask to be born?"
Dominant Director Parent: "If you had, my answer might have been no!"

When they don't get their way, Dominant children often try to take charge of the situation. For instance, one child tried to gain control over the baby-sitter by holding his breath until he turned blue. Parents often describe Dominant Director children as headstrong or difficult, but understanding the child's need for near-complete control over his environment can yield surprising benefits. Allowing Director kids to have authority over pets, toys, their own rooms, or other personal activities can channel their natural need for control in a positive way. Otherwise, they may frustrate their siblings in an effort to parent them. Jessica usually pipes up, "Mom, he thinks he's the boss and he's not!"

When he was almost 13 years old, Jason pumped out one too many verbal abuses (from his mother's perspective). They had a discussion that resulted in a deal: He'd talk politely and civilly to her and she'd stop talking sarcastically to him. This seemed to work fine for two days. When she announced, "Dinner is ready," Jason hurried upstairs and said, "I'm ready." Then he waited. "Gee, Mom, I could have sworn you would have said, 'Yeah, you're ready all right'!"

"Not any more. We made a deal, remember? You're much more pleasant to be around now that you're watching your mouth, so I'm monitoring my sarcasm."

"I guess so, but you know what, Mom? I kind of miss it!" Why? Because, whether they admit it to themselves or not, Dominant Director children (and adults) often enjoy confrontation. As one acquaintance told us, "This (dealing with a Dominant Director child) is definitely not the *E* ticket at Disneyland."

D's deal with tangibles

Since Dominant Directors often view themselves as *results specialists* working towards the realization of tangible goals, they may like to get the family together to elicit what everyone's doing. They can monitor subsequent progress and accomplishments. They typically like giving suggestions. "I'll bet you could do even better if you studied 15 minutes more every day." Or initiating games to develop particular skills. "We'll play this word game to help you build up your vocabulary," or, "We'll practice catching so you can become a better baseball player."

If their helpful hints are accepted as such without arousing anyone's negative emotions, Dominant Directors can maintain a rather high activity level with their families. Being concerned about everyone's feelings drains them of energy, so they prefer to direct conversations toward more tangible, less abstract topics.

Negotiation can become a way of life

Seldom can a family member ask a question of a Dominant Director without meeting with some sort of rebuttal. A simple, "Would you like to go to the movies?" seldom receives a yes or no answer. "If we see Beaches sometime this afternoon, I'll go. Otherwise, I'm not interested." Or, "Okay, if we go to University Town Center. Then we can look at the wide screen TV's in The Television Shack." Dominant Directors often structure their responses in a controlling cause and effect mode. "If you (first) do so-and-so (something I want), then I'll do this (something you want)." Translation: "It needs to be this way, or I won't play." Why? They want to win, or at least have the final controlling say so.

Dominant Directors may favor parallel activities with their spouses and children. They may want everyone under the same roof, or in the same room. Other than that, they frequently have no further need for personal control and may be satisfied letting others do their own thing. One may build model airplanes, another read a book, someone else talk on the phone, and yet another study for an exam. So long as everyone is physically there, without necessarily overlapping or conversing, the Dominant Director is often content. This is because when positively motivated, the D need for control is more focused, limited only to the number one priority at that time, rather than wanting to control everything.

D's compliments have power

Dominant Directors have the dubious distinction of being the least natural listeners among the four types. Why? Partially because they've probably already arrived at an answer. Additionally, they are often too impatient to listen to long explanations or personal, emotional concerns. They also tend to find it easier to give criticism than to provide positive feedback to others. But all Dominant Directors have to do to make giant strides forward are to positively tip the scale in the direction of (1) giving more reinforcement, while also (2) listening more to increase their level of understanding and to communicate shared interest.

Health and relationship alert!

They also frequently report problems with two other areas of their lives—their relationships and their health. They often have high divorce rates and as someone half-jokingly says, their children may call them *Uncle Daddy* or *Aunt Mommy*. Even when they're home, they may be there physically, but not always emotionally.

Regarding health, they may fall prey to heart attacks as part of their Type A behavior pattern. The good news is they usually don't get ulcers. Instead, they give them. They're carriers. Because of their self-imposed busy lifestyles, this type may figuratively have to pencil in *Romance the spouse tonight* on their to do lists. Then they can cross it off when they're done.

Dominant Director Marilyn's natural inclination was to manage her daughter and point out what she would do now, tomorrow, and next week. Then her husband observed that all day long, Molly was, in effect, being ordered around. Marilyn did find herself saying, "Molly, let's go swing," or, "Here. I'll help you onto the seesaw." So she consciously stepped back and allowed Molly an hour of personal choice. What better place than the relatively child-proof playground to give her daughter some emotional breathing space?

D's can find mutually acceptable solutions

Marilyn and her husband Joel also have four long-haired, indoor cats. One day, Joel fumed, "I can't stand those cats in the house any more. Their hair gets all over my suits, they have accidents on the stairs, and today I found a fur ball next to my shoes. They've got to go."

But Marilyn was determined to find an indoor solution. "They can't go outside because they're declawed. And I'm not getting rid of them. Let's find an answer where we both agree." They decided to convert their family room to a cat motel. They've already made arrangements to replace the carpet with tile (impervious to hair, accidents, and fur balls) and add doors to the family room to separate it from the rest of the house. They arrived at a workable compromise for each

Remember . . .

DOMINANT DIRECTORS' FAMILY BEHAVIORS

- Favor the role of authority in the family system . . . with them in charge
- Like doing activities on their terms
- Want the freedom to spend extra hours working
- Involve themselves in specific family activities that mean something in terms of concrete results

DOMINANT DIRECTORS' PREFERRED FAMILY SITUATIONS

- Being the undisputed head of the family
- Deciding what's what, when, and how
- Not having to deal with everyone's emotions
- Having the personal freedom to do what they're interested in doing
- Negotiating better deals, when possible
- Seeing family members stretch and grow
- Getting results that the whole family can feel good about

Action Plan ⸱⸱⸱

HOW DOMINANT DIRECTORS CAN ADAPT THEIR BEHAVIOR WITH FAMILY/CHILDREN

- Allow the family to do things without being controlled by the Director's preferences
- Accept not being in charge all the time, moving toward a more democratic family system
- Verbalize positive emotions and encourage family members to do likewise . . . enjoying both in the process
- Learn to laugh at the lighter side of life
- Openly admit mistakes and say "I'm sorry"
- Unconditionally accept their family at face value

HOW YOU CAN HELP DOMINANT DIRECTORS MODIFY FAMILY BEHAVIORS

- Point out other family members' perspectives
- Trade off activities: "I'll do this if you'll do that"
- Voice your concerns gently, but firmly
- Politely refuse delegated duties, when appropriate
- Encourage them to verbalize praise and compliments to others
- Gently remind them to laugh and take life less seriously

of them, where neither had anything to lose except the money invested to satisfy one another.

And more mutually acceptable solutions

Because of Dominant Directors' focus on personal control, their family's suggestions may initially fall flat. "Why don't we all drive up to Alpine on Sunday?"

"No," the Dominant Director may respond from behind the newspaper.

"Why not?"

"I don't feel like it."

"It's only Wednesday. How do you know that on Sunday you're not going to feel like it?"

"Because I don't like going there. It's a waste of time and there's nothing to do when we get there. I'd rather stay home and relax."

"Well, we're all part of this family, too, and we want to do something together in the fresh air on Sunday. So why don't we all think about some suggestions and we'll talk about them in an hour, okay?" Under these kinds of circumstances when he realizes some outing seems inevitable, the Dominant Director may take the initiative to try something that is mutually acceptable. "Well, if you really want to get some fresh air, maybe we can go to Mission Bay Park and fly kites. Then I can bring my magazines."

Interacting Socializers' and Their Family Interactions

Family fun

This type favors fun with family members. Even if he can't avoid his least favorite relative's annual Thanksgiving visit, he can usually find positive, diversionary activities to dull any unpleasant sensation he may feel. There are always group tours of the city, trips to the zoo or beach, or a group restaurant experience—all large enough arenas for separation within group activities.

I's live in the moment

Interacting Socializers enjoy sharing the moment, and projecting more shared moments into the future. They dislike most solitary activities and want to perform them with their family or friends. "Let's go for a swim!" or, "How about taking a walk with me?"

They like to feel that their family is close-knit and can solve most problems by verbalizing their feelings. When a family member hurts their feelings, they typically withdraw from them to recover, seeking solace in other family members or friends who can caringly listen to them vent their emotions. They tend to feel overburdened with secrets or with having to hold in their feelings. If they dislike a close relative's behavior, they usually verbalize it. But unless they are aware of the difference between hating the person and hating the act, they may say regretful things if they are deeply hurt.

"Can we talk?"

The Interacting Socializer likes to go with the flow, but in an impulsive, spontaneous manner. He wants to talk about anything and everything, from current events and how they affect him and others, to more personal subjects family members may not want to discuss. He likes enthusiastic greetings, hugs, squeezes, and outward displays of affection, especially if other people are around to see how much his family loves him. In fact, outside witnesses who tell others about his family's outpouring of emotion for him can make an Interacting Socializer's day. His status needs will be bolstered by these external factors (people testifying about his popularity).

Interacting Socializers, more than the other types, have that youthful quality of keeping in touch with the child within themselves. They often feel less inhibited than others about discussing both their triumphs and their warts (as they perceive them) with their families. "Yes, I did some stupid things in junior high school, Sam. I smoked cigarettes in Kathy's attic before her mom got home from work and once I even set fire to an overstuffed chair. Was I ever petrified! So I hope you won't act as dumb as I did and can learn from my mistakes."

About I children

Interacting Socializer children typically hear things like, "You don't have to tell anyone about the fight Daddy and I had last night." Otherwise, the entire neighborhood may know the family's life history. For this behavioral type, talking about any experience, good or bad, is almost as natural as breathing. As one observer pointed out, "Generally speaking, the Interacting Socializer may be *generally speaking*."

Young Interacting Socializers may get reprimanded for talking with friends at school, often while the teacher competes with him or a Dominant Director child for the class's attention. Solitary activities bore them unless they learn to view them as games or socially related experiences. Of the four types, Interacting Socializer children respond the most spontaneously to treats and rewards when they've memorized their spelling words or correctly played a musical piece. On the other hand, anything that smacks of potential stardom attracts these children like bees to flowers. Plays, recitals, pageants or anything that draws special attention to themselves command their interest.

Unlike Dominant Directors, Interacting Socializers often respond positively to anyone's and everyone's attention almost from day one. Interacting Jessica gurgled and smiled at anybody within view, many of whom commented on her precocious flirting. According to Jessica, the world was populated by no strangers, only potential friends and allies.

People can help an Interacting Socializer deal with this need for universal approval by gently reminding him no one can please all the people all the time, not even him! For instance, the Interacting Socializer child who gets lost in a department store may continue wandering away without realizing it, enchanted with the unending array of toys or games, talking excitely to anyone who'll listen.

"This will hurt me, too"

Although few parents enjoy dispensing discipline, Interacting Socializers often feel literally as badly as their children when they dole out punishments. "Barry, I hate to have to do this, but you ate candy after I told you not to. So no more

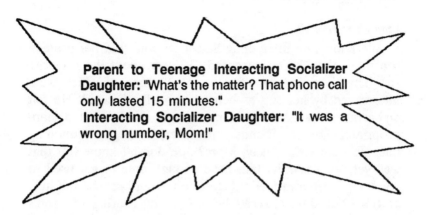

Parent to Teenage Interacting Socializer Daughter: "What's the matter? That phone call only lasted 15 minutes."
Interacting Socializer Daughter: "It was a wrong number, Mom!"

sweets or TV for the rest of the day." Five minutes later he may return to Barry's room and ask, "How are you doing, Buddy? Do you want to go outside and practice soccer for awhile?" Or better yet (from the Interacting Socializer's point of view), he'll point out Barry's unacceptable behavior to his wife and ask her to take care of it.

Peaks and valleys

This type tends to experience wide mood swings ranging from feelings of ecstasy to agony. There often doesn't seem to be much middle, smooth ground between the peaks and valleys. In this sense, they tend to live by their feelings. As a result, neutral feelings are equivalent to no feelings for Socializers. This perception fails to provide them with a needed gauge for determining what they want to do (that leads to increased good feelings) or avoid (because of the bad feelings which they experience). This stimulating, external orientation and sense of confusion results in overemotionality and a sense of rational confusion when they're under more intense pressure. "Can't you see I'm busy? Go away and leave me alone!" Or, under normal circumstances, they can be just plain emotional and sentimental. "Oh, Jamie, that's the most beautiful valentine I've ever seen!" In either case, I's seldom feel neutral about anything!

Enough is enough

We know one Interacting Socializer who told her preteen son more than he ever wanted to know about the opposite sex. This extended to off-color jokes, some of which were interpreted by her son as being personally directed. He felt embarrassed by his mother and thought she had acted inappropriately. Before friends came over, he began cautioning her, "Just say hello, okay, Mom? Joe doesn't know you that well yet, so please let him have enough time to get used to you." With her own feelings close to the surface, she felt hurt at first, but then cheered herself up by sharing her son's comments with her husband and sister. By viewing his request through the eyes of humor, she came to better understand her son's point of view.

"Oh, no! I didn't check!"

Of all the behavioral types, Interacting Socializers are the most likely to forget about things—ranging from class plays to PTA meetings, special dates, personal appointments, etc. Because of this natural tendency, they can benefit by coordinating their family, work, and social activities on one calendar or pocket organizer so they don't disappoint family members and themselves. Gentle reminders to Interacting Socializers can help them anticipate a family event. "Remember, Howard, Sarah's birthday party is this Saturday at noon. Let's make sure we get ready early so we get all the preparation out of the way, okay?"

Sometimes this type may respond to hearsay and, typically, not check before they reach a conclusion:

Socializer Linda: "Harry, I'm not happy that you told Martha that I've gained weight!"

Husband Harry: "Linda, that's not correct. What I said was you thought it made you look heavier than you are. Isn't that exactly what you told me?"

They may leap before they look

Interacting Socializers often need to look before leaping. This extends to openly addressing their children with emotionally weighty questions. "Jimmy, I heard a very disturbing

Remember . . .

INTERACTING SOCIALIZERS'
FAMILY BEHAVIORS

- Shared activities with informal discussions..now and later
- Togetherness, which may include people outside the family in the fun
- Varied family activities in stimulating environments
- Spur of the moment decisions
- Focus on emotions and how family members feel about various matters which arise
- Tend to talk up or talk down others

INTERACTING SOCIALIZERS'
PREFERRED FAMILY SITUATIONS

- Talking about their innermost joys and fears
- Sharing warm, emotional moments
- Laughing, joking, and acting silly together
- Feeling accepted by the family for being dynamic and fun-loving
- Relaxing and not having to deal with conflicts
- Feeling acknowledged as friends as well as spouses and children

Action Plan . . .

HOW INTERACTING SOCIALIZERS CAN ADAPT THEIR BEHAVIOR WITH FAMILY/CHILDREN

- Monitor their natural tendency to jump to conclusions and wait for all the facts to come in
- Discipline their children when appropriate, instead of succumbing to the fear that the children won't like them
- Understand that there are times when they can benefit by toning down their feelings of excitement
- Write down significant dates and events
- Better organize activities (or motivate someone else to do them)

HOW YOU CAN HELP INTERACTING SOCIALIZERS MODIFY FAMILY BEHAVIORS

- Express appreciation and compliments first, suggestions second
- Pitch in and help them rearrange (or get rid of) their clutter
- Show them how a little more efficiency can free them to do more fun things
- Temper spontaneity with some family planning
- Talk to this type privately about perceived challenges and areas which require improvement

rumor. Is it true you've taken drugs?" This could be toned down to something like, "Jimmy, I heard a rumor that I think you want to know about. I'm not going to let myself get upset, so just talk to me and let me know what is going on with you, since we have always cared about each other enough to be open and honest about our feelings, right? Is there any reason for me to be concerned about drug use when you go out places with kids?" In this example, the parent asked open-ended questions while reassuring her son she was aware of her own tendency to get tense about situations and relationships that are important to her. The message was, she knows she has a problem to work on. Now she wants to know if they have a problem to work on—namely, drugs.

If the rumor is wrong, she will have both saved face and avoided accusing her son without justification. If her suspicions are confirmed, she can reassure Jimmy that she still loves him, but cannot accept the behavior (which can harm him, someone whose well-being she cares about). Then she can help him identify a course of action that will enable him help him to solve the problem without harming his self-esteem or jeopardizing their relationship.

Steady Relaters
and Their Family Interactions

"Like a bridge over troubled water"

Part of the Steady Relater appeal is that they tend to naturally accept and tolerate others, warts and all. Edith Bunker, a Steady Relater for all seasons, illustrates this type's tendencies to soothe the entire household. Even though Archie clashed with the Meathead, Edith got along beautifully with both of them. She occupied the role of *A Bridge Over Troubled Water*, the heart of the family unit. In her dealings with Archie, Michael, Gloria, and George Jefferson (the neighbor), she genuinely enjoyed their differing positive traits and also succeeded in overlooking the negatives. She personified the considerate, neighborly, and predictable behaviors of the Steady Relater: the *teddy bear* personality among the four types.

Today's events are tomorrow's memories

Steady Relaters are often collector types. They like to accumulate personal treasures, photographs, and souvenirs that aid them in reflecting about the way things were. They may balk at throwing any of these articles away because of the memories and sentimentality associated with them. "I know the image has faded on this photo, but it meant so much to my mother I just can't part with it." On the other hand, Dominant Directors may go through things once a year and throw out junk they haven't used. "We never look at these travel folders any more, so let's get rid of them." By contrast, Interacting Socializers count themselves lucky if they can find some of their old keepsakes. "I know my high school yearbook is here someplace."

Similarly, Steady Relaters often want to do things with family members in which they both share and have opportunities for making reminiscences. "Remember the time we all went to Aunt Agnes's and Uncle Joe's farm for a week? You milked a cow and rode the horses." At times, Steady Relaters can overdo their affiliation with family routine and become possessive. "But we always go to John's and Mary's for the holidays. Why do we have to go somewhere else this year? After all, for me things just won't be the same—it'll be like missing out on these holidays altogether."

About S children

Steady Relater children often try to please almost everyone with their easy, go along temperament. Their parents typically say, "That child never gave me a bit of trouble," or, "What a good baby!" Relater children tend to ask for permission before touching breakables, TV sets, or food in the refrigerator—filling their parents with pride when the family visits someone else's house.

This is very unlike Dominant Directors and Interacting Socializers who may make themselves right at home. By comparison, Steady Relater children seem quite easy to raise.

They are more likely to take naps when told to, do their homework on time (but may avoid doing extra work), and seek peace and quiet. Their *Yes, Mom,* and *Yes, Dad,* responses have such an endearing ring.

Young Steady Relaters like to both participate in and watch the world go by. Even as infants, they enjoy going for walks in their strollers, whether or not their parents stop to look at things or talk to people. And they would stay in their cribs or playpens much longer than the other three types, without complaining. When admiring on-lookers compliment your Steady Relater toddler, he may smile, but also blush and bury his head in Mother's rib cage. He likes attention, but he prefers occupying a seat in the audience to playing a starring role. Later, he may become a true team player, acknowledging everyone in his group with helping to reach the goal. A Steady Relater is not likely to accept, at least publicly, 100% of the credit.

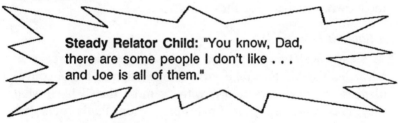

Steady Relator Child: "You know, Dad, there are some people I don't like . . . and Joe is all of them."

Let's keep things as they are

Moderation in all things tends to be another theme this type often lives by. Everyone could relax under the same roof, doing the things they like best, but following the accepted guidelines of family structure. In the best of all possible Steady Relater worlds, little would age or change. No dissension, anger, or even elation would enter their family's lives. Continuity from the past to the present, projected into the future, is important to them.

It's a family affair

For the Steady Relater, preparing and conducting outings and vacations is a family affair. They like input from everyone concerned and prefer to map out the details of the schedule ahead of time. If they are not required to follow more rigid guidelines, they'll want to include easily paced schedules and relaxation time breaks. They generally want everyone to get involved in the pre-planning stages of the actual event. If Susie can't take part in a group meeting, Steady Relaters try to represent their interests by including something special for them. "We'll be close to the Hopi Indian reservation. Susie would love to see the Kachina dolls."

Show Steady Relaters you care

They appreciate feedback on favors they've performed. "Oh, boy, Kachina dolls! That sounds great, Mom!" or "Dad, did you fill my car with gas? That was really nice of you." But, Steady Relaters prefer that significant others notice their thoughtfulness without prompting. So, this type, especially, may not feel comfortable posting notes about impending birthdays or holidays. They prefer the family to remember on their own, just because they care.

A little bit of home

Steady Relaters may even begin their packing weeks in advance. They like to take extra things (such as home conveniences or emergency items) with them so they'll have what they may want at their fingertips. When Paula puts her suitcase together, she includes not only her clothing and accessories, but snacks, band-aids, a small sewing kit, nail polish remover, cotton balls and swabs, plastic bags, large garbage disposal bags (in case it rains), vitamins, antiseptic, and anything else that she thinks her family may need.

"First I did this, then . . . "

Steady Relaters can sometimes be too set in their ways. Their literal mind-sets often think one step at a time. When a son, daughter, or spouse asks, "What did you do today?" the answer may become a chronology of the day's events: "I got up, exercised, showered, drove to work." Sometimes a simple, "I really didn't do anything out of the ordinary today," is sufficient. Additionally, they can learn to communicate in ways that aren't intended to elicit orderly recitations of similar blow by blow descriptions from other family members.

Unspoken needs

Communicating directly with loved ones about what may be bothering them can be a real problem for this type. Since they often make sacrifices and act as peacemakers in the family unit, they may inwardly expect acknowledgment and thanks, but fail to say anything about it. Taken to an extreme, this reticence about voicing their concerns, coupled with their modesty, sometimes places Steady Relaters in the tenuous position of martyrs or victims.

When they've had enough

For instance, Dominant Director Dick thought something was amiss in his relationship with his wife Sharon, a Steady Relater, but he never broached the subject. One morning Sharon cleaned out her drawers and began tossing her clothes into crates, cartons, and assorted luggage.

"Hey, what are you doing? We're not going on vacation," Dick said, in his Dominant Director way.

Since her Steady Relater's book was virtually brimming with check marks, she said, "We never go on vacations. That's one of our problems."

"What about three years ago when we had the quiet vacation at home?" countered Dick.

"You call that a vacation? You stayed home from the office and brought a briefcase full of work with you. That's all you did!" Sharon said. "I'm leaving you, Dick. I just can't stand it any more!"

"What are you talking about?" Dick pursued, wide-eyed in his disbelief.

"If you don't know by now, I'm not going to enlighten you," Sharon retaliated.

"I know!" Dick said angrily. "Sharon, tell me the truth. Is there another man?"

"There just has to be somewhere!" sighed Sharon, slamming her suitcase shut. With that, she left. When a Steady Relater

Remember . . .

STEADY RELATER FAMILY BEHAVIORS

- Generally, tend to be naturally group-oriented
- Want to do things together for the personal satisfaction of being with others
- Enjoy customary family events: "Every Thanksgiving, we go to Grandma's house."
- Like regularly scheduled and planned participative activities—"On Wednesdays, we all go bowling."
- Want to be shown sincere appreciation for all they do

STEADY RELATERS' PREFERRED FAMILY SITUATIONS

- Their ideal families show how much they mean to them by expressions of warmth and displays of personal appreciation
- Like to help implement family decisions
- Home life is a well-structured and peaceful retreat where stresses seldom occur
- Live in the same, or similar, neighborhood
- Enjoy a lifestyle which is comfortably organized with predictable, routine schedules and activities
- No big surprises or changes disrupt them

Action Plan . . .

HOW STEADY RELATERS CAN ADAPT THEIR BEHAVIOR WITH FAMILY/CHILDREN

- Communicate more in abstract terms; i. e., at times, accept less explicit, more generalized answers, when appropriate—such as exploring the big picture, new ideas, or the point of the matter
- Make decisions on their own, or take the initiative, when appropriate
- Recognize that change is inevitable
- Speak up when they're upset about something, rather than keeping silent until they've accumulated a list of grievances and pent-up frustrations

HOW YOU CAN HELP STEADY RELATERS MODIFY FAMILY BEHAVIOR

- Encourage a mutual dialogue on thoughts and feelings . . . good and bad
- Stress that not all situations/comments are personally directed
- Enlist their input in suggesting what tasks they can do and goals they can set on their own
- Tap their talents and encourage them to develop and grow; perhaps even seeking public recognition for them
- Help them assert themselves, when appropriate

closes the door, you may never get your foot in it again. Dick certainly never did.

S's Speak out

Like Sharon, Steady Relaters can benefit by realizing that those close to them may need reminders to thoroughly understand and be responsive to their needs, wants, and expectations. But if those needs and wants are only hinted at, not directly verbalized, spouses and children may not grasp the importance of meeting our personal expectations. Steady Relaters can learn to say, "Jim, Timmy is your son, too, and it bothers me when you don't take more of a part in spending time and taking care of him. For instance, when you're home from your business trips, I think you could give him a bath once in awhile and read him a bedtime story without my having to suggest it."

"The times of our lives"

When it's time for Junior to go to college, Steady Relaters like to become an integral part of the proceedings. For instance, they may want to share in studying or otherwise preparing for exams, filling out college applications, or assisting with composing essays. They tend to view these mutual moments and tasks as the stuff memories are made of. Participating in situations like these can also help Steady Relaters better adapt to impending changes. In this case, the son will leave home in September, so sharing the *times of our lives* can ease the transitional period for the Steady Relater parent between the more comfortable, known past experiences and the less comfortable future ones.

Cautious Thinkers
and Their Family Interactions

Cautious Thinkers proceed carefully

At times, this type's concern can be overdone. For instance, Cautious Thinker Ed was so fire-conscious he bought fire extinguishers for his two-bedroom home—one for the hallway and one for the bathroom. He organized fire drills for his family so that everyone knew what to do in case of an emergency. "Remember to crawl on your hands and knees so there's less chance of being overcome by smoke inhalation." Ed's caution carried over to other aspects of family life. If anyone expected to drive more than five miles in the car, he'd throw up the hood and tinker around inside, making sure everything was safe before starting out.

Other types may detect faulty communications and deal with them directly. But Cautious Thinkers are often uncomfortable with interactions gone awry. As Raymond says, "If I can just put it out of my mind, then maybe it never was 'real' to begin with." They may just sweep those thoughts under the rug and try to forget about them. "Maybe it will go away," they may think. When Raymond experiences strong emotions, he tends to step back initially and analyze them. He likes to figure out what's wrong first, then express it. "I like to work out strategies before I act. When I get angry, it's difficult for me to confront somebody to express it. I do not express anger readily. The stronger the emotion, the less likely I am to deal with it directly."

Fix mistakes, downplay emotions

Although he strongly dislikes making mistakes, Raymond says now he's more likely to admit that he does make them. "I apologize more now and try to fix it, if necessary." He admits this behavior did not come naturally to him. He learned it during his 17-year marriage to Gail, an Interacting Socializer.

On one occasion, Gail commented on the tense, strained atmosphere when they visited Raymond's brother Len. She wanted to discuss it with Len. Raymond tried to dissuade her from making a big deal out of a little deal, but she insisted. "I don't like to jump to conclusions," Raymond says, "so I'm likely to give people the benefit of the doubt." He talked with Len, a Dominant Director, about Gail's concerns, but "I didn't enjoy it," Raymond said. "I prefer to let it fly with him. After all, it didn't turn out 'rosy' with him like it usually does when

I talk things out with Gail. He let me know he didn't appreciate the fact that I brought those things up."

Different interests

Cautious Thinkers typically gravitate toward practical
hobbies and interests. They often enjoy computers, novels or
educational subjects, collections (stamps, art, music, etc.), and
other pursuits that involve more private individual involvement. They may prefer that the family share their interests,
but many will continue enjoying themselves alone, having
learned their hobbies lean toward the esoteric. Raymond
admits that he tends to be a real individualist, so he's had to
consciously work at getting more involved in shared family
activities. He likes to go hiking with Gail and his two daughters, but he also truly welcomes chunks of time alone that
enable him to rid himself of stress. "It helps me clear my
thoughts just to have such quality thinking time," he says.

About C children

Cautious Thinker children often seem to be more serious
than the other types, partially by showing signs of organization
and order at an early age. They stack their toys, keep their
puzzle pieces together, and generally favor places for everything and everything in those places. Like Steady Relaters,
they like to watch and observe, but Cautious Thinker children
hold their emotions within themselves. These are intense
children who may lose themselves in activities and often are
seen, but not heard. In fact, they can become so involved in
what they're doing they may not even hear others speaking
to them.

Individuals who fit this type often do well in school because of their many compliant-appearing traits. They may find
it hard to accept behaviors they see, such as children failing
to finish their assigned homework or refusing to study ade-
quately for tests (which tend to make this type nervous). They
like to know the expected structure, the emphasized information, and how to derive the correct answers. Often, Cautious
Thinkers intuitively invent their own structure, method, or
model for understanding and processing what they need to

know or do. Of all the types, these kids *don't want to be caught dead in public* for not complying with commonly accepted standards of behavior, let alone those which they additionally expect of themselves!

Heidi, a 12-year-old Cautious Thinker, usually compiles a list before taking a family trip. She packs by laying her clothes out on the bed for her mother to check before putting them into the suitcase. This year, she made a two-sided list: one naming all the items, the other specifying color coding the day she plans to wear each outfit.

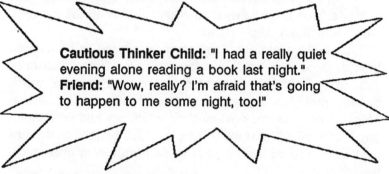

Cautious Thinker Child: "I had a really quiet evening alone reading a book last night."
Friend: "Wow, really? I'm afraid that's going to happen to me some night, too!"

Individual time with loved ones

Camille is not comfortable with large public or family gatherings. Rather than shun these events, she has learned how to associate with those few people who make her feel most comfortable. Of course, she politely and briefly touches base with others. But she'll go off by herself to just be with another person so they can talk privately without intrusions. Camille, like other Cautious Thinkers, usually keeps secrets quite well. She has an uncanny memory for being discreet in sorting out what individuals may do with information—avoiding any possible complications that may result.

Need to be right

Cautious Peter carefully loaded his family's luggage on top of the station wagon by methodically placing it in what he viewed as the best areas for each suitcase. However, after a half hour of jostling around winding drives, a piece of luggage suddenly fell off the car and onto the side of the road.

"Let's put it inside this time," his wife Mary suggested. "There's plenty of room in the back."

"Well, the kids need quite a bit of room in back," Peter answered.

"But they have enough room. We'll get there quicker if the luggage goes inside," Mary persisted.

"I know these will fit on top if I just load them right," Peter pursued.

Irritated, Mary said, "Well, apparently you didn't tie them right before."

"Well, I'll make sure to this time," Peter said, resolute now in his decision to properly load every suitcase on the car roof. He'll show Mary who's right!

Like Peter, Cautious Thinkers have a need to be correct. In fact, more than any other fate, this type fears criticism of their work or efforts. Since they gauge their personal worth by their precision, accuracy and amount of activity, Cautious Thinkers pride themselves on their efficiency and perfectionism. But, if taken to its worst extreme, such perfectionism runs the risk of turning into nit-picking, faultfinding, or even thick-headedness.

"Read my mind"

Because they tend to be more comfortable thinking about their feelings rather than expressing them to others, Cautious Thinkers may expect people to know what they think, especially those who know them well. For 47 years, Cautious Thinker Helen agonized over the fact she had taken care of her mother-in-law since the beginning of her marriage. She expected her sister-in-law, Grace, to volunteer to house *Nana* for a few years. But Grace never offered. Helen's Interacting Socializer daughter finally asked her, "Well, did you ever discuss this with Aunt Grace?"

"Of course not!" Helen answered. "It was obvious what was going on. She just didn't want to take care of your grandmother."

"How do you know she felt that way if you never discussed it with her? Maybe she just assumed that was how you wanted it," the daughter pursued.

"She knew and didn't do anything about it," Helen said.

According to her, Grace had let her down, but Helen had never mentioned a word. Helen's *thinkings* got hurt. Sensitized Cautious Thinkers may sever relationships like this because, "Of course So-and-So must have known better! After all, I would!" But, the facts of human behavior tell us that unless So-and-So, too, was a Cautious Thinker, she may very well not have understood.

Self-discipline and logic

"I guess I'd like to be the boss because I like to have things my way, but it doesn't often work, so we usually have to compromise." By talking, however reluctantly, Raymond and Gail have arrived at common rules for disciplining the children. "I like self-discipline. I expect a lot from myself and those around me, but I've learned to be clear about my expectations. If they don't measure up, I tell them. "Look, I told you to clear the table and you didn't do it. You've started another task. First, finish clearing the table before creating another mess."

Cautious Thinkers sometimes are perceived by others as too picky. They ask lots of questions. "What about this, what about that?" One observer who married a Cautious Thinker says that sometimes their questions may even seem like an inquisition to others. She commented, "When something bothers them, count on at least 20 questions. Maybe they'll spread them out over the day, but they're still there."

Non-Cautious Thinker Wife: "Let's go to the movies tonight."

Cautious Thinker Husband: "What's playing?"

Non-Cautious Wife: "I think the new Robert DeNiro movie began Friday."

Thinker Husband: "Where is it?"

Wife: "I don't know, but almost anywhere is fine with me."

Thinker Husband: "Well, what time does it start?"

Wife: "I don't know what time it starts!"

Thinker Husband: "How can you expect to go somewhere when you don't have any kind of plan? Besides, what will we do with the kids?"

Wife: "I'll tell you what. I'll go to the movies and you can stay home with them."

A more productive dialogue

This malfunction in communication could have been prevented if the couple had been more responsive to each other's needs. The wife, recognizing the fact that her husband needs data, could have supplied him with some. "The movie begins at 7 p.m. at the Garde Theater. Maybe your sister can watch the children." Or she could have enlisted his help in figuring who could baby-sit or asked, "Do you have another option?"

The husband, observing his wife's stressful, emotional state could have acknowledged her feelings, "You seem emotionally drained. Do you want to talk about it?" or, "It does look like you might want to get out for awhile. Am I correct?"

Like Dominant Directors, Cautious Thinkers can become even more effective dealing with people by demonstrating greater concern and appreciation for others. A useful technique for accomplishing this would be sharing feedback, such as: I really appreciate that," or, "How thoughtful of you! Thanks!" Cautious Thinkers can also benefit by learning how to deal more directly with difficult people and situations. This includes quicker adjustments to disruptions, deviations, disorganization, or errors. They can concentrate on turning things around rather than dwelling on frustration responses like "I told you so," or "I knew it all along," or "What can you expect?"

Nobody's "perfekt"

Cautious Thinker adults can become more productive in interactions with their children by admitting to their youngsters it's natural and expected that people will make mistakes—even themselves. "Steven, I want you to look at this algebra problem I just did. The first time, I made an addition error. That's one of the reasons I'm more comfortable checking." Examples like this one can serve to help a child gain a more realistic perspective about the limits on all types of people. It also

Remember . . .

CAUTIOUS THINKERS' FAMILY BEHAVIORS

- Although they're naturally more stiff and formal with strangers, they can be quite demonstrative with their family
- They are most comfortable when family members exercise caution and look before they leap
- They carefully guard the safety of their family
- They keep mistakes at a minimum
- They practice self-discipline and the pursuit of quality
- Spontaneity and emotionalism take a back seat to caution and logic

CAUTIOUS THINKERS' PREFERRED FAMILY SITUATIONS

- Their home environment is organized, neat, and efficient
- Their family behaves logically
- Other people in the home adhere to their (Cautious Thinker) standards
- They can choose to interact or not, and their family will understand
- They want to be right; when mistakes happen, they prefer to 'fix' them
- They prefer individual time with loved ones

Action Plan . . .

HOW CAUTIOUS THINKERS CAN ADAPT THEIR BEHAVIOR WITH FAMILY/CHILDREN

- Accept the fact that no one is right all the time . . . not even them
- Vocalize their feelings more often (or what they think about their feelings)
- Occasionally behave spontaneously
- Voice their disapproval or criticism in a caring way
- Lighten up and not act and think so seriously at home

HOW YOU CAN HELP CAUTIOUS THINKERS MODIFY FAMILY BEHAVIORS

- Encourage them to verbalize positive thoughts and feelings about family members
- Help them lower their perfectionistic standards for some things
- Calmly explain that caution can sometimes be overdone
- Gently prod them into seeing the humor in their own foibles, and those of others
- Mix occasional spontaneity with planning and organization
- Help them view life less critically and more optimistically

explains to the child why the Cautious Thinker parent behaves the way she does toward others.

As natural critical observers, Cautious Thinkers may also practice easing up a little on what their children may perceive as *raining on their parade*. When the neighborhood kids go roller skating, perhaps it isn't necessary to analyze their skates for near-perfect wheel alignment and performance capabilities. Children need to experience some aspects of life spontaneously, otherwise their capacity for just plain having fun may be snuffed out.

People Smart Principle #10—The Principle of Acceptance-Resistance: "When you treat people only your own way, it increases the tension-resistance level between you."

Chapter 10
Romance, Romance!

One person's attraction is another's distraction

Just as each behavioral type has different needs and fears in other life settings, they may also have different general patterns and relating preferences in a romantic relationship. Visualize a Dominant Director, Interacting Socializer, Steady Relater, and Cautious Thinker you've dated, known, or would like to know more intimately. Then apply these general romance enhancers to maximize your next encounters with people of each personal style, based on your newly found insights about their wants and needs.

Dominant Directors and Romance

D's usually know who they want

When Dominant Director Rory sees someone he's enamored with, he goes after her. After meeting Jane, he decided he wanted to win her love. Since he's going to graduate school and, consequently, studies for hours in the library, he often asks Jane to come along so he can spend more time with her. Then he assigns her chores: searching the subject and authors' indexes for books, locating newspaper articles on microfiche, and running out to pick up sandwiches for lunch.

Even in romance, Rory uses his Dominant Director tendency to delegate. Unless he's specifically told otherwise, Rory assumes it's okay to take the initiative. From his perspective, Jane can say no, if she wants to, so if she doesn't object, he assumes she wants to do various things he requests.

And what they want

His assumptive behavior extends beyond delegating duties to Jane. For example, if he's double dating with Jane and another couple and feels like getting a back rub, he'll just directly ask for one. If Jane refuses, he'll ask his friend's date. Once while eating in a restaurant, Rory even startled people when he complained, "My toes have cramps in them. Will you crack them for me, Jane?"

Embarrassed, Jane replied, "Here? Now? You've got to be kidding!"

"Why is it disgusting? They really hurt, Jane." His roommate's date Sylvia made eye contact with Rory, so he pursued, "Sylvia, can you please just pull my toes a bit for me?" Not knowing what to say or do, Sylvia, a Steady Relater type, reluctantly submitted to his insistent request.

Rory's roommate Walt, another Dominant Director, uses a somewhat similar approach. He and Rory routinely inquire all around their apartment house for someone to type their college projects—free, of course. "If they don't want to do it, they can always say no," Walt and Rory contend.

If a man calls Dominant Director Holli to say, "I'd like you to come with me to La Jolla Shores on Saturday. I'll pick you up at 11:00," she understandably wants some input regarding time and place. She says that in these situations, she's tempted to say, "Hey, wait a minute. Why La Jolla Shores? I'd rather go up to Del Mar. And another thing, how about picking me up at a time that's convenient for me, too, rather than just you?"

When D's make up their minds

Dominant Director Melody chased Stan until she caught him. When she met him, she decided, "This is it." Even when Stan told her the relationship would never work, Melody was determined to convince him they were a good match. For months she fielded his objections, saying she had a clear picture in her head of the two of them together. Finally, he, too, began to see what she had seen all along. Melody describes her iron will like this: "When I make up my mind, I'm like a little terrier dog chewing on a slipper. You can shake me and try to grab that slipper away, but I hold on no matter what. And do you know what? I've always gotten what I wanted that way."

But sometimes the Dominant Director's will doesn't square with the logic of a situation. For example, when John went skiing for the first time with Maureen, he thought skiing looked easy. A self-professed natural athlete, John just knew he'd be good at it. Far be it for him to allow a little thing like never having done it before to keep him off the advanced slopes. Besides, if Maureen could do it, surely he could. So down he went, shooting out of his chair lift full speed ahead. Multiple bruises later, John learned the hard way that some things do require more than the self-proclaimed attitude, "Of course I can do that."

Love Me, love my alma mater

When Don took Ann to visit his old college alma mater, he expected her to mirror his enthusiasm about the place, even though the temperature was 35 degrees, the wind whipped through the campus, and rain pelted them as they walked around the football stadium. "I scored the winning touchdown here in my first game," he told her. "What a welcome that was!"

"Don, I'm soaking wet. Can we go through someplace indoors now?" Don made hard eye contact, then withdrew, hardly speaking a word the rest of the afternoon. "Are you angry with me because I didn't want to go outside while it was thundering and lightning?" Ann finally asked.

"I can't believe you don't share my thoughts and feelings about this campus, Ann. I'm really disappointed."

Ann, perceiving this as the beginning of the end of their romance, asked, "Are you trying to tell me that we won't be seeing each other any more?"

"No, I just wanted to tell you how much this means to me, that's all," Don answered. "I'd like you to get excited about it tomorrow."

In this example, Don succeeded in saying exactly what he was thinking, communicating the information to Ann, and verbalizing the importance of her sharing his enthusiasm about the campus. Dominant Directors may blow off steam, feel better, then want to pick up where they left off as though nothing happened.

D's can learn to relinquish control . . . once in awhile

Dominant Director Holli says she can benefit by learning to allow her date to take control some of the time. Since she typically likes to call the shots in her relationships, she could profit from permitting more mutual give and take. She admits when seeing evidence of her date wanting control, at first she tends to view that trait as a negative.

She also says more benefit could be derived from trusting her dates more. Since Holli was and is an independent woman, she's used to doing things the way she wants. Consequently, she often has to consciously force herself to do things according to someone else's perspective. Since this type is generally very comfortable making unilateral decisions, they may unwittingly leave out the other person's point of view altogether. They may naturally continue this behavior in the dating world, unless someone gently enlightens them about this personal blind spot.

Dominant Director: "Enough about *me*. Let's talk about *you*. What do *you* think of me?"

They let others know

This type tends to make strong requests. "Requests?" Al said to Mary. "You don't make requests, you make demands. You say it like it's an order!"

"Well, how do you want me to say it?" Mary asked.

"Like I have some choice. It seems clear that when you make up your mind, there is little or no choice."

"Give me an example," she said.

"All right. I'd like to go to the beach this weekend, but I'm open to suggestions. That still leaves me an option."

"That sounds reasonable. I'll try it this time," Mary responded.

Dominant Directors may want to tell love interests some things 'for their own good'. But the recipients of these words of wisdom may not respond in kind. Al says, "Mary has learned not to put her fingers in the gears."

This means now she asks first. "Do you really want me to tell you the bottom line?"

"If he says yes, then he has to deal with it. So now we're both more turned in to the results both of us want," she says.

They tell it bluntly

So brace yourself for direct comments from a Dominant Director. If the answers to certain sensitive questions may result in hurt feelings, it may be advisable to ask less blunt ones, instead. Even when they try to be tactful, Dominant Directors waste no time in telling their opinions. So when Veronica asks, "Mark, do you like my new outfit?" Mark may say, "Are you sure you want to know?"

"You don't like it?" Veronica inquires.

Naturally blunt, he may say, "No, not at all."

"Why not?" she asks.

"It looks cheap. You look like you just stumbled out of a thrift store." Of course, his lack of tact may be unwelcome, but most significant others know just where they stand with a Dominant Director. If the Dominant Director gets his or her way—and of course, they're more than likely to try—their dates will at least seriously consider their advice.

An enjoyable evening?

Dominant Director Matthew may initially find it difficult to yield to his dates' visions of a pleasant evening. When he asks her to a specific restaurant, he may automatically balk if she suggests dinner at an alternate place. "Boy, that must be a half hour drive. I'm on the road all day, so I'm really not looking forward to driving again," he may protest. But if she offers to drive, he may capitulate. Why? They're natural negotiators. If Dominant Directors contemplate giving in, they typically want something in return. That way, they still get that key result they want.

In pursuit of the bottom line

Ryan, another Dominant Director, has to force himself not to complete his dates' sentences and thoughts. He interrupts to get to the bottom line quicker. "Why waste time searching for the words when I'm right there to supply them?" Others may interpret this behavior as his version of filling in the blanks. But who wants to think of herself as a blank? Besides appearing rude, Ryan risks not really knowing how his dates think or feel about matters. He could learn to count to 10 (at least) and let others say what they want at their own pace, in their own way.

"I'm the manager"

Dominant Director Christine's latest love interest lived 12 miles away, so she decided to find another apartment for him that was within walking distance. "Guess what? I've found an apartment for you and Gil just two blocks from mine."

"But we don't need another apartment. We like it here," Chad protested.

"You know how you hate getting up early, right? Well, this summer you're going to have to get up an hour and a half earlier to commute for your internship. If you live here, you can take the train and leave a whole half-hour later. Plus, you'll be closer to me," Christine explained in her most charismatic voice. (Dominant Directors can be quite forceful and charming, if they want to be).

On moving day, Christine choreographed the traffic flow, duties, and pace for both Chad and Gil. If they wanted to sit down, she chided them, "You'll get done quicker if you save your break until the first load is hauled off."

Remember . . .

DOMINANT DIRECTOR
DATING/ROMANCE CHARACTERISTICS

- Seek results-oriented relationships—"What's in it for me?"
- Like to assume the role of pursuers
- Want to set the unwritten rules for the relationship
- Like winning over the other person and reaching their relationship goals
- Are likely to ask for whatever they want
- Want to take control of the relationship
- Often delegate duties and concerns

DOMINANT DIRECTORS' PREFERRED
DATING BEHAVIORS

- Special arrangements by the date to be available for them
- A lot of control in deciding where to go and what to do
- To say what's on their minds
- Not being asked questions whose answers may harm their chances of meeting their needs (desired results)
- To negotiate—"I'll concede this if you'll do that"

Action Plan . . .

HOW DOMINANT DIRECTORS CAN LEARN TO ADAPT IN DATING SITUATIONS

- Compromise occasionally, instead of insisting on doing things their way
- Accept other viewpoints as valid, too
- Participate more, delegate less
- See themselves in a more light-hearted way
- Not to interrupt
- Make requests instead of demands

HOW YOU CAN HELP DOMINANT DIRECTORS MODIFY THEIR DATING BEHAVIOR

- Gently remind them when less desirable behavior surfaces
- Use shared humor to help them laugh at their own imperfections
- Calmly tell them how their behavior makes you feel
- Speak non-judgmentally and stick to the facts
- Try negotiating, yourself—"Next time I get to choose"
- Repeat, when necessary: "I'm not comfortable with that situation."
- Explain that you want a voice in decision-making, too
- Let them know that you appreciate it when they listen patiently

"Christine, you're really beginning to bug me. What exactly are you doing, anyway? Besides giving orders, I mean," Chad asked.

"Why, I'm managing this entire project, of course," Christine said.

"Well, stop managing and start lifting," Gil and Chad laughed, handing her one of the heaviest cardboard boxes. "How does it feel to be one of the slaves, instead of their overseer?" Gil smiled.

Christine smiled, too. But Gil's analogy flashed into her brain as a new, heightened glimmer of self-awareness. "I guess I can come on strong sometimes, but at least I've cultivated a sense of humor about it," she said.

Romance and Interacting Socializers

There's a party going on

The Interacting Socializer's favorite dating, and date prospecting, spots tend to include places with party atmospheres. If he doesn't go to an actual party, then comedy clubs, dances, concerts, galas—almost anywhere where he can see and be seen—will do. Joyce and Joe are two such party animals. Although not romantically involved, they often drive to a *happening* together, then mingle with the rest of the singles, working the crowd as they explore interesting possibilities. Each has perfected the process of zooming through the room for prospects, scanning from a distance, and then finally emoting up close and personal when they get that magic feeling. They even jokingly refer to themselves as *Spuds* and *Studs*.

Putting on a show

Flirting by an Interacting Socializer is likely to appear quite obvious. Other types may almost imperceptibly crinkle up the sides of their mouths and consider that flirtatious behavior. Not so for Interacting Socializers. They may grin, wave, wink, hold hands, or otherwise leave no doubt that they're interested when they make up their hearts, rather than their minds, about pursuing someone.

The idea of meeting a new potential love interest fuels them for putting on a good show. This type of person, more than any other, can act his perceived part and then project himself into the audience to sense the impact of his own theatrics. Tuning into other people's positive reactions to him serves to reinforce notions of his own desirability. Think of Bruce Willis of TV's MOONLIGHTING or Bette Midler— both larger than life, and *on* at a moment's notice. They exude and often captivate their audience with outspoken charisma. Whether the performance consists of dancing, telling jokes, sharing anecdotes, or posing in an eye-catching outfit, observing their Interacting Socializer behavior while on the prowl is an entertaining experience.

They may play the field

As a group, Interacting Socializers are likely to enjoy dating lots of different people. To paraphrase a quote from the classic movie *The King and I*, Interacting Socializers can behave like bees—flitting from flower to flower to flower. They tend to feel comfortable with a rather active, or even hectic, dating schedule. "Let's see, I'm going to a play with Ralph Friday night, then off to the beach with Scott on Saturday afternoon, miniature golfing with Ted Saturday night, and then a cocktail party with Ralph again on Sunday."

Falling in and out of love

Of all the types, Interacting Socializers report succumbing more to falling in and out of love (or, at least, fascination with others) than their counterparts. They may become quickly smitten, then almost as suddenly transfer their affections elsewhere. Since they are comfortable with newness and change, it's rather natural for them to keep their options, and their eyes, wide open. Yet they're impulsive. "Yes, let's get engaged!" At the extreme, this practice can lead to later regrets and fanciful thoughts of what might have been; and possibly a roving eye. But when someone really very special comes along, they're also likely to fall faster, harder, and more passionately than others.

Flattery may get you far

Flattery may carry you a long way with Interacting Socializers. They enjoy glittery compliments more than the other types, even when they perceive them as sounding a bit much. Similarly, they may freely compliment others. "John, I wish I had a shirt like that. It's so soft and it makes your body look great." At times this rather uninhibited behavior may be interpreted by more restrained people as a come on, whether the Interacting Socializer intended it that way or not. Interacting Socializers may view these comments merely as part of a socially acceptable behavior between two people of the opposite sex, especially if they share a repartee filled with humor and wit. Interacting Socializers tend to admire quick, witty minds and enjoy verbal jousting, as long as the other person avoids sarcasm at their expense—something they're guaranteed with long-time friends.

I's may have telephonitis

Since they tend to be natural conversationalists, they usually like social telephone interactions, too. Their calls can stretch into hours. We even know one who liked to play Golden Oldies via the phone while he filled the role of deejay. "Wait till you hear this one. It's a classic," he'd voice into the mouthpiece. Then he'd spin the record (or play a tape) for about 30 seconds while his girlfriend played the role of a contestant on NAME THAT TUNE.

The burden of boredom

When George asked Interacting Socializer Jean to accompany him on some errands at the Motor Vehicle Department, bank, and hardware store, she said, "Gee, George, those things are boring, boring, boring! How about if I go shopping while you run around to get your duties done. Then we can meet for lunch." This tendency to want to escape from confining, uneventful circumstances is typical of this type. She apparently wants to see George, but not necessarily under just any circumstance.

Interacting Socializers are likely to want time off from the potentially smothering one-on-one pairing to go out with friends or otherwise participate in some activities without their *main squeeze*. Sometimes, just the thought that they have the option to go out with the girls or guys, if they want to, is sufficient to satisfy their need to freely flap their own wings.

I's like excitement and surprises

Non-Interacting Mel: "Eileen, about our date Saturday night. There might be a problem."

Interacting Socializer Eileen: "Uh, oh, what kind of problem?"

Mel: "My cousin just flew in from Jacksonville and will only be here through Sunday afternoon."

Eileen: "And the problem is?"

Mel: "Well, he's already seen the movie we wanted to go to. I haven't seen him in so long, maybe we can postpone our date till later in the week."

Socializer Eileen: "We can go to the movies any time. If you'd like, I'd love it if your cousin came along with us. I could fix him up with Cheryl, or we could go sight-seeing. I don't care. It would be an adventure to play tourist. I'm sure I could help him have an even better time than usual."

While some types tend to look forward to a particular event, Interacting Socializers like Eileen often welcome less ordinary activities. Whatever their reaction, their emotions generally come through loud and clear for their dates to read. In fact, parents may caution grown Interacting Socializer sons and daughters, "You wear your heart on your sleeve. Why don't you first consider whether keeping some of your reactions to yourself may be more appropriate, at times?"

Naturally flirtatious

While on dates with Steady Relater Corinne, Interacting Socializer Ken continually flirted with other women. He'd smile and say hello to perfect strangers—all female, of course —and make approving guttural sounds when a good-looking woman passed by. Noticing that Corinne was uncharacteristically quiet, he said, "Aw, Corinne, you're not mad at me for having a little fun, are you? C'mon now, where's your sense of humor? I'm just trying to have a little harmless fun."

"A sense of humor!", Corinne snapped. "This has nothing to do with a sense of humor. This has to do with being rude and hurting my feelings. I don't behave that way when I'm with you, and I think at least you could have the decency to reciprocate."

"Wow, Corinne! You sure are touchy tonight!" Ken mumbled.

"Look, you're the one who asked me out, Ken. It's really insulting to me when you flirt with other women right in front of me. If you've got to do it, reserve it for sometime when you're with the guys, okay?"

Since other dates had also displayed negative body language when he acted friendly and had even said they were busy the next time he called; when he later reconsidered what Corinne had said. He realized her observations may have been, unfortunately, right on target. Later he called her, saying, "Thanks for straightening me out last night, Corinne. Of course, I really didn't mean to hurt your feelings. I don't particularly like negative feedback, but I guess you're right after all. I'll try to be more considerate from now on, all right?"

Notice that Corinne expressed her concerns in terms which Ken could clearly understand—her feelings—and how his behavior affected them. If Interacting Socializers perceive that they've made someone feel badly, they'll usually prefer to know about it, if it will allow them to smooth things over and make their relationship *right* again.

Remember . . .

INTERACTING SOCIALIZER
DATING/ROMANCE CHARACTERISTICS

- Seek approval and admiration from the date
- Like excitement, variety, and light-hearted fun
- Enjoy the thrill of the chase (romance)
- Tend to look for a socially acceptable match that may provide the bonus of favorable attention
- May want to date many people simultaneously or play the field
- May become rather easily infatuated, experiencing love at first (or at least second) sight

INTERACTING SOCIALIZERS'
PREFERRED DATING BEHAVIORS

- Unexpected situations and surprises tend to energize them
- Their dates pay obvious attention to them, in private and in public
- Like to share fun activities with their companions, but will go to extremes to avoid duller, routine tasks
- Prefer a date who lets them know how much he or she is admired
- Like to laugh and maintain a light-hearted tone
- May want universal approval from past and present dates; they like to remain on friendly terms
- May want space in their relationships to satisfy needs to socialize with those who are important parts of their lives

Action Plan . . .

HOW INTERACTING SOCIALIZERS CAN ADAPT IN DATING SITUATIONS

- Downplay their openness and, at the extreme, flirting or showing off
- Focus more attention on their date and less on themselves (or the impact they're making)
- Tone down their tendency toward gushiness, a trait that can cost them some credibility
- Censor their words, rather than say whatever pops into their heads at a moment's notice
- Commit, when appropriate, without accompanying feelings of confinement

HOW YOU CAN HELP INTERACTING SOCIALIZERS MODIFY THEIR DATING BEHAVIORS

- Warmly explain that quiet moments are sometimes appropriate
- Offer to assist them in getting more organized
- Pitch in and help them finish one thing at a time
- Share in making small changes; instead of bigger, more impulsive ones
- Plan some things, proceed spontaneously with others
- Don't trample their dreams, but mentally divide their ideas by half
- Specify secret information

Romance and the Steady Relater

They aim to please

When Steady Relater Sid attended a hockey game with his date Shelley, he brought fresh snacks galore, offering Shelley cantaloupe wedges, bananas, grapes, and orange slices. "Is there any more cantaloupe left?" she asked.

"Oh, no," Sid said, "I'm sorry, but I just ate the last slice. If I'd known, I would have given it to you. Would you like my orange instead?"

"No, thanks. My taste buds were set for cantaloupe, but it's no big deal."

"I know you must be hungry. How about half the orange?"

"No, thank you, really," Shelley answered.

"What if I peel it for you?" Sid persisted. To a Steady Relater, service is his business. He literally aims to please as a way of satisfying his own need for amiable relationships with others.

After a positive first encounter, Sid will pursue from there, trading off preferences. "This first time let's do what you want, then next time maybe what I want, okay?" He likes a reciprocal dating situation, even though you can see that it's a lot harder for him to assert himself in developing one.

But will this last?

After the relationship has endured for a year or so, this type slowly begins to think that it may last. Steady Relater Cecelia actually dated her boyfriend for 11 years, thinking he'd eventually feel ready for marriage if she just waited long enough. However the time for the big decision never did arrive.

S's tend to stick with their dates

At a party, Steady Relater Polly felt as though she would devote most of her attention to her date. Unless he knows people there, Polly's inclined to stay with him, even if her close friends happen to be there, too. She wants to make sure her date has a good time.

Polly says that if she decides to flirt, she does it subtly by smiling gently, telling stories (perhaps even about herself, but never about him), while acting helpful and pleasant. Even if she thinks wonderful things about him, she doesn't tell him so until later in the relationship. Her brother Ken, another Steady Relater, concurs.

Less is more

Steady Relaters often shy away from anything that smacks of being too overdone. They're basically more middle of the road people who like things on a steady, even keel—No extreme hairstyles, obviously overdone make-up, ultra-flashy clothes, or embarrassing dating prospects for them.

Price consciousness

Steady Relaters tend to view dating behavior as located between extremes. Consistent with this relative reservedness and comfort with moderation, they are typically more price-conscious. Consequently, Steady Relaters may be very aware of what a date will cost. At a restaurant, they may think twice before ordering the most expensive thing on the menu, even if they might be really tempted to risk this splurge. When invited to a school dance, they almost immediately think in terms of the finances of each step toward the big night: formal attire, $_?_; hair styling, $_?_; accessories, $_?_; transportation, $_?_. Then they add up all these prices ($-?) against how much they want to attend with that person ($+?).

S's take things personally

As with other areas of the Steady Relater's life, he prefers that others discover him. Taking most things personally, he may particularly fear rejection in the dating market. He doesn't bounce back as quickly as some of the other types, so he prefers to hold, "Would you like to go to out for a drink or bite to eat?" until he's more assured of getting a yes answer.

If their friends say so

Many Steady Relaters entrust their friends with looking out for their romantic interests. If Ray and Sally say that Jack or Jill is great, then they're apt to go by their friends' recommendations. They prefer to meet the person with the friend who recommended them. An informal introduction at their house, a party, or a movie makes the Steady Relater most comfortable. Collective dates with friends allows them the security of knowing they're likely to have a more pleasant time, whether they hit it off with the date or not.

"Chase me"

Steady Relater Ken says he often likes the woman to make the first move. He also appreciates her setting the pace for an intimate relationship, as long as she doesn't come on too strong or too soon. If he perceives he's being overpursued, he may become uncomfortable and deal with the situation by avoiding her. When she calls, he may not be there, or at least create the illusion he is gone. He'll arrange to have already made other plans or be busy on a project whenever she wants to get together with him. In typical Steady Relater fashion, he likes to avoid confrontation and wounded emotions, hoping she'll get the hint he isn't interested by his avoidance behaviors. As Ken says, "If I'm not ready, I'm not ready—and pushing me isn't going to get me ready any sooner, whether people think so, or not!"

S's like their dates sunny side up

Steady Relaters like their dating partners to exhibit a good sense of humor and a mild, easygoing disposition. Their ideal date generally is a person with a sunny disposition who laughs readily, smiles easily, perhaps knows a few good jokes or stories, and just enjoys spending time with them. This type wants to be sure their romantic interests think they're special and worth another person's time. Toward this end, they may choose to go along for the ride if the date just wants their company, sit in a doctor's office while the other gets some treatment, or even wait in the car while the loved one does some errands. Togetherness in this way appeals to them more than any of the four types.

Hum-drum for some, but fun for S's

They like constancy, those things they can count on doing week after week. In this respect, Steady Relaters tend to be creatures of habit. For example, Saturday night may be reserved for going out, Tuesday, for dinner at home. And Thursday is probably for double dating at the movies with close friends. As with other aspects of their lives, they favor relatively smooth progressions in their dating routines. Although this type naturally prefers a minimum amount of stress, when they commit to someone, they want to make things work out. They often are willing to lend support and help their loved one weather the hard times by showing evidence of their loyalty and concern.

"You choose;" "no, you choose"

Since Steady Relaters often tend to accommodate their date's wishes, they may give in to the date's preferences without voicing their own. "Oh, any restaurant you like will do. You pick, okay?" At the extreme, when Steady Relaters allow their dates to make decisions for them, they may unknowingly set themselves up for victimization. Too much acquiescing can make them appear wishy-washy or opinionless, as well as contribute to their own feeling of being trapped. They can benefit by learning to speak up occasionally, saying what they'd really like to do instead of allowing someone else to dictate until it gets out of hand. By doing this, the problem often can be avoided in the first place.

S's hesitate to hurt people's feelings

By the end of a date, even though many Steady Relaters may decide that the person was not for them, they might go to the date's place anyway. When Steady Relaters are invited home, they typically don't like to appear too rude or brash. But if one thing leads to another, then the situation may accelerate to the point of becoming difficult to escape from the date's apartment, all to spare the other person's feelings.

Remember . . .

STEADY RELATER
DATING/ROMANCE CHARACTERISTICS

- Tend to cooperate and accommodate
- Like identification with the significant other
- Give and like to receive sincere attention
- Naturally operate on a one-to-one basis
- Want to familiarize themselves with the unwritten rules regarding the relationship
- Tend to view dating in a more conservative, progressive, stepwise manner

STEADY RELATERS' PREFERRED
DATING BEHAVIORS

- Seek approval and some sincere, steady pursuit by the other person
- The dating process proceeds in a relatively routine, expected, uneventful way . . . with few unpleasant surprises
- Prefer to participate in the different facets of the loved one's life
- Generally want to share time according to a regular, slower paced schedule
- May prefer to avoid a stressful relationship in favor of a calm, predictable one

Action Plan . . .

HOW STEADY RELATERS CAN LEARN TO ADAPT IN DATING SITUATIONS

- Voice their opinions and thoughts, instead of deferring to their dates
- Say no, when appropriate
- Somewhat reduce their servicing tendencies to limit other person's dependence on them
- Accept some changes in relationships as natural
- Attend more to their own thoughts and feelings
- Act more assertive, when appropriate
- Understand and deal with other types' natural behaviors

HOW YOU CAN HELP STEADY RELATERS MODIFY THEIR DATING BEHAVIOR

- Encourage them to aim higher
- Support them in verbalizing their thoughts and feelings
- Share in developing more assertiveness skills
- Help them plan for some disorganization in their lives
- Show them that disagreement does not necessarily equal an argument
- Assist them in speeding up, at times

"No, maybe, all right"

The same holds true for declining dates. Steady Relater Cindy says that even if she had a miserable time on the first date, she'd say yes to subsequent ones. Why? She didn't want to make him feel bad. Back in the days when *going parking* was a common practice, she found it difficult to say no, even to the boys she hoped she'd never see again. Since then, Cindy says, "I've wised up and learned to be more assertive, to escape my *doormat* mentality." Yet another Steady Relater, Mary Agnes, says that except for a horrible first-time date, she usually will go out with someone who doesn't really appeal to her another time, just to confirm that her initial impression was right. After that, she'll avoid him by saying she's busy or by postponing telling him about the decision she's already made. "Check with me next week or so and we'll talk about it, okay?" If her avoidance is successful, he won't call again and she'll be reprieved from putting him off yet another time.

Why trade the known for the unknown?

Steady Relater Randy has been a widower for 13 years. He confesses that he misses a real family, but he isn't sure he's yet found the person he wants to settle down with for the rest of his life. He's been seeing his receptionist Wanda steadily for six years, but doesn't feel he's actually in love with her, so he's still on the lookout for Miss Happily Ever After. Yet he can't seem to break off his existing relationship for a potentially more productive one. His attitude amounts to, "Why disrupt a sure thing?" Meanwhile, Wanda persists in the possibility that he'll make her the final offer.

Cautious Thinkers and Romance

C's prefer long-term statistics

The way to Cautious Thinkers' hearts is through their logic. Even with love, they tend to use a rational approach. "Before I let myself go, how realistic is it to be infatuated with this person?" They look at the long-term probabilities for a possible match-up. Forget about what the person says; what does he or she actually do to indicate what they're really like? Cautious Thinkers are the most naturally reticent and doubting of the four types, as well as the least verbal. *Show me* is their motto. Like Steady Relaters, Cautious Thinkers need time to establish a relationship. But they may also want to check your track record to predict the odds.

When Cautious Thinker Kathleen meets a romantic prospect, she likes to verify that they have common interests—job, movie, book, or vacation preferences, for instance. To Kathleen, someone interesting means a man who is low-key, quiet, conversational, and doesn't talk a lot about himself. She dislikes game playing and wants everything clearly spelled out. "If he says he'll call and doesn't, I'll give him one more chance and that's it." Compliments don't impress her. She wants to hear a sincere, "I'd really like to spend more time with you." "Wooing is not for me," she adds. Cautious Thinkers' logic can extend to gift giving. Often, they may give practical presents that fit the known, personal interests of the recipient—a small set of tools, a local road map, or a how-to book—instead of more romantic, personal items. Those are reserved until a much deeper, long-standing relationship has evolved.

C's use diplomacy

Cautious Thinker Ralph says dating is hard work. All that energy poured into pursuing a potential date drains him. He likes women to go after him, but, like his Steady Relater counterpart, turns off to women who are too aggressive. "I try to be diplomatic. If a woman I'm not interested in keeps going after me, I'll be roundabout in telling her I don't want to see her any more. Maybe I'll make an excuse, like—I'm going to a wedding." Cautious Thinker Paul used this ploy and became trapped when his erstwhile date discovered he had told her a white lie. So Paul wound up going out with her one more time. This turn of events triggered enough assertiveness to tell her, "No more, please."

Hard to get back in their good graces

When the Cautious Thinker makes up his mind to break up with the significant other, it may take awhile before he can build up to it. The essence of the message is usually akin to, "I've given this adequate time and opportunity and this is just not going to work." When pressed, they're probably able to tell you why, but not likely to do so unless assured it won't add fuel to the fire that keeps things burning, or even smoldering. Remember, they like dealing with specifics. And if forced into telling their former dates what's on their minds, they may beat around the bush anyway. Finally, when this type closes the door, they usually padlock it. So once they've made their decision, it's very difficult to get back in.

Do they care what you think?

One difference between the Cautious Thinker and Steady Relater is that the S type cares what you think; the C isn't generally as concerned about this. So Cautious Thinkers may not make an effort to get along with someone they dislike. They'll simply keep away from them or become even more quiet and reserved. Withdrawing is their way of coping when they're not having a good time. Here's a lesson: When dating a Cautious Thinker, keep your word. If you want to keep the relationship moving forward, be where you're supposed to be when you're supposed to be there and seek their feedback on how you're doing.

Does the world seem absurd?

Ralph says, "I think Woody Allen is funny. Groucho Marx had a perverse quality that I like. And Monty Python has a keen sense of the absurd. I guess I like people who see the ridiculous. Ultimately, the world is a ridiculous place." John Lennon, another Cautious Thinker, seemed to share a similar tongue-in-cheek view of life. Whether true or not, from their viewpoint life is seen from a quite different and comparatively unique perspective. Of all four types, they are the ones who most often truly march to the beat of a different drummer.

C's are likely to know quality places

Often, the Cautious Thinker can contribute helpful suggestions regarding where to go and what to do. This is an area where his emphasis on quality can really shine. "Soderman's Restaurant in Old Lyme has good seafood and reasonable prices. Or Jake's is good for chicken fried steak, Yankee pot roast, and grape nut custard pudding." Like Steady Relaters, they often opt for a proven favorite over a new place that may not meet their known standards.

And, of course, the proverbial icing on the cake is when the date acknowledges, "Andrew, you were absolutely right about this restaurant. The gravy on that chicken fried steak alone was worth the drive. What a well-kept secret! How did you discover it?"

They want to do things right

En route to the destination, the Cautious Thinker typically will have already found or called for exact directions, possibly writing them down while consulting a map. Cautious Thinkers usually become nervous and worried when they're with a person who wings it and isn't sure of where they're going:

Cautious Thinker: "Why don't we stop at that gas station and ask how close we are to Laurel Street?"

Non-Cautious Thinker: "There's no need for that. I know it's somewhere around Poplar and Elm."

Cautious Thinker: "But we only have two minutes to get there. Our reservations are for seven o'clock."

Non-Cautious Thinker: "Do I look worried? Don't fret, we'll be there soon."

But to a Cautious Thinker, getting there at the right time is important. This type often is very precise with exacting standards. Therefore, a Cautious Thinker may view a seven o'clock dinner reservation as a seven o'clock sharp deadline. Left to her own more self-disciplined preferences, she would have shown up on the dot, if not even sooner.

The sound of silence

When Cautious Thinker Darren and his long-time date Celia go to their favorite diner, conversation between them may sound like this:

Celia: "Well, Darren, what are you going to order tonight?"

Cautious Darren: "The usual." (Silence)

Celia: "Did you read about the air crash today?"

Cautious Darren: "Yes."

Celia: "Isn't it horrible? All those innocent people!"

Cautious Darren: "Yes, it is." (More silence)

Celia: "Would you prefer being alone?"

Cautious Darren: "No. Why do you ask?"

Celia: "Because I feel like I'm talking to myself. Pulling one-word answers out of you isn't much fun."

Cautious Darren: "My answers have been more than one word."

Celia: "That's not the point. The point is I feel like I'm cross-examining you. Try keeping up your end of the conversation, okay?"

Cautious Darren: "You know that I'm a quiet person of few words."

Celia: "Quiet is one thing; uncommunicative is another. I need you to talk with me, not just respond to my talking, all right?"

Cautious Darren: "All right, Celia. I'll try to do better. Am I talking more now?"

Celia (laughing): "That *IS* better, Darren. At least you're asking me something now."

To Celia, talking is an important part of togetherness. To Darren, sharing the same activity may be enough. In this example, Celia tells Darren her specific needs. Darren, in turn, responds to those needs by talking more and asking her a question. By behaving uncritically, both can more easily see the positive side of their natural differences and learn to appreciate one another and develop a deeper, more mutually satisfying relationship.

Excited on the inside

Because Cautious Thinkers are, by nature, difficult for others to read, it's helpful if they say what is truly on their minds. Typically, they may throw in a quiet suggestion that can become overridden by more boisterous dates or small groups who may literally not hear the Cautious Thinker's comments. Since this type seldom discloses their real feelings and thoughts—except to a trusted, long-term friend or date, they sometimes hesitate to protest what the group decides. Sometimes they may think, "My opinion probably won't change the outcome anyway," so they hesitate to share their views. Then they may remain quiet because they resent their own compliance. Mustering up enough assertiveness to make sure their opinion is heard can contribute to a more successful group experience.

As in other aspects of their lives, they firmly control their emotions, so once romance has been offered and accepted, it's doubly important that they express their feelings. Otherwise, the date may wonder if the Cautious Thinker still feels and thinks the same way about him. "Audrey, remember what we talked about last night? You seem so quiet, I'm just wondering if something's wrong."

"No, really, everything is fine," Audrey assures him.

"Well, you don't seem very excited about being in love."

"Of course I am," Audrey elaborates. "I just don't show my excitement as much as you do. But I'm actually excited on the inside, even if it's not apparent to you."

Like Audrey, Cautious Thinkers tend to get inwardly enthusiastic. This can be frustrating for more talkative types, but is more easily tolerated when the feeling of excitement (or anger, happiness, warmth, etc.) is verbally communicated. Picture Clint Eastwood or John Wayne in their typical movie roles. When they're interested in *getting the girl*, they usually pursue her in a less verbal, more emotionally controlled, and painstaking way. They leave a lot to the woman's imagination. "Does he or doesn't he care for me?"

Their feelings for the loved one are usually shown by what they do for the heroine, not by what they say or promise. They seem to live by the axiom: "Talk is cheap. Let's see what

Remember . . .

CAUTIOUS THINKER
DATING/ROMANCE CHARACTERISTICS

- Seek acknowledgment that they are right
- Want to share quality time
- Usually prefer to date only one person at a time
- Think about the possibilities for the relationship before falling for someone
- Look objectively at the loved one
- Proceed in a cautious, rational manner
- Look at probabilities and variables to determine if a relationship will last

CAUTIOUS THINKERS' PREFERRED
DATING BEHAVIORS

- Dislike unexpected situations and surprises
- May want close to exclusivity in their relationship, doing most social things as a twosome
- Prefer a date with substance and depth
- Want some freedom in their relationship for alone time
- Observe and mentally collect 'date data' to help them make decisions

Action Plan . . .

HOW CAUTIOUS THINKERS CAN LEARN TO ADAPT IN DATING SITUATIONS

- Accept the other behavioral types for themselves, without expecting them to become more like them
- Reveal more about themselves and their feelings
- Give and receive sincere compliments
- Participate more, go off by themselves less
- Behave less critically and more light-heartedly

HOW YOU CAN HELP CAUTIOUS THINKERS MODIFY THEIR BEHAVIOR

- Gently remind them that human errors can be reduced, not eliminated
- Help them tap their sense of humor by pointing out funny observations
- Encourage them to let their guard down, occasionally
- Support them in developing more direct behaviors
- Help them verbalize their feelings
- Calmly point out that life consists of gray areas . . . not just black or white ones
- Demonstrate by your actions that you care about them—right or wrong

you do." Even when they appear emotionally hooked, they sometimes don't realize it until late into the film. Emotions, after all, are an area of less familiarity than things for Cautious Thinkers. And getting their emotions right can prove to be a greater task than they at first envisioned.

Once committed, though, Cautious Thinkers often become intensely involved in the relationship. They may even reach the point of overprotection of the time, the activities, or even the relationships of their mate with others.

Birds of a feather . . . or opposites attract?

So which type is best suited for which? Which axiom applies: Birds of a feather or opposites attract? Actually, any type can be well suited to another if both make an effort to learn what is important to the other—and if they acknowledge their own, as well as the loved one's, natural strengths and weaknesses. If the two appreciate and accept each other, despite their respective natural limitations, they'll be on the way to a successful love relationship founded on mutual understanding and respect. The important thing to remember is that each behavioral type has needs which they strive to fill. But when both people in a romantic relationship put themselves in the other's shoes, then the potential for a more productive, mutually beneficial match increases significantly.

Dominant Director plus Dominant Director

Two Dominant Directors can try to dominate each other and become stubborn, impatient, and tough. "I'm the boss." "No, I'm the boss." At worst, this basic tug of war over the need to be the top dog can ruin a budding relationship before it ever really begins. A sense of humor, verbal expressions of each other's admiration, and win-win usage of those natural negotiating skills in an accepting, understanding atmosphere can go a long way toward cultivating a romance between a Dominant Director duo. Like Stan and Melody, they can learn to listen to each other and come up with mutually acceptable solutions that allow them both to win.

Dominant Director and Steady Relater

Negatively, a Dominant Director and a Steady Relater can also result in a persecutor/victim type of unfortunate relationship in which each person becomes trapped in a nightmare of pace and priority differences. More positively, they can share a complementary pairing in which each one accepts and appreciates the different strengths which the partner possesses. This blend of types also gets a possible vote as the match made closest to heaven if adaptability exists. That is, the Dominant Director needs to compassionately listen to and draw out the Steady Relater and learn more about the Steady Relater's feelings and opinions. Similarly, the Steady Relater has to understand the Dominant Director's need to get up off the couch and do things in the process. They can also benefit by learning to accept, versus stand up to, the Dominant Director's take charge positions.

Dominant Director plus Interacting Socializer

A Dominant Director/Interacting Socializer match-up may result in an activity filled, risk-taking, dynamic duet. Or it can be a combustible battle of the century pitting will against ego. In its workable form, this combination can become a fast-paced balance between business and pleasure, with each type enhanced by the other. For this to happen, the Interacting Socializer has to learn to accept the other's discomfort with discussing feelings at the expense of actual facts. The Dominant Director can learn to recognize the Interacting Socializer's natural priority for personal and shared feelings which may otherwise cause them to filter out problems and complexities. Dominant Directors can use their negotiation and delegation resources. Interacting Socializers can use their seemingly unending supply of enthusiastic ideas and positive energy to help both of them find common solutions to challenges that come along. Otherwise, each type may engage in a frenzied competition for *what I want* that leads in two different or opposing directions.

Dominant Director and Cautious Thinker

When Dominant Director meets Cautious Thinker, their mutual task orientations and inclinations for not verbalizing feelings can bond them. But their conflicting paces, quantity versus quality preferences and Direct/Controlling versus Indirect/Controlling lifestyles, can clash like an atomic blast. The fast-moving Dominant Directors can slow down their pace and learn to tolerate the Cautious Thinker's natural need for caution. On the other hand, Cautious Thinkers can recognize that Dominant Directors may become impatient and blunt, at times, and learn to verbalize their discomfort with those traits. Both want different types of control, but Dominant Directors go about getting it directly, while Cautious Thinkers do it indirectly. A move toward redefining their shared expectations and concerns assures them their desired results will be achieved. It can be the foundation for a powerful and unique type of bonding relationship between these two self-determined types.

Interacting Socializer plus Interacting Socializer

When two Interacting Socializers get together, they have been known to try making life a perpetual party. Or they may engage in a bitter rivalry, each trying to outdo the other. They may even attempt to foist work onto each other. Since both prefer to deal in the realm of their feelings and the big picture, who will deal with the nitty-gritty details? The one who feels more comfortable with them may write tasks down for the other and help the loved one to get more organized. "Where there's a will, there's a way."

Whatever the creative solution, chances are these two will want to entertain each other and have fun along the way, not to mention talk about virtually everything that pops into their minds. However, for this relationship to flourish, they have to first explore together and then agree about *TCB*—how they'll take care of the business that must be achieved for them to keep feeling good about each other.

Interacting Socializer plus Steady Relater

A Steady Relater/Interacting Socializer duo often provides a warm, emotive, mutually supportive combination. But it has also been reported to end with the Steady Relater's resenting the partner's search for center stage, universal approval, and flurries of activity—often in the absence of the Steady Relater. In this scenario of conflict in natural chemistry, the Interacting Socializer may feel squelched by too much routine, steadiness, and boredom with staying put. Their relationship could result in a more flexible set of optional routines for fun and games (including wild card options), thereby better meeting the needs of both.

The Interacting Socializer has to realize that the Steady Relater is more private, safety-seeking, and organized. Those traits could have a stabilizing effect on the Interacting Socializer if the Interacting Socializer agrees to meet the Steady Relater halfway. Similarly, the Steady Relater has to learn to accept the Interacting Socializer's natural spontaneity, persuasiveness, and sociability. While both enjoy people—including their own companionship—the issues to resolve primarily focus on who, how often, when, and for what mutually derived purpose?

Interacting Socializer plus Cautious Thinker

An Interacting Socializer and a Cautious Thinker are another set of intriguing individualists with quite different tendencies. This can result in a complementary relationship where each partner makes up and compensates for the less developed strengths of the other (which can certainly simplify matters, since they have such obviously different preferences). However, it can also intensify each other's stress levels with the suppression of their differing paces, priorities, and approaches. The pairing of these two results in two intuitive types combining in a potentially creative, innovative relationship.

The Interacting Socializer needs to understand the Cautious Thinker's private lifestyle and desire for a deeply private relationship, including their discomfort with having to socialize. The Cautious Thinker has to learn to accept the Interacting

Socializer's need to be with people and their disinterest in dealing with messy details or complications. They must also understand the Socializer's desire for varied recreational activities—whether watching TV, going out to eat, calling on friends, or going to movies or sporting events. By working out and appreciating their individual differences and providing each other the space and time for these to co-exist, they can become a productive combination—with each compensating for what the other naturally lacks.

When Steady Relater meets Steady Relater

With another Steady Relater, this relationship tends to become a paragon of consideration and stability. However, sometimes it also decays into stagnancy and over-predictability, with neither party taking any risks or doing much out of the ordinary. As with any match-up of the same types, they might share a lot in common, but each may also tend to view life in such a similar way that they have to stretch beyond themselves to attain growth and balance. Since both parties generally are pleasant and tolerant-acting, problematical issues may remain hidden, with neither one wanting to initiate a possible confrontation. But someone ultimately has to take charge of the harsher realities and assume more control. Given Steady Relaters' natural propensity for perseverance, they, more than the other types, may stick it out, hoping they can make it work. The real challenge for this couple involves how they will successfully manage adverse situations—with significant differences in their personal values systems being the most threatening of all to the stability of their relationship.

Steady Relater plus Cautious Thinker

A Steady Relater and a Cautious Thinker share a slower pace, but Steady Relaters are somewhat more people and feeling-oriented than Cautious Thinkers. Steady Relaters support others; the Cautious Thinkers subtly control people and situations. Steady Relaters prefer a more casual, relaxed atmosphere of involvement with people; Cautious Thinkers prefer a more formal one with the option of being left alone to do their own thing. Both strive for peace, calmness, and tranquility. Both typically take an organized, though indirect approach. If they can agree to discuss important, but uncomfortable, issues and feelings, they can encourage each other's further growth and development. Neither one is naturally assertive. The Cautious Thinker might find greater success initiating tasks, while the Steady Relater can perform the social activities, personal discussions, and follow-up implementation required.

Cautious Thinker plus Cautious Thinker

Two Cautious Thinkers have been known to harmonize beautifully; however, the two have also been reported to become so task-oriented and detached from common objectives that their relationship suffers dramatically. Again, a match of the same type can result in a wonderful sharing of similar thoughts and actions, but it may also stymie those areas where a bit of stretching is required—assertiveness, directness, socializing, and expression of feelings. If two Cautious Thinkers choose each other, they'll typically want to make the relationship right and may proceed with extreme caution. They share perfectionism, thoroughness, creativeness, and an intellectual approach to viewing life. Their relationship could be organized and workable for them. However, it could also become rigid with both being convinced that their priority or their way is the only way to go—leading to a cataclysmic, or even irreversible, battle of unspoken differences.

How to make any and all combinations work

Each combination of types can make or break their own relationship according to how accepting and adaptable they're willing to be in their dealings with each other's natural needs, fears, strengths, and limitations. The crucial difference in a relationship is in tolerating and shrugging off each other's irritating traits—and recognizing when it is appropriate to modify one's own natural behavior. Then, increasingly more acceptable solutions can be reached which result in the mutual satisfaction of their individual needs. The issue here is not so much compatibility as it is commitment. Commitment calls for mutual respect and trust of another person, despite individual differences and weaknesses. People who stay together communicate and reciprocate with each other in the context of shared commitment. They affirm strengths and appreciate the partner's individual uniqueness as they adapt their style to meet the other person's needs. Understanding and applying these People Smart principles can make the difference for the individuals they and you want to love.

Part Four

Custom-Fitted Personal Patterns

People Smart Principle #11—The Over-Dependency Principle: "Too much of anything can become a liability that works against your own best interests."

Chapter 11
Mixed (Acquired) Styles

When you are yourself, your core behavioral type shows

As we mentioned earlier, people have their own special way of doing things—an identifiable and predictable behavioral type. Behavioral type is a pattern, or group of recurring habits, resulting from the way you typically do things, the way you deal with people and situations. It's your naturally comfortable way of behaving most of the time when you relax and just act yourself. Usually, your off the job behavior is the closest to your core behavioral type.

Which style have you acquired?

Everyone has a basic core type—one of the four discussed throughout this book—which we gravitate toward when no one makes demands of us. Besides our basic core behavioral type, we usually also have an acquired style which we may have adopted to function better in life's various arenas. Acquired styles are unique, more in-depth explanations of human behavior.

Core plus acquired styles represent 95% of the people

Acquired style includes those additional tendencies which most of us consciously add to our core behavioral type in order to function better in our social, personal, or work environments. Field research has shown the combination of these two traits results in 15 common, classical patterns. This accounts for 95% of the population. The remaining 5% don't fit these most common classical patterns. Rather, they make up other less natural combinations of the core four.

"Can I be a combination of all four?"

Most of us are combinations of two or, at most, three of the patterns. True, we may exhibit behaviors from all four during the course of the day. Yet we behave most naturally and comfortably in our core style, our personal home base. Usually we spend many hours using our acquired styles, too, especially when we deal with other people and varied tasks. Often, people demonstrate one style at work and a different, more natural core-related style at home where we have more freedom to simply be ourselves. By contrast, our work style is usually a learned one, where we have adapted to perform many roles that meet not only our own individual expectations, but also those of others (e.g., co-workers, boss, organization, customers).

Self-perception versus how others see us

"How do I know the way I see myself is the way I am?" For some of us, our behavioral pattern represents the way we strive to be, rather than the way we typically act in a given environment. That is, our self-perception includes both how we intend to act as well as how we actually think or feel we do act. However, from the point of view of those who observe our actions, they usually know much less about our intentions. Instead, when asked to describe us, they base their conclusion on what they actually see as our typical behaviors! By being aware of possible gaps between these two views of ourselves, we can further increase our personal, interpersonal, and group effectiveness.

When seeking this feedback from others, there are certain advisable guidelines. Feedback can vary significantly in its degree of accuracy, including our actual behavior! So whether you wish to ask others how they see the basis of the *Personal Assets Inventory,* or a more general assessment based on a review of the four basic patterns (and the 15 common combinations among them), we recommend some tips.

When asking others to give you feedback to compare with your self-perception and increase your level of personal awareness, make sure these individuals are familiar with your behavior in a particular environment and that they fill out the questionnaire accordingly. Also have them respond anonymously so they describe you the way you really are, without projecting some more idealized portrait they may feel expected to provide. Regarding the temptation to whitewash, remember there is no good or bad inventory profile pattern. The purpose of the inventory is to arrive at this simple reality: Each of us has his or her own unique set of natural and learned personal tendencies which this tool will reveal.

Finding your own classical pattern(s)

Which of the 15 types is most like you—at work, socially, elsewhere? Up to this point, you have achieved the following new insights about yourself and other people:

#1 – a multi-faceted understanding of the daily behavior of the four basic types of people,

#2 – a more clear-cut understanding of those types of behaviors which are most like you as well as those tendencies which are least like you,

#3 – a wide variety of insights of how to more effectively adapt your own personal behavior as well as your actions in dealing more effectively with each of the four basic types of individuals in various common situations (e.g., at work, in sales, as leaders or managers, socially, at home, and in romance).

You can build upon the foundation of these three key breakthroughs to double your People Smarts. Add further insight to each of these three achievements by simply looking at the same dimensions of behavior—but from a slightly different, more powerful dimension. In the rest of this chapter and in the final one, we will focus on the 15 more commonly found, and comprehensive combinations, of the four basic behavioral types. As a result, you'll increase your potential level of precision with as many as 95% of the people you encounter!

Now you can get started tuning in to the 15 combinations! These classical patterns explain our observable behaviors and the inner goals and fears which direct our patterns of behavior. Additionally, they show how each of these individuals— ourselves or others—can become even more effective in life. Use the *Personal Assets Inventory* tool located at the beginning of Chapter 2, as your initial guide in this process. For a more precise measure of your classical pattern, we recommend the *Performax Personal Profile System* and related in-depth audio-based self-study programs (availability noted in Acknowledgments).

At this time, return to your completed copy of the inventory. Look at your scores for each of the four individual total boxes (D-I-S-C). The number contained in it will allow you to determine the specific classical pattern which best describes you overall. Note: Remember, you can follow this same process later to see how your classical pattern may change in different environments, situations, or viewpoints (others' perceptions).

If You Only Have One High Score

If you have a score of 12 to 20 for only one of the four columns, your pattern is:

"D" Column = Classical Pattern #1 (Developer)
"I" Column = Classical Pattern #5 (Promoter)
"S" Column = Classical Pattern #9 (Specialist)
"C" Column = Classical Pattern #13 (Objective Thinker)

If You Have Two High Scores

Or, if you have two column scores, each ranging between 12 to 20, your pattern is:

Highest "D" Column score, with

"I" score which is almost identical = Classical Pattern #3 (Inspirational)

"I" score which is lower, but still 12 or more = Classical Pattern #2 (Results-Oriented)

"S" score which is lower, but still 12 or more = Classical Pattern #11 (Achiever)

"C" score of 12 or more = Classical Pattern #4 (Creative) Highest "I" Column score, with . . .

Highest "I" Column score, with

"D" score which is lower, but still 12 or more = Classical Pattern #6 (Persuader)

"S" score which is lower, but still 12 or more = Classical Pattern #7 (Counselor)

"C" score which is lower, but still 12 or more = Classical Pattern #8 (Appraiser)

Highest "S" Column score, with

"D" score of 12 or more = Classical Pattern #11 (Achiever)

"I" score which is lower, but still 12 or more = Classical Pattern #10 (Agent)

"C" score of 12 or more = Classical Pattern # 14 (Perfectionist)

Highest "C" Column score, with

"D" score of 12 or more = Classical Pattern #4 (Creative)

"I" score of 12 or more = Classical Pattern #8 (Appraiser)

"S" score of 12 or more = Classical Pattern #14 (Perfectionist)

If You Have Three High Scores

Or if you have three column scores, each of which is between 12 to 20, then your pattern is:

For scores in the "D", "S", and "C" columns = Classical Pattern #12 (Investigator)
For scores in the "I", "S", and "C" columns = Classical Pattern #15 (Practitioner)

For all other combinations, refer back to the two highest scores as shown above to determine the closest classical pattern.

For future reference, we have included a handy quick-reference guide to the classical patterns, the *Classical Patterns Master Chart*, for both your own personal development and for application with people you know.

Increasing Productivity With the Patterns

The guiding principle of People Smart management is to reinforce the positive and productive behaviors in both your own and in others' patterns. To do this, respond first and most strongly to the person's primary, or strongest, drive. For instance, the Results-Oriented person has a basic Dominant Director (D) need for control, so react accordingly. After that, focus on the secondary drive(s), when appropriate. With the same Results-Oriented individual, remember the secondary need for the Interacting Socializer (I) to influence. Simply refer to this *Classical Patterns Master Chart* for a quick and easy reference that identifies these primary and secondary motivations in each of us.

Classical Patterns Master Chart

Classical Pattern	Primary Drive	Secondary Drive
Developer	D	(none)
Results-Oriented	D	I
Inspirational	D	Nearly = I
Creative	D	Nearly = C
Promoter	I	(none)
Persuader	I	D
Counselor	I	S
Appraiser	I	Nearly = C
Specialist	S	(none)
Agent	S	I
Achiever	S	D
Investigator	S	C and D
Objective Thinker	C	(none)
Perfectionist	C	Nearly = S
Practitioner	C	I some S

Dominant Director = D   Interacting Socializer = I
Steady Relator = R   Cautious Thinker = C

You can benefit by reading more about any of these personality types to further your understanding and acceptance of the reality of each pattern's unique needs. By doing so, you will improve both your effectiveness in dealing with them and the quality of your relationship with them in a particular setting (work, social, home, or romantic).

DOMINANT DIRECTOR (D)
Behavioral Patterns

#1: The Developer

A Dominant DIRECTOR style
- Want to win
- Fear boredom and routine
- May think their way is the only way
- Seek new challenges
- Want to find their own answers
- Interpret rules
- Accept responsibility for mistakes
- May manipulate people and situations
- Under pressure, do things alone; can become belligerent

Developers want social power and influence

The Developer is best described as the core Dominant Director, which, like all Dominant Director patterns, has a common basic drive towards personal power and influence. Their tendencies may be summarized as Direct and Controlling. The unique goal which motivates these people is new opportunities. On the other hand, the basic fear which tends to lead to a direct type of fight response is loss of control. Consequently, this person typically speaks his mind. What others are afraid to say, the Developer often says for them.

Developers are less concerned with others' opinions of them than are many other styles. This relative disinterest in what others think about them allows them to take more risks, free from the burden of potential ridicule. "Let them laugh. I'll show them," may be their creed. They tend to take credit, and often responsibility, for their own actions without including or blaming anybody else. "The buck stops here," with the Developer.

Often question authority

Developers often look for their own answers, instead of seeking them from so-called higher authorities. They go to the source—primary references or documents—rather than ask bosses or colleagues. Even when they look outside themselves for answers, they seldom take the expert opinion as gospel. They prefer to arrive at their own conclusions based on the facts at hand. Eventually, their view may concur with the expert's or the boss's, but Developers seldom go along just to conform or to avoid rocking the boat. They reach their own conclusions (sometimes unilateral ones) in the same manner they tend to generally conduct themselves independently. In this sense, they often question authority and, at times, may need someone to remind them of more appropriate steps toward results.

They make things happen

Similarly, they may not follow accepted procedures to reach their goals. If this style thinks they may have to endure a lot of red tape, they may ignore the rules and prepare to suffer the consequences. For instance, if company policy is to check out reference books from the office, Developers may just walk out of the building with them, rationalizing, "I'm going to bring them back Monday." For Developers, *borrowing* things may seem a lot easier than going through established protocol.

At the extreme, Developers may tend to manipulate people and situations. They want things to come out so that they win. We know one former president of an association who is now a board member. Even though he has no vote, Graham makes it a point to attend meetings so he can steer the others around to his way of thinking. Since he is a virtual association legend, many of the current voting members go along with his recommendations. In Graham's mind, the suggestions are already decisions. He thinks the ends justify the means, regardless of which means arrive at the conclusion he has in mind.

When someone tells Developers something is hard, or impossible, they usually can't wait to get started, the sooner to conquer that insurmountable obstacle. "All right, so where's this parcel of land that nobody's been able to buy?" Then, step aside and watch those Developers charge into action. They also tend to show excitement and that rarin' to go quality in a pinch. They're the batters who like to step up to the plate when their team trails 3-0, with two outs and bases empty. They may even point to where they plan to direct the baseball.

When individuals who fit this pattern think they know how to do something, that's usually good enough for them. Consequently, they may ignore or reject instruction and advice. Then they may build an invisible, protective shield around themselves to ward off persons or situations that stand in the way of winning their goals. This shield also protects them from different opinions and viewpoints. When they go after other people's advice, that's typically a sign of extreme panic, stress, and desperation.

An interview with a Developer

Interviewer: "I'm here today talking to a very successful executive with a Developer pattern. What do you think is your greatest strength or the biggest benefit you've received as a person with this Developer pattern of behavior?"

Ted: "I guess it's my ability to cut through the details and get to the meat, the things that count, the stuff that's going to impact the final outcome. I don't get bogged down. I don't let things that aren't related get in the way of making quick decisions."

Interviewer: "How long have you worked at this position?"

Ted: "About three and a half years. For me, that means it's time to start looking around. You see, I've had about a four year cycle. My boss understands that. By about the fourth year, I've usually accomplished what I want and become not only bored, but also very, very restless. But just before I was ready to quit my last job, my boss surprised me by tossing me into the middle of a big new project and BAM! I was off and running again with my motor revved up and powered with full steam ahead."

Interviewer: "And you liked that?"

Ted: "Of course! Suddenly there was another new challenge. And that's the exciting thing about opportunities—you never quite know how it's going to develop and turn out. I may have to move. It may result in boom or bust, but one thing's for sure, never a dull moment. And another great thing about it is that you never really fail. You just keep changing the rules as you go. Over the years I've developed a lot of self-confidence in my ability to get things done."

Interviewer: "What happens when you make mistakes?"

Ted: "I just pull things back on course. You see, you've got to know how to control things and keep everything running on schedule and in the right direction."

Interviewer: "What about the people you supervise?"

Ted: "One of my greatest frustrations is the energy it takes to move people to get things done. I sometimes get so frustrated with people that I jump into the project and do things myself just to get it done. Needless to say, a few of my managers don't like me butting into their projects. And then that becomes frustrating for all of us."

#2: Results-Oriented

An Interacting DIRECTOR style

- *I can do it* attitude, whether they've done it before or not
- Don't willingly give up; persistent
- Stand up for their rights
- Prefer that others get things done quickly
- Naturally independent and dominant
- Self-confident that they can accomplish and make a difference
- Achievement-oriented; show annoyance when goals are thwarted
- Fear others taking advantage of them
- Under pressure, may become critical and resistant

Results-Oriented people want dominance and independence

As Dominant Directors with many Interacting Socializer traits,

Results-Oriented behavioral tendencies can be summarized as Direct, Controlling, and somewhat Supporting (except under pressure). Their unique motivating goal is dominance and independence, while their characteristic fear is that others may take advantage of them or beat them to a goal; they tend to be wary and distrustful of others who show these same characteristics. They may display well-developed egos, prompting them to show impatience and annoyance with others, especially if people don't measure up to their standards. They are usually unwilling to sacrifice their own wants for those of others, so people may view them as haughty, at times. "She thinks she's better than we are," detractors may say.

They like who they are

Results-Oriented styles' high self-dependence involves more than just achievements. They seem to naturally like who they are. This innate sense of self-importance often enables them to make mistakes and still feel good about themselves. Setbacks and disappointments are typically short-lived. "So what if I can't spell well. The secretary can fix my misspelled words before my correspondence goes out." They downplay mistakes and focus on their success rate.

They frequently make judgments based on how quickly others accomplish tasks, sometimes at the expense of quality. "Hurry up, hurry up," this style may say. They want to see output—quantity. Some styles neither function well under pressure nor naturally focus on quick results, so hurrying them often causes more mistakes.

Overstepping conventional bounds may not deter Results-Oriented individuals. They often like confrontation and may challenge authority figures by making demands or imposing their wills. "Your department is slowing down the production of our computer discs." Opponents may feel the full force of their determination because Results-Oriented people tend to stand firm and take responsibility for their actions. Like the Developer style, these individuals may barge through protocol, cutting corners to reach a goal the fastest way. The adventure of it all fuels Results-Oriented people to pursue victory. They may prefer to teach themselves what they need to know and often gravitate toward situations where they can be more independent.

An interview with a Results-Oriented person

Interviewer: "Today we are talking with a very successful Results-Oriented individual who is the general manager of a heavy equipment company. Sam, can you tell us what you feel is your greatest asset as a person with this Results-Oriented pattern?"

Sam: "Absolutely! It's the ability to get things done—not be afraid to attack a task, any task."

Interviewer: "Would it be accurate to say that you don't want anyone getting in your way and slowing you down?"

Sam: "Yeah, that's right. I don't like to mess around. I just get it done and get it over with."

Interviewer: "Do you work with people who mess around and take longer? And if so, how does this affect you?"

Sam: "Sometimes I try to avoid them."

Interviewer: "Can you give me an example of what you mean?"

Sam: "When I give one of my staff an assignment and he doesn't carry it out as rapidly as I like, I just get away because that puts stress on me. I realize that others usually take longer than me, so if I delegate it, then I walk away. Otherwise, I get frustrated."

Interviewer: "You mean if you stood there and watched, you might end up even more frustrated?"

Sam: "Yeah. For example, when my kids do the dishes, I leave the room. They come and tell me when they're finished. I don't want to see how they do it because they take too long and they don't do it my way, anyway."

Interviewer: "Because of the impatience you have, you like to speed up the process; for instance, by having people move quicker?"

Sam: "Sure. It's hard for me to just sit here patiently."

Interviewer: "Is that why you took the tape recorder out of my hands when I first came in for this interview and you said you'd handle it? Was I moving too slowly for you then?"

Sam: "Yeah. You were fumbling with it and I'm good at mechanical things like tape recorders."

Interviewer: "You just said you were good at mechanical things. Are you aware that some other types of individuals would consider that statement a bit arrogant?"

Sam: "Look, I state my achievements freely and I'm not shy about what I can do. If others think that's arrogant, I guess there's not much I can do about it."

Interviewer: "Has anyone ever mentioned it to you before now?"

Sam: "Well, no one has called it arrogance. A few people have told me that I act like I really think I'm important. But it's not really that I'm arrogant. It's just that I don't take much time with people. It takes a lot of time and patience to handle people's feelings and I want to get things done faster and quicker. And I am confident of my abilities. I decide what I'm going to do, then I do it! I say, 'Yes, I can do it.' And then I do it, no matter what the situation."

Interviewer: "It sounds like you enjoy the challenge or opportunity provided by antagonistic circumstances, that is, situations where others might hesitate, fall down, or even just give up altogether."

Sam: "Yeah. It's like fighting through to the finish on things."

#3: Inspirational

Dominant and Interactive DIRECTOR style
- Accept competition and even aggression from themselves and others
- Appear to reject affection (on the surface)
- Want to control the environment
- Judge others by how effectively they project strength and power
- May leap before they look
- Tend to overuse pragmatism (The ends justify the means)
- Fear seeming too soft and dependent
- Under pressure, tend to argue and become belligerent

Inspirationals want to control environment and people

The Inspirational style is a Dominant Director type with nearly equal Interacting Socializer characteristics. He is a combination of Direct, Controlling, and Supporting characteristics, depending on what the situation seems to call for. He is motivated to be a master people-mover since his goal is to control his environment or audience. He may appear undirected, at times, but can surprise others with sudden bursts of enthusiasm and energy, especially when he has an audience. Sometimes he entertains and focuses as much on making an impact with his spectators as on the task at hand. This may result in his rejection of outward displays of affection as seeming to be a weakness or appearing too *soft*.

Inspirational people seem to naturally understand that nobody can be nice every second, and they accept lapses from pleasant behaviors in themselves and others. They fight for what they want and often respect opponents who act similarly, without holding grudges. They also seem to naturally realize that different strokes appeal to different folks. This insight can help them to better motivate and deal more effectively with others.

Ah, authority!

This type typically looks up to people who project power—especially if they have succeeded in overcoming obstacles to reach that position. If the Inspirational person perceives others as weak or subservient, he often dominates and gets them to comply with his wishes. But he has difficulty respecting them. He admires people who persist until they get what they want, regardless of how they get there.

Inspirational individuals tend to shape their environments, and, like the Developer and Results-Oriented styles, often act without first asking, "Is it okay if I do such-and-such?" Instead, they usually plunge in full force, and may suffer repercussions later. They may not even realize they're in over their heads until late in the game. When mistakes happen, they may blame other people or circumstances, rather than themselves.

An interview with an Inspirational

Interviewer: "Today we are talking to a 38-year-old Vice President in the banking industry. What would you say is the benefit of having an Inspirational profile like yours?"

Inspirational: "Well, I guess it's that I can get others to do things. I don't particularly like the word inspire. It's more like my enthusiasm and energy for getting things done seems to turn people on to want to get things done. They get excited about what I'm excited about and then they want to do what needs doing. It's kind of like they catch the *fever* or spirit or whatever you prefer to call it."

Interviewer: "You like seeing people . . ."

Inspirational: ". . . Excited. It's natural for me to sell the people I deal with."

Interviewer: "According to the research on this Inspirational pattern, it predicts that you like to control your environment, to run the show. Does this sound like you?"

Inspirational: "I'd say it sounds like me 100%. I've seen that as far back as my high school years and then into my adult life. In high school I was always involved in taking the initiative to lead a lot of activities and organizations. But sometimes it can become a problem."

Interviewer: "What do you mean?"

Inspirational: "I think there are times I get carried away and seem to need to control something. Sometimes it can be a sensitive situation because when I try to control things I can be threatening to others, particularly men, who aren't confident or secure. I can be pretty intense at work, but I try to relax at home. My husband reminds me to slow down and relax, be less intense, and stop trying to run the *master control panel*, especially with our teenagers."

Interviewer: "People with the Inspirational pattern are said to fear being too soft. Is that true of you?"

Inspirational: "That's true. I agree with that. In fact, I can give you an example of it that happened last week. One of my colleagues who I've been working with for the last four years was surprised to discover I have three children."

Interviewer: "What happened?"

Inspirational: "Well, I had a telephone call from my teenage daughter while we were in my office. After I got off the phone I was upset and told him about the situation. He was really surprised. He even said, 'Well, I guess you aren't really a superhuman after all.'"

Interviewer: "Wow! How'd you take that comment?"

Inspirational: "I thought it was sort of intriguing and funny. Since then our interactions have improved. I've always separated my personal and professional life. Since that experience, I think I'm now a little bit more aware that it's okay to relate on a gut level now and then. But I prefer a more professional level and I guess not being soft is part of that. It's just that I'm concerned about really coming across as being vulnerable and losing control that I need to be certain things will turn out okay."

#4: Creative

A Cautious DIRECTOR

- Want to change the way things are done
- Answer to their own personal ideas and standards
- Want to influence others, or may sulk
- May control outward emotions and expressions
- Strive to accomplish the unusual
- Need tangible recognition
- Critical of selves en route to becoming stars
- Fear they won't reach their standards
- Under pressure, can become bored or blue

Creatives want unique accomplishments

The Creative person is a Dominant Director with a somewhat higher or lower Cautious Thinker pattern. She is quite Controlling, though somewhat both Direct and Indirect, depending on the situation. Her quick thinking, inventive mind may be restrained by her inner need to analyze all options before making decisions. This type both asks herself questions and supplies the answers, often internally. The goal which naturally motivates her daily behavior is dominance, especially regarding unique accomplishments. On the other hand, she fears not being influential or successful in reaching these outcomes. Even if she reaches her goal, she may not be satisfied unless the process used in attaining that goal meets her specifications. As a result, she also fears failure to achieve her standards, both by her or anyone else. She is simultaneously sensitive to criticism (consistent with the Cautious Thinker pattern) and blunt in her criticisms of others (Dominant Director pattern). At the extreme, she may tend to dish out more than she herself wants to take.

One eye on the future

When positively motivated, Creative people focus more on the future than they do on either the present or the past. From their perspective, keeping an eye on the future facilitates accomplishing the unusual—a primary motivator for this style. To them, the opposite of the unusual is routine, and they will do almost anything to avoid the boredom which they associate with business as usual. So, they may prefer to think of different things to do each day to facilitate larger changes toward that future orientation.

While working toward this end, they often demonstrate their unique ability to consider both the past and present in preparation for tomorrow. This relates to their propensity to view tasks in relation to the whole, and to figure out how those tasks influence the results. Better yet, they may prefer to alter some of those tasks so the outcome becomes somewhat different than before.

Whatever their techniques, Creative individuals are change agents who seldom leave or continue things as they found them. For example, they tend to pitch in and start tasks without waiting to be told how they're supposed to do them. This approach often generates change.

An interview with a Creative

Interviewer: "Today we're talking to a very successful vice president in charge of marketing. She is a Creative with the D higher than the C. (She shows more Dominant Director traits than Cautious Thinker ones). Sue, would you tell us what you see as the greatest strength in your own Creative pattern?"

Sue: "I think it's my ability to size up and solve a wide variety of problems. I look at problems in different ways, analyze them, and come up with answers that make sense to me, solutions that have often never been tried before. I enjoy doing things differently and I constantly am on the lookout for different ideas. I'm one of those people that wake up in the middle of the night and say, 'Hey, I know a better way to do it.' Although I think this is one of my strengths, at times it can also become a personal weakness that works against me."

Interviewer: "What do you mean?"

Sue: "Well, let me see if I can think of a specific example. Oh, I've got one that just happened. I hired someone to wallpaper one of the rooms in my house. When he finished the job, I was dissatisfied with the results. I didn't think he'd matched the patterns where they met as precisely as it could have been done. Every time I looked at the wallpaper, I knew I could have done a better job. I even stayed up a few nights reading about wallpapering, until I came up with a better way of doing it. I think I figured out my own way of measuring that will make sure a pattern matches—even if your walls are uneven. Of course, then I had to repaper the wall to see if I was right or not."

Interviewer: "And, were you?"

Sue: "Yes! Not only that, but I've talked to a large wallpaper company about printing a booklet explaining my new method."

Interviewer: "Does that critical quality make it hard for you to work with others?"

Sue: "I like being involved with people when it comes to some things, but I prefer working alone or with one or two people on a long-term basis—people who I've carefully selected."

Interviewer: "I'm not sure I completely understand what you just said. Did you say you like being involved with people or not?"

Sue: "Well, it's not that simple. You see, I like it when they present me with problems and then leave. You know, get out of my way so that I can concentrate on solving the problem. Every once in awhile, I'm presented with a problem that several people have worked on and no one else can come up with an answer. It makes me feel great when I can come up with the correct solution."

Interviewer: "Would you say you also like public recognition?"

Sue: "Not really. I like recognition when it's from people I really admire. But, most of all I like to do things that are hard or difficult for most people to do and be able to work on them until they're right. Then, with a new, better way of doing things, everything is likely to work smoother."

Interviewer: "You didn't say you like easy things."

Sue: "That's right. Easy things anybody can do. Personally, I find it boring to be saddled with such easy or routine and ordinary matters. That's it! I like to be an extra-ordinary person!"

INTERACTING SOCIALIZER (I)
Behavioral Patterns

#5: The Promoter

An Interacting SOCIALIZER style
- Seek approval from others and are motivated by their acceptance
- Naturally Direct and Supporting
- Fear loss of social acceptance and resulting loss of self-esteem
- Give both time and emotions free rein
- Like to jump from one activity to another
- Operate emotionally
- Prefer to start many activities, but do not necessarily finish them
- Under pressure, can become sentimental and careless

What Promoters want

This pattern is the core Interacting Socializer behavioral type. Naturally Direct and Supporting, the Promoter has a common drive towards gaining social approval from others. Since a Promoter seeks popularity, she often learns good sportsmanship as a means towards this end. Although winning feels better, she can often muster a hearty sounding, "Great job," to the people who actually get the promotion she wants or, "We were terrific" to acknowledge her own runner-up group.

She makes people feel comfortable with her easy friendliness, chit-chat, and flattering comments and she doesn't hesitate to mention up-and-comers and people who may be too modest to tell others about their accomplishments. With her natural tendency to meet people, she often learns where to go in the company to find particular services. She may act as an unofficial ombudsman. "Oh, you could talk to Helen Watts about the Scandinavian brewery account. She just got back from Copenhagen and made a lot of contacts there."

Promoters are natural communicators!

A natural talker, she relies on speech to let others know where they stand with her. Similarly, she expects others to respond in the same way. If people don't verbalize their thoughts and feelings to her, she can feel confused and left out. Consequently, when another style doesn't open up to her, she may respond by increasing her talking in an effort to draw them out. Less wordy styles, especially those of the Cautious Thinkers, may withdraw even more under what they perceive as a verbal tirade.

Over-complimenting is another way she achieves her goal of attaining recognition. But she needs to monitor her tendency to overpraise, giving sincere compliments only when they're deserved, not just to make the other person feel good. Otherwise, some people may view her as a brown-noser or sycophant who tells others, especially the boss, what they want to hear.

If she loses any sort of perceived popularity contest, she can view this loss as a major setback. She may feel temporarily crushed and unaccepted, but will typically bounce back when others show her they still approve of and like her.

Promoters have big hearts!

Naturally more accepting than many other styles, Promoters can often overlook physical, emotional, political, and philosophical differences that others may not. She often sees handicaps, annoying habits, radical or ultra-conservative views, and other discriminating factors which may alienate other styles as relatively minor considerations. "So what. He's a great person and a fine friend." She adjusts to varied work approaches and to diverse ways of doing things. "I don't care if you come in the office at four in the morning or nine at night, Fred, just as long as you complete this project by Monday morning." This acceptance shows itself in the forms of warm eye contact, touching, and verbal bouquets.

An interview with a Promoter

Interviewer: "Today we're talking with a manager of a mid-sized company on the east coast. Jay, you're a Promoter pattern and according to our research, Promoters are motivated by a personal goal of approval and popularity. Does that fit you?"

Jay: "Absolutely. I don't think there's any question about it. You see, without approval or recognition it's pretty hard for me to stay motivated. Approval and popularity are very important to me. I can't imagine anyone doing anything without wanting approval from people."

Interviewer: "Is it also true that you have a natural tendency to overuse optimism?"

Jay: "Well, I certainly can't deny that. I set some pretty high expectations for myself and the people that work with me. Just recently, as a matter of fact, I set some goals for a new product to be completed last June. I suppose the goal was a bit too ambitious, when I stop to look back on it. We just about killed half the people in the department to reach those goals. At times, I think that I can get carried away with my optimism. In hindsight, we could have had a similar degree of success if I had more realistically determined the typical work output of the people who work for me—and then either added more staff or changed my game plan."

Interviewer: "Are you quite aware of how hard your people are being worked?"

Jay: "You know, I don't like it when people who work for me say, 'I'm so busy that I've got too much to do.' I like to think that I can see that. I don't need to be told that they've got too much to do. I like to keep them challenged and busy. But, I don't want to keep them so swamped that either they or the decisions they make will suffer. But I can tell how busy they are. Yes, I'd say I'm very sensitive to what's happening with my people."

Interviewer: "Could you be more effective with a sense of urgency?"

Jay: "Well, as a general rule, I don't like to have to work from a list of priorities developed every day. But on occasion, I can get sort of side-tracked and misjudge priorities. When this happens, I've been known to spend too much time on one item or promotion or product that I'm particularly concerned about. I can sort of shuffle up the priorities if I really like something a whole lot better than something else. So my boss occasionally has to take a look at what I'm doing, but hopefully not too often. But he does take a look at the priorities I set for myself and if they seem a little bit out of whack—then he usually lets me know about it."

#6: The Persuader

A Dominant SOCIALIZER style
- Collect status symbols
- Admire how well others express themselves
- Fear routine and the same old thing
- Cultivate friendliness and openness
- Look at life positively and enthusiastically
- Persuade others to pursue a common vision with their optimism: *That woman could sell eggs to a chicken!*
- Have inherent trust in others
- Under pressure, can become soft and persuadable

Persuaders want authority and prestige

The Persuader is an Interacting Socializer with many Dominant Director traits; so he is Direct and basically Supporting, but can also be somewhat Controlling. He is motivated by his personal goals of authority and prestige which provide him with a variety of status symbols, such as a high salary, being on a first name basis with the boss, and other tangible items that may encourage people to comment on his prestige.

Give Persuaders freedom

On the other hand, his primary worry or fear in life is a fixed environment, including complex relationships which can limit both his retention of, and continued growth in attaining, social approval from new experiences. *Don't Fence Me In* describes the Persuader's attitude toward the limitations imposed by both people and things.

Confinement or restriction of freedom makes him uncomfortable and may give him *itchy feet*. "When Mel gives us an evaluation next week, he'll say the same things he says every month. What a waste of time! Maybe I can arrange to be elsewhere." He may respond by avoiding the situation or by literally putting it out of his mind. Since Persuaders tend to be free spirits who hear the beat of a different drummer, they need to participate in setting their own limits for tasks, schedules, and family considerations. Otherwise they may rebel against being told what to do.

Eternal optimists

Persuaders tend to admire people who they feel can express themselves well and hold their own. At times, they can become overly helpful with less verbal individuals and actually complete their sentences for them or say something like, "John is trying to tell you that we're just not interested." Often, this trait is intended as assistance; other people seem to recognize this in many Persuaders and often grow to accept their openness.

This style's trust level exceeds that of most of the other styles. Even when things go wrong or when people disappoint them, Persuaders tend to remain optimistic, to the point of rationalizing excuses for the situation or for others. "Carol can't help it if her mother fell down the stairs. We'll just have to work a few hours extra to catch up this time." They can overdo this characteristic and are tapped as easy marks by some individuals.

Full of confidence!

Despite their inherent faith in others, Persuaders typically have a high level of confidence that can withstand others' negative reactions. "Well, Harry, I know you think this project is a lot of wasted energy, but I feel strongly that we'll come out ahead on it." They don't require others' good wishes to maintain their enthusiasm, which at times can become excessive. For example, they naturally pitch people and products and may overdo this behavior. When colleagues are already sold on an idea, Persuaders need to know when to quit selling and be temporarily quiet.

Persuaders tend to act young at heart. They are often able to view each new person and situation as interesting and new, and carry on with energy and excitement. This ability to perceive life as continually fresh keeps them from becoming cynical. Since they can become aggressive at times themselves, they anticipate and accept the same behavior in others, and are usually not put off by it. They seem to naturally accept the bad with the good. "Everybody has their share of setbacks. We've done it before and we can do it again."

An interview with a Persuader

Interviewer: "I'm here interviewing a very successful sales manager. Steve, what do you think is your greatest strength or biggest benefit you gain from your Persuader pattern of behavior?"

Steve: "On the job, I'm considered a supersalesman. I even have a plaque to prove it. At our last sales meeting my sales group chipped in and bought me this huge plaque. Visualize it for a moment. It must be a foot and a half long. Do you know what a plaque like that would sell for? The engraving is at least half an inch high. It says something like: 'To the

Super Salesman of the Year—tops in selling products, tops in selling service—and, most of all, tops in selling!' You see, I'm always telling my salespeople that they sell our products and services, but I sell them on selling. It's true. Nothing in this business happens until a sale is made. I really love my work. I just like being with people. Selling simply follows as a natural result of this process."

Interviewer: "According to research, the goal of the Persuader pattern is prestige and the authority that accompanies a variety of status symbols. Does this fit you?"

Steve: "Yes. I called it 'being motivated by pins, points, and plaques.' In our company we have a wide range of sales incentives. When I was in straight sales, I made sure I got all the awards. I still have them up on my wall."

Interviewer: "Do you ever see yourself overusing some of these strengths?"

Steve: "Well, sometimes I have to be careful not to overwhelm people who are naturally quieter and more low-keyed than I am. I can come on so strong that I kind of knock them over with my high-powered energy and enthusiasm."

#7: The Counselor

A Steady SOCIALIZER style
- Tendency to empathize and understand; this can be overused so that others take advantage
- Can become overly attached to those they care about
- Act dependable, caring, and responsible
- Naturally good listeners
- Tendency to trust others
- Prefer indirect actions
- Like to keep everybody happy
- Under pressure, can become too intimate and, possibly, gullible

Counselors want friendship and acceptance

The Counselor is basically an Interacting Socializer with many Steady Relater characteristics. She is essentially a Supportive type of person who is primarily Direct, although she can become somewhat Indirect under less favorable circumstances. Her personal goal is friendship, especially as it results in acceptance by others. Her related fear is being perceived as harming others. This explains her natural dislike of pressuring or otherwise telling people what to do.

She typically listens when others air their ideas and grievances, and often sincerely empathizes to the point of almost experiencing the other person's feelings herself. Counselors can behave so considerately that they may even feel reluctant to ask a friend to return an item by a specific time. They don't want to inconvenience them.

Lots of friends

Counselors share the Steady Relater's trait of seeking close, personal, one-to-one relationships instead of popularity per se. They tend to have wide ranges of friendships and acquaintances. This style makes them available if a friend needs them; tasks can get done later because "Kevin needs to talk to me now." When Counselors experience pressure and stress, they may want to talk about their innermost fears and problems. Similarly, when others seem troubled, Counselors may feel compelled to help them, sometimes encouraging a climate for the divulging of intimate secrets. At times, this results in a compromise of the Counselor's loyalties. For example, if she knew her partner (a dentist) had contracted AIDS, she would likely become torn between feeling responsible for both her partner and his patients.

Counselors are there when the going is tough

One Counselor we know is, literally, a counselor—a social worker who deals with troubled teenagers. Linda is so attuned to people in need that she sometimes takes strangers home with her. Once she spotted a woman crying behind the wheel of her car in a supermarket parking lot. The woman told her that her husband had taken their children and changed the locks on the house. Linda invited her home, let her sleep in the spare bedroom, and lent her $200 to help tide her over. Because of tendencies like these, Linda's friends often refer to her as the Good Samaritan.

An interview with a Counselor

Interviewer: "Today we are talking with a sales manager who is a Counselor. Nancy, in your opinion, what's the greatest strength of your Counselor pattern?"

Nancy: "Being able to communicate. Being able to understand exactly what people are saying and then relating that to my own optimistic outlook of the opportunities in life for all of us. I'm basically a people-oriented, relationship type of person. I love people and find it easy to be with them—even strangers."

Interviewer: "Have you always been that way?"

Nancy: "Yes, I guess so. My mom and friends say I was the kind of kid who'd give you the shirt off my back if you were my friend, especially if it would keep you as my friend. But that wasn't meant to buy friendship. It's just that I've always enjoyed my friends and I like to share with them."

Interviewer: "You hold your friends in high regard?"

Nancy: "Yes, I do. Material possessions don't matter to me as much as my friends do. My friendships are the greatest thing in the world to me. If my friends began to turn their back on me because I'd messed up, I'd be really hurt. As a matter of fact, I have been hurt by that."

Interviewer: "You said you're a people person. There's research that's been done on the Counselor pattern that says both the *I* (Interacting Socializer) style and the S (Steady Relater) style are relationship-oriented. And the I and the S are your primary and secondary motivators. So according to this research, relationships are very influential to you. What I'd like to know is—have you ever relocated in your life? And if so, what did you do about staying in contact with your friends?"

Nancy: "Well, I have moved. But that didn't mean I had to lose my friends. For instance, last week I was in New Orleans for a sales manager training program. I lived in New Orleans for four years, so I have a lot of friends still there. The training classes lasted from nine in the morning until nine at night. I mean they were long days. We'd get a break at 3:30 and come back at 6:00. The days were full. But, every night after class I'd still go and visit friends until 12:00 or 1:00.

I was really tired by the end of the week but it was worth it to have been with my friends again."

#8: The Appraiser

A Cautious SOCIALIZER style
- Want to win and/or get results with flair
- Judge others by their ability to start activities, i. e., make things happen
- May overuse authority and position
- Fear losing
- Want to do things the best way
- Naturally enthusiastic
- Under pressure, may become restless, aggressive, and impatient

Hard to predict

The Appraiser is an Interacting Socializer with many Cautious Thinker traits. In many ways, this style can take on qualities like those of a chameleon. Although he is basically Direct, he can just as quickly become quite Indirect. Similarly, it's even harder to predict whether he will be Supportive or Controlling from one moment to the next—though he prefers to be both. However, he's not that hard to figure out if we look at the more predictable goals and fears which drive his actions.

Won't step on others

Appraisers have a goal of winning (with people) with flair, while they fear looking bad to others. They perceive winning as a black or white situation—either you win or you lose. Although they want to win, they don't want to win at any cost, or at the expense of hurting others' feelings. Taking shortcuts may smack of cheating to Appraisers, so they'll tend to try to avoid those behaviors to maintain social approval.

They apply ideas (those of others plus their own) to move closer to a winning position. When given a choice, Appraisers often opt for the best way (in their eyes) if that way significantly tips the scale in their favor. They're willing to work harder if extra work means a potentially bigger payoff. Of course, given their preference for working with at least one other person, those other workers may actually shoulder the majority of the work while the Appraiser builds their morale —painting vivid verbal pictures of the bonus they'll receive when they finish. "I'm telling you, this is practically in the bag already!"

They dive right in

Appraisers can become impatient with others who put off getting started. "Okay, we've been asked to make a chart of our daily activities for one month. Let's get going!" Other styles may want to gather more information first. Or special marking pens, or poster board, effectively framed. But Appraisers typically want to plunge right in.

They may even turn the day into a series of mini-competitive games to motivate them to carry on with their customary enthusiasm. "I'll bet I can make 10 phone calls by 9:30," or, "If I close the O'Connell account today, I'm treating myself to dinner at the Plantation House." Or, "I figure I can write 20 pages on the proposal today and still get it in the mail in time to catch the Nordstrom's sale."

Appraisers can even get so involved in getting a job done that they may embellish the truth a bit. "The boss says he wants the new territory developed according to . . ." Maybe the boss didn't exactly draw out the details, but the Appraiser feels sure if he had, it would come very close. He can become entangled in his own verbal web which others may even interpret as a lie. "I heard Mr. Shenkel, too, and he didn't say anything of the kind, Andy. You're either an unreliable source, or worse." In this instance, Andy has overstepped (or overspoken) his bounds. Now the pressure is on because his fear of social rejection has been activated.

Emotions may temporarily rule

When Appraisers' visions don't materialize, they can become impatient, sometimes lashing out at others or generally overreacting to situations. They know this puts others off, but at these times their emotions rule and they can't seem to control themselves. After an outburst, they may later say, "I don't know what's wrong with me today. I overstated my case about Mr. Shenkel, but I didn't do it maliciously. I just got carried away by the sound of my own voice, I guess. Sorry about that and about those other things I said in anger, Tom," he may say, slapping Tom on the shoulder and vowing to monitor future behavior.

An interview with an Appraiser

Interviewer: "We are here today talking to Jack, a successful consultant. What do you see as your greatest strength or asset as a person with this Appraiser pattern?"

Jack: "I can really tune in to people and their problems when I want to. I get excited about helping them get the outcomes they want, but my feelings are not naive. My positive feelings are typically a result of my use of logic and the implementation of more effective behaviors they take to reach the outcomes they want. When I've reached that goal with my clients, then I like to treat myself by socializing with them. After the hard work, I like to just enjoy their company —no problem-solving—just socializing and enjoying each other's company. I find that it not only meets my own personal needs, but also can be invaluable in building our relationship since they then can come to see me as a real person—just like themselves."

Interviewer: "Jack, how about telling us more about the degree of fit between the Appraiser's personal goal of results and your own unique pattern of behavior?"

Jack: "As I noted earlier, one of my strengths is how I tune into people and situations to diagnose problems and opportunities. And I can do that fairly quickly, if needed. So you see, I can size up a client's problem quickly and start working right away with the client on how to handle conditions to get their desired results. However, sometimes my own desire to focus on getting to the possible results through my quick thinking, intuitive leaps can backfire on me."

Interviewer: "What do you mean—It can backfire on you?"

Jack: "I've learned that some people are a lot more comfortable holding onto their problems than I am, and therefore they aren't as ready to address them in a hurry. They just want someone to listen to them talk about the problems. And some other people need more time to understand their problems before they are comfortable doing anything different. These people want to take their problems out and slowly look at them and review them. I can jump in, analyze a problem that they've sometimes had for years, and come up with effective solutions in a very brief period. When I do that, some people get mad at me, or resentful. And still others become even more dependent on me than before—which is counter-productive to the whole idea of helping them learn how to better help themselves. They're not yet ready to have their problem solved. Realizing this and how to deal with this reality in others has been an ongoing growth process in my life."

STEADY RELATER (S)
Behavioral Patterns

#9: The Specialist

A Steady RELATER style
- Want and are motivated by acceptance, respect, and organization
- Naturally reserved and supporting
- Fear loss of security
- Follow established procedures and traditions
- Like to stick to limited activities at a time and follow through until completion
- Think logically and realistically
- Prefer tangible, identifiable tasks
- Under pressure, they comply

Specialists want stability

Specialists comprise the core Steady Relater style, so they are both Indirect and Supporting. Like each of the four Steady Relater behavioral patterns, her common drive is toward personal stability in her life. In this respect, her more specific goal can be described as maintaining the status quo or stability state in her life environments—whether at work, home, or elsewhere. Her basic fear is disorganization, including change, which may destabilize her relationships or her accomplishment of work tasks.

Specialists naturally look before they leap. More accurately, they look before they step. Before acting, they think about it and plan ahead. Sue tends to follow an established pattern when she works and likes to see projects through to completion. She's usually willing, and sometimes even insistent, on "doing things the way I've always done them." She typically likes others to ask her how to complete a task. Assuming the Specialist has done it before, she'll probably show the questioner an organized, step by step procedure that *works for me*. Otherwise, she'll seek out the accepted way to do it.

Specialists accentuate the positive

When a Specialist works on a task, she usually goes about it in a predetermined manner and with a rather easygoing approach. She knows what she has to do and she does it, usually without becoming side-tracked. Her consistent, pleasant work style also sets a consistent, pleasant environment for co-workers. In this way, Sue contributes her organization and relaxed manner to the group effort.

Specialists naturally want to provide services and favors for people. For instance, they're generally willing to assemble parts and materials for a project, saving others time and footwork. They like to see people getting along, regardless of the environment. In their goal to keep relationships stable, Specialists can be especially tolerant and accommodating of others' behaviors. They tend to give people the benefit of the doubt. "Carl must not have gotten a good night's sleep, he's so edgy this morning," or, "This is the first time since you've worked here that you've handed a report in late. I know you have a good reason."

Since Specialists often look at the bright side and seek the best in people, this trait, when exaggerated, can have negative repercussions. A Specialist friend or boss may cover up for someone's unacceptable actions, choosing to overlook the possibility that the person may be taking advantage of her. Any behavior, including viewing others as potential friends and treating them accordingly, can be taken to an extreme.

An interview with a Specialist

Interviewer: "Today we are talking with a customer relations specialist. Coincidentally, she is also a Specialist in the classical patterns of behavioral styles. Joyce, what do you think is your greatest strength concerning your Specialist pattern?"

Joyce: "I suppose it's a willingness to listen to others. I get a lot of people calling with problems and I hang in there and listen to them. I don't jump to conclusions because, if I did, I'd miss what the real problem is."

Interviewer: "So, you consider yourself an accommodating person?"

Joyce: "Yes. I've been told that I'm very patient."

Interviewer: "Have you recognized that maybe you accommodate others too readily?"

Joyce: "Yes. For instance, I'm sometimes too willing to concede when I'm talking to my boss. I recognize that there are times when I might say something like, 'Hold on. We need to look at this a different way.' But that's very hard for me to do—especially if he says something very forcefully. I have a co-worker who tells me that I'd be better off to use sentences like, 'Here's an approach I think we might consider.' But most of the time I end up saying things like, 'I don't know if this would work but I suppose we could, perhaps, try . . . ' The amazing thing is no one says anything about my idea. Then later someone else will bring up what I said as their idea and everyone will like it. I end up thinking, 'Why didn't it seem like a good idea when I said it?' So my co-worker thinks I could be more forceful when I give my ideas so I get credit I deserve for them."

Interviewer: "How often do you disagree with your boss?"

Joyce: "I don't really ever disagree with him. I just want to get better at presenting different ideas to him. It's a stretch for me to speak up to him because his style is one that doesn't seem to want me to. I try to accommodate him."

Interviewer: "You seem to like a more controlled, structured work environment?"

Joyce: "Yes, I do. I enjoy a work environment where I can make my plans and then have them work. You know—without a lot of confusion or changes. Changes or modifications are okay if they are definitely needed, but only where necessary for efficiency and stabilizing things. I like everyone having a clear understanding of what's expected. If there isn't a clear plan, then it's demotivating for me because I can't positively contribute to the situation without knowing what direction we're going in. So having kind of a game plan to go by and letting everybody know what's expected is my perception of what I mean by a controlled environment to operate in."

Interviewer: "What's your opinion of people who don't prepare or aren't organized?"

Joyce: "I've thought about them a lot because I have to deal with people like that all the time. First, I just can't understand how they can possibly function with things in that state of disarray. And second, I feel a need to help them. I usually try to help them put things together and follow through in an organized fashion."

Interviewer: "You talk about concrete results quite a bit. Are other people aware of how motivated you are to get results? Are others even aware of the kind of results you accomplish?"

Joyce: "To your last question, no, I probably don't toot my horn enough. I guess I'm just too modest—to where others might not see the results of my personal efforts. I do get a lot of satisfaction out of doing and finishing things, but I've always thought that our results speak for themselves. I suppose there's two sides to it."

Interviewer: "Two sides to?"

Joyce: "To how people see me and what I feel about things. It's important to work with other people and achieve things together. But, that doesn't mean I need to always have people tell me that they like me or how to do something. I simply want the people I'm involved with to appreciate me because I get done what I set out to do!"

#10: The Agent

An Interacting RELATER style

- Display loyalty and expect the same from others
- Like displays of affection/approval; dislike aggression
- Naturally giving and friendly
- Work toward mutual harmony
- May overdo helpfulness and empathy
- Want acceptance
- Under stress, can stand up for rights if backed up with appropriate information

Agents want to be wanted

The Agent is a Steady Relater with many Interacting Socializer characteristics. Basically, he is a very Supportive person who is also more Indirect than Direct, even though some of both characteristics are evident in his daily behavior. His personal goal is acceptance and approval—being a person who is wanted and needed by others. While all people, from time to time, have a need for acceptance, this is the primary, ongoing focus for Agents. This can further be understood by their related fear of dissension or conflict, both within themselves and with others. They sincerely appreciate thoughtfulness, words of encouragement, and expressions of friendship. They often project a warmth and acceptance that make many people feel at ease.

Agents are often sensitive to others' emotional or physical pain, and may try to comfort or reassure the person by offering signs of understanding and friendship. Although all four Steady Relater styles tend to be good listeners, Agents take the prize in the listening category. They have the patience to actively respond to someone's problems. They tend to function better as sounding boards for venting frustrations rather than as solution givers. Their natural focus is to help the person make do with the current situation and circumstances, not offer suggestions for change.

If a friend asks, an Agent may accompany her to a hair salon while she gets a permanent, listen for hours to a rehearsed speech, go along for a ride 100 miles away, root for her at a softball game, and otherwise give companionship and support to the friend's interests and little victories. This type is also likely to remember birthdays and anniversaries with a card, letter, note, or carefully chosen gift. They also typically make a point of learning and remembering spouse's names and jobs, children's names and ages, and something about the daily life of the people they get involved with.

An interview with an Agent

Interviewer: "We are talking with Dave who is a manager and has an Agent pattern. Dave, what do you think is your greatest asset as an Agent pattern?"

Dave: "I'm a natural listener. I find it easy to gather information, organize it and then relate to the task and people involved in a situation."

Interviewer: "Do you like to plan things?"

Dave: "I find it very difficult to operate without a short-term plan."

Interviewer: "Let's talk about your relationships at work. Are they important to you?"

Dave: "Very important. But, I have a hard time when a conflict exists. I like everybody to get along and I'm a peace-maker. If I see people in conflict, I try to go in and smooth things out so that we can get back to things running nice and easy. You know, predictable and without a hitch—or any unnecessary upsets in the process."

Interviewer: "How do you think the Agent pattern benefits you in your role as a manager?"

Dave: "I think I can empathize with an employee's situations. I have a sensitivity to what makes them function and how they like to be treated. I put that to good use in order to help all of us achieve goals."

Interviewer: "So, I guess you use your people skills for a variety of aspects of your job."

Dave: "Yes. For example, I empathize with members of my team and then I can smooth things over so that everything runs on an even keel."

Interviewer: "According to our research, the Agent influences others through friendship and offering understanding.

Does this fit for you?"

Dave: "Yes, I do offer a lot of friendship and understanding. The way I do it is by listening well—and when I understand what their needs or wants are, then I try to be responsive to them. I also try to help people through understanding to better know what their goals are, or what they want to accomplish."

Interviewer: "Do you think you're patient enough to do that with people?"

Dave: "Probably too patient."

Interviewer: "It appears to me that this behavior has paid off for you."

Dave: "Well, yes and no. I think this behavior works well for me in terms of people who are peers or report to me. But I think that some of the people running the business see my behavior as a sign of weakness at times. Or sometimes they think my listening and concern for others is a lack of real tough management approach."

Interviewer: "What kinds of things could you learn to do to be more firm and assertive?"

Dave: "To say no when it's appropriate. But, I really am focused towards the business aspect of relationships. I still offer support and understanding, but I do cut it off before it becomes a social experience. I have a friend who turns managing into counseling. I'm not like that. And, I also think that I'm starting to promote myself more. That's new for me. I've never done it in the past. I've done some excellent work every place I've been, but I seldom took credit for it. I was always very willing just to let the credit go by unnoticed, thinking that it would be noticed. I learned it definitely is not noticed—unless you beat your own drum a little bit. I was even shocked to discover other people were taking and receiving the credit for things I had done. But that's in the past and I'm much wiser now."

#11: The Achiever

A Dominant RELATER style

- Busy and industrious work style
- Responsible for their tasks; pull their own weight
- Break jobs down into smaller sections and complete them one by one
- May do too much; have difficulty delegating
- May show impatience and frustration with self or others
- Want concrete results
- Fear looking bad because somebody else did something wrong
- Under stress, become frustrated and impatient

Want personal accomplishments

The Achiever is a Steady Relater type with many Dominant Director traits. She is instinctively a more Indirect individual who can give the appearance of being somewhat Direct, especially with key tasks or roles in her life. She tends to be Supportive at the start of a situation or relationship, but becomes much more Controlling as time goes on if the results have not yet been achieved. When this happens, the Achiever may show frustration and impatience with others and end up doing the job herself. With her pattern of high Steady Relater and slightly lower Dominant Director characteristics, the Achiever's goal becomes personal accomplishments. These are often at the expense of the group if her needs have not been satisfied. Her primary fear is other individuals with competing or *inferior* standards who are likely to become barriers in the process of achieving her desired results.

Achievers pre-think their steps

Achievers often naturally take many variables into consideration before accepting and beginning a task. While other styles may not have counted on all the time and physical exertion to get that job done; achievers have usually already thought out the steps. Then they proceed to complete those steps, one at a time. They tend to view work as a series of parts. When they understand how to execute those parts, they're ready to start. While they're involved in the task, they often become immersed. They may stay up all night to complete a paper or shut others out of communication to finish a project.

Independent and self-reliant

Achievers also demonstrate a large measure of self-reliance. Since their natural tendency is to work independently, they tend to want to do things themselves, their way. Some non-Achiever co-workers and acquaintances may not agree with a determined Achiever's one-sided decision for the group.

An interview with an Achiever

Interviewer: "Jim, we heard quite a bit about how industrious the Achiever pattern is. Do you expect that same level of effort from others? In other words, how do you evaluate others, especially the people you work with?"

Jim: "Well, I'm very practical. I look at the concrete results of the people I work with. You see, it's fairly easy to focus on the goal and then simply measure the progress by the results achieved. When I say results, I mean the specific and measurable things like the number of products, the quality of services, or the number of units sold. I don't have much time for people who just want to talk. I really have a strong personal need to see results."

Interviewer: "When you look for the concrete results exclusively, don't you miss out on those areas where results are not as easily demonstrated? For example, when hiring, or working with people, if you select only those people who agree with your perspectives, then you will overlook talents that are different from your own. And the fact is that each of us needs people who complement us because of their different interests and skills. For example, the doer type of Achiever, who prefers to take action rather than talk, might need a person who prefers to talk. A person who has developed the skill of speaking about various subjects."

Jim: "Hmmm, I'm beginning to understand what you're telling me. When I think about it, it makes sense to me that people who have different goals and skills can be useful in handling various tasks. But, to be quite honest with you, I find myself naturally evaluating others by the concrete results they achieve. Maybe that's the reason why I prefer to rely on myself instead of trying to convince others of something. I know the results that I can and can't successfully deliver."

#12: The Investigator

A Steady, Cautious, and Somewhat Dominant Relater style
- Prefer a logical approach
- Hang on until he gets the answer; tenacious
- Like one-on-one, small group settings
- Can become blunt and seem unfeeling
- Carry grudges, but often don't verbalize them
- Dislike and fear large groups and intangible ideas
- Keep emotions on an even keel; don't outwardly express euphoria or rage
- Under stress, may turn inward and think of wrongs done to them

Investigators want official power roles

The Investigator is a Steady Relater with many Cautious Thinker and Dominant Director characteristics. A person with this pattern is basically an Indirect individual who may appear to be Supporting initially, but as time goes on, proves more Controlling—though usually in a very subtle way. The unique goal for the Investigator's less commonly found behavioral pattern is the power provided by formal role positions. His related basic fear is involvement in less controlled circumstances—such as dealing with many different types of individuals or with abstract situations which can ultimately lead to difficulties—and may lead to loss of position.

Investigators view life dispassionately

The Investigator is typically a self-disciplined person who prefers a logical, unemotional approach. He can usually be counted on to maintain his composure in emergencies and to factor out feelings to get at the facts. "You never called Jill a loser before. I think the real reason you're angry is because she's going out with your old boyfriend." This style's dispassionate insights can open our eyes in ways we hadn't counted on.

Investigators often show an organized, pre-structured quality that other styles may lack. When they agree to meet with you at 8 a.m. two months from today, they'll be there. If you don't show up, they may telephone to remind you. "Gosh, Ira, we talked about meeting for breakfast so long ago I forgot." Ever persistent, Ira the Investigator is likely to offer to wait while his disgruntled companion scrambles to meet or otherwise accommodate Ira. Even mutterings or excuses are unlikely to dissuade Ira from his mission. He's fully capable of listening unemotionally to a barrage of complaints and even some verbal abuse without acting ruffled. Since he naturally factors out the feeling elements in life's scenarios, little seems to outwardly disquiet him.

Investigators keep on

Without wasting their time on emotions, Investigators prefer spending it on some meaningful, premeditated activity. They usually are determined to reach their goals independently. "I think I can do a better job by myself." They like to figure out where they're going and how to get there. Investigators tolerate negative conditions from others because of their almost uncanny persistence and their belief that they're right. "I'll stay up all night, if I have to, to finish this. My idea is a good one and I'm going to prove it." As frustrating as this trait can sometimes be for the other styles, Investigators are often correct. In turn, this can arouse negative feelings in others, like, "Isn't that guy ever wrong?"

Reason, logic, and self-discipline

Since this style's propensity for rational thinking often predominates over feelings, the Investigator leans toward a natural bias for logical processes in others. At the extreme, he may overlook or down play people skills in favor of specialized technical skills; he tends to gravitate toward reason and orderliness and move away from situations which involve much human interaction.

Individuals with this style behave in such a disciplined way that we know one who was placed in charge of explosives in his army battalion. He could handle the nitroglycerine and TNT with hardly a tremor—a much needed prerequisite for dealing with munitions.

People may describe Investigators as "cool under fire" or as "Rocks of Gibraltar." Their projection of calmness can reassure others that everything will turn out all right.

An interview with an Investigator

Interviewer: "We are here talking with an individual with the Investigator pattern. Sherry is a manager of the Claims Department for a large insurance company. How many people do you supervise?"

Sherry: "In management—four."

Interviewer: "According to our research, people with the Investigator pattern are typically very determined. Would you say that describes you?"

Sherry: "I think it describes me quite well. Particularly when I have something that I want to get accomplished. I don't stop until I've gotten permission to get it into full motion."

Interviewer: "Can you give me another example of how your determination has made a difference?"

Sherry: "Well, when I was a kid, I earned every one of the badges available through the Girl Scouts. I've never heard of anyone else who did that!"

Interviewer: "Thank you. That's a very clear example. Do you prefer working with things or people?"

Sherry: "Definitely things! I even like to refinish antiques for a hobby."

Interviewer: "Our research reveals that Investigators can be blunt with people at times. Would you say this describes you?"

Sherry: "Yes. I think that describes me pretty well. At least, that's the way my first husband would have described me. After several years, I told him he'd have to change if he was to stay married to me. I guess you could call that blunt."

Interviewer: "Okay, let's talk about the fears of an Investigator. According to the research, Investigators don't like to be involved with a lot of people or abstract ideas. Does that fit for you?"

Sherry: "The fear of having to deal with lots of people is very real for me. In a previous job I had to conduct large sessions for as many as 300 people. When I first started doing it, it was horrible. Fear is a good word to describe how I felt. Later, it got easier for me to do it, but I never liked it. I prefer working with a small group of people or even one on one. I can work with large groups, but I don't prefer it. Why, I don't even like going to large parties."

Interviewer: "How about the abstract ideas?"

Sherry: "I'm not really very comfortable trying to sell what you call an abstract idea. For example, we have a new quality control program. And management is supposed to sell our employees on the idea of quality service. Everybody is supposed to be excited about this idea. But I really don't get it. Quality control is an issue for the production line. Everyone has a job that they're being paid for. That job is supposed to include quality. That's not an exciting idea that anybody has to sell. Quality is a concrete fact, not an issue for open discussion and debate!"

CAUTIOUS THINKER (C)
Behavioral Patterns

#13: The Objective Thinker

A Cautious THINKER style
- Concerned with appearances
- Naturally process-oriented
- Seek quality control
- Fear irrationality and loss of emotional control
- Need to be right
- Tend to act and think logically
- Naturally geared toward reasoning and intellectualism
- Like to acquire data
- Under stress, they tend to worry

Objective Thinkers want to control accuracy

Objective Thinking individuals comprise the core Cautious Thinker behavioral type. As such, they are both Indirect and Controlling. Like each of the three classical Cautious Thinker behavioral patterns, they seek the control that assures them of getting personal accuracy.

As an individual with this single strong Cautious Thinker need driving his behavior, the Objective Thinker's unique goal is his concern for correctness. His core fear is irrational actions, including the ridicule and criticism that would be attributed to him personally for such mistakes. So they often ask questions and test ideas to ensure that they're on course. Consequently, this type is right much of the time.

Objective Thinkers are considered by many to be the most complex and difficult to understand among the four basic behavioral types. They are essentially driven by this controlling force in the form of self-direction. This is through compliance with their own personal or inner standards (which, of course, may not be the same as those of another person, their group, or even the organization in which they work). In other words, they strive to please themselves and satisfy their own standards of quality.

How they differ from Dominant Directors

They tend to be somewhat similar to the Dominant Director (D) patterns. Their actions are typically more Controlling than Supportive. The essential difference between the two is the inner-directed, more private desire for personal autonomy and privacy. This contrasts with the more outer-directed style of the Dominant Director patterns which seek to meet their personal needs by directing others toward the results they desire. Objective Thinkers reject and avoid conflict and aggression, often seeking a quiet, private place to regain a sense of calmness.

An interview with an Objective Thinker

Interviewer: "Today we are talking with the chief financial officer of an electronics company. Melanie, what do you view as your greatest strength with respect to your Objective

Thinker pattern?"

Melanie: "I take a job and work at it until I have it all done—completely and properly."

Interviewer: "What do you mean by completely done?"

Melanie: "Everything is done in a precise manner. Everything checks out. There are no errors. Everything checks out to my satisfaction."

Interviewer: " It sounds like you put in a lot of time. Has anyone ever told you that you work too hard or spend too much time on your work."

Melanie: "Yes, my boss and my children have mentioned it."

Interviewer: "You mean they say things like, 'Hey, you're working too hard. Let it go and stop working overtime on things'?"

Melanie: "That's right!"

Interviewer: "Why do you think you do that? Couldn't you just say, 'I'll let it go until later', or, 'Tomorrow's another day?'"

Melanie: "Well, I take a lot of pride in getting the job done. It gives me a lot of satisfaction to do it thoroughly. And, besides, I don't like to be interrupted when I'm in the middle of something that's important to me. It interferes with my thought pattern and sometimes I have to start all over again. And then I really lose even more time."

Interviewer: "Are there any particular kinds of projects that are more meaningful or enjoyable for you?"

Melanie: "Right now one that comes to mind is a new system that will correct or improve, actually, a lot of things that I've been concerned about. I make sure the system works. It's up to me to find any bugs that may cause problems before we actually implement it."

Interviewer: "What part of your work do you like best?"

Melanie: "I like reconciling all the general ledger accounts."

Interviewer: "How do you feel about having to check up on something for a long period of time, and while you're doing that you're not able to interact with people?"

Melanie: "Oh, that doesn't bother me at all. I can shut off the world completely and just work at what I'm doing sort of like an artist does when she goes into seclusion to work on a project."

Interviewer: "Do you ever have a tendency to overuse some of these aspects of your personality? For example, do you ever check up on things too much?"

Melanie: "Well, some people have suggested that I might check up too much."

Interviewer: "I heard a little laugh there. Is there something that can be amusing about this tendency?"

Melanie: "My boss would rather be off several dollars than spend extra time finding the minor mistakes. He doesn't see how I can sit there and try to find the small errors. He thinks it's a waste of time if it doesn't involve 'big dollar amounts'. But I've found that where there's one mistake, there are sometimes more. I've worked here 13 years and in the beginning he didn't understand why I kept looking for mistakes to make sure there weren't even more hidden errors or omissions."

Interviewer: "Your preciseness, your accuracy, your wanting to be correct—have you been this way all of your life?"

Melanie: "Yes, at least as far back as I can remember."

Interviewer: "What do you think you could do as an Objective Thinker to become even more effective?"

Melanie: "I think, perhaps, be better at interacting with people."

Interviewer: "How do you think that might help?"

Melanie: "Well, sometimes I just work, work, work and I feel maybe if I interacted more openly and often with people I could delegate more work—and become more successful in coaching and supporting their own development."

#14: The Perfectionist Pattern

A Steady THINKER style
- Want to be in charge of quality control
- Go by the book; follow established rules, if they were formed by people they respect
- Want to get things done right
- Pre-think procedures and attend to details accordingly

- Masters of diplomacy and tact
- Dislike opposition and hostility
- Want stability and security—no surprises
- Under pressure, they become tactful

They want predictable, steady accomplishments

Perfectionists are Cautious Thinkers with many Steady Relater characteristics. As such, they are Indirect and basically Controlling, though also somewhat Supportive, people. Their goals are predictable accomplishments in a steady manner. Similarly, their essential fear is antagonism. This fear can take place socially, as interpersonal or group conflict. It can also be work-related, in the form of opposing their priorities or processes. Fear can also include virtually any unknown or uncontrollable changes in the environment which are likely to lead to turmoil, thus reducing the likelihood of achieving their identified objectives.

Perfectionists prefer to follow proven practices. Once they know the correct procedure, they may painstakingly perfect it so they do as good or better a job than their instructor. Their precision may carry over to impact others' actions. For instance, when Perfectionist Sybil sees a colleague reading another's report, she may want to say: "Mr. Nevelle said that we're supposed to show him our reports before anyone else sees them." Instead, she may give the offender a sharp look, or pretend not to see what's happening.

When quality is at stake, Perfectionists may take risks to ensure that the finished product will be better. "James' idea about designing computer graphics to illustrate our proposal just may swing the Melrose account in our favor. I vote that we do it."

They are often conscientious and comfortable with tasks, but may not be as comfortable with people. Perfectionists may behave quietly and privately around others, waiting for them to initiate relationships.

An interview with a Perfectionist

Interviewer: "We are talking with a vice president who is responsible for market research. In your opinion, what are some of the assets of this style of behavior?"

Pat: "According to the results of the *Performax Personal Profile System*, I am a Perfectionist pattern. One of the greatest assets of having this style is that I gather data so that I can make good, reasonable, sound business decisions based on the latest, most complete information that's available for this purpose. Making sure everything is always done the right way is my job."

. Interviewer: "Okay, what particular benefits do you derive from your Perfectionist pattern?"

Pat: "People have told me I do excellent work. People rely on me for information."

Interviewer: "Do you derive any other benefits?"

Pat: "Yes, I always feel good that I have done the best I can. I always feel like I save time and energy by doing it the right way the first time, so I don't have to come back and do it over again."

Interviewer: "According to our research, the personal motivation of the Perfectionist is focused on stable, predictable accomplishments with secure, reassuring results. Does that fit you?"

Pat: "Yes. I like to know exactly what I'm doing. I like to know exactly where I'm going. If I'm given a project, I want to know what the project is going to be used for and how and when it is going to help us get where we are going."

Interviewer: "By the way, are you also a Perfectionist at home?"

Pat: "Yes, some of my friends make fun of me when they come over because my garage is cleaner and more organized than most homes. All of my tools are nicely hung on pegboard. Like I said before, everything has a place and every place has a thing that belongs there. It frustrates me to have to look for something unnecessarily. I can't stand it when that happens. When I go to the third drawer on the right side of the cabinet, I expect to find my Phillips screwdriver there. I know that's where it will be. That's where I keep it. When I go there and my wife has moved it, you know, I go *Grrrr*. So, my wife and I have worked out a very pleasant arrangement. She tries not to bother my things; and when she does disrupt my things, she puts them back. If she doesn't, then I try to remind myself that she's not a Perfectionist pattern like I am—and she doesn't necessarily care where those things go. So then I politely go and ask her, 'Honey, where is my Phillips head screwdriver? Did you use it? It's not in its place.' And she says, 'Oh, yeah. I left it upstairs when I used it on the lamp up there. Do you want me to get it?'"

Interviewer: "Are other things in your house also organized?"

Pat: "Yes. I have file cabinets where everything is neatly labeled. And all my clothes are hung in a certain order. Long-sleeved shirts are on the far right. Short-sleeved shirts are toward the left. Pants are in the center and belts are to the left of the pants. It's convenient to look in and know exactly where everything is."

Interviewer: "Do you ever overuse this kind of behavior—at work, for instance?"

Pat: "Yes, I'll spend too much time on a project. I spend too much time fretting and worrying that it's not going to be right. I can't take the project and show it to anybody until I'm sure it is right. I've got to get all the information. I know that I spend too much time at some things that I work on, but they're not perfected yet, so I need to keep working on them until they are. And then I will inspect things at least one more time to make sure everything is in perfect order."

#15: The Practitioner pattern

An Interacting, somewhat Steady THINKER style
- Think they can do better than others
- Have high aspirations and ambitions
- Expect high level of expertise from others, as well as themselves
- Dislike criticism, especially regarding their expert ideas
- Cultivate self-control
- Good problem solvers

- Want others to value them for being exciting, unique, and proficient
- Under pressure, they may become restrained and sensitive to criticism

Practitioners want personal growth

Practitioners fit into the Cautious Thinker style with some Steady Relater and Interacting Socializer traits. They are fascinating studies as social chameleons. They tend to shift from one of three characteristic behavioral tendencies to another in response to other people. When allowed to act on their more natural preferences, however, they are more Indirect than Direct and somewhat more Controlling than Supporting. The Practitioner's unique goal is her relatively high ambition for personal growth, compared to the other classical behavioral patterns. Her primary fear is lack of recognition, being just one more predictable member in the mainstream.

Since Practitioners are motivated to advance themselves, they want others to recognize them for their accomplishments and knowledge. They often work at becoming experts at their chosen specialties. Practitioners usually develop special problem-solving skills and cultivate specific areas of expertise toward the end of achieving. They often know the rules and how to get a task done and can explain these procedures to others. Consequently, their natural problem-solving strengths and typical stored information can benefit others, too.

These folks dream ambitious dreams, but those aspirations are usually attainable through hard work and self-control. Similarly, this pattern often judges others by how self-disciplined they are, sometimes showing little patience with those who lack that trait.

An interview with a Practitioner

Interviewer: "This morning we are talking with a very successful advertising professional. Please, Gary, can you tell us about your own personal ambitions."

Gary: "My personal goal has always been to keep moving ahead. And that means I have to always keep learning, whether it's in the same job or by changing jobs. I like to increase my knowledge and skills in whatever I decide to do. And I like to explore opportunities and interests that are related to my job. But I also like to get as much information about as many different things as I can."

Interviewer: "Do you think you give the impression of knowing something about lots of things?"

Gary: "I don't consciously try to do that, but based on the comments people have made to me, I guess I naturally do give the impression of knowing about many different types of things. For example, here's a physics magazine with an article on quantum physics. I'm reading it just for the fun of it."

Interviewer: "So you do have a natural desire to know about a lot of subjects. Do you manage to work your most recent insights into your conversations—so that people might gain a more favorable impression of you and what you know?"

Gary: "Well I haven't found that many opportunities to talk about quantum physics yet. But, on the other hand, who knows when it might come in handy. After all, you only need one good chance to pay off in diamonds."

Interviewer: "Well I did notice that you managed to work it into this interview. Maybe a 'trial balloon' to see if I had some interest in quantum physics?"

Gary: "Yes, I suppose I do that. I will find ways. If I just learned some new information, I will try to weave it into a conversation so that I can make good use of what I know. But I also keep a lot of stuff to myself, not simply because I want to, but because it's simply not the right type of opportunity to risk it. But I don't think I go overboard or am obnoxiously overbearing in finding ways to show people what I've learned. Instead, I try to discreetly slip it in to enrich or sweeten our interaction."

Interviewer: "Can you give me an example where you sort of steered the conversation in a direction that you thought was more meaningful?"

Gary: "Sure, last Saturday night. I definitely turned the conversation or, rather, started a different conversation where I could relate some information I had just read. I thought these people would find it truly fascinating. But after I did start it, I was really worried whether they'd even give a hoot about what I told them. Luckily, one person had read something about it, too. And they all were interested. The conversation went on for at least another 20 minutes. It was a real hit, but it was also somewhat risky."

Interviewer: "According to our research, the Practitioner may overuse a superior attitude, at times. Does that sound like you?"

Gary: "I don't think so. I usually know what I'm doing is right, but I don't flaunt it or rub it in someone's face."

Interviewer: "Let me, perhaps, ask this in a different way. Do you have a relatively high opinion of your own opinions?"

Gary: "Yes. You see, I do a lot of checking and thinking before I actually implement things like procedures. And if people discount what I think is best, I can get very critical. Then I'll turn it around on them and have to be shown or proven wrong. I don't have a very open mind about going about things in ways that don't fit what makes perfectly logical sense to me. I suppose that's what you were suggesting by the term superior attitude. Well it is something that I'm trying to perfect. After all, I wouldn't want to have an inferior attitude towards myself or things I do."

Note: Carlson Learning Company has graciously allowed us to use the previous interviews from their Classical Library audio program. Each dialogue captures the essence of the 15 mixed styles. The authors wish to acknowledge and thank Carlson Learning Company and its Performax Network Division for their support in supplying information on the needs model of behavior—DISC. For more information on mixed styles and other learning instruments, contact Carlson Learning Company, Carlson Parkway, P.O. Box 59159, Minneapolis, Minnesota, 55459-8247; or call (612) 449-2856.

Chapter 12
Keys to Unlocking Personal Effectiveness

Self-Managing Your Fears and Anxieties

Now that you know more about your own core and mixed behavioral styles, what will you do with all this information? How do you maximize your interactions? You can significantly increase your personal effectiveness by adjusting your core behavior so you emphasize your more positive, productive traits and downplay the less positive ones. Those less productive characteristics often emerge when something triggers your fears and anxieties. By self-managing your behavioral type, you can simultaneously cultivate your natural tendencies while monitoring your less developed strengths.

The Dominant Director Patterns

#1 — Developer

A Dominant DIRECTOR pattern
- Want to win
- Try to control people and situations
- Fear boredom and routine

#2–Results-Oriented

An Interacting DIRECTOR pattern
- *I can do it* attitude, whether experienced, or not
- Don't willingly give up; persistent
- Achievement-oriented; show annoyance when goals are thwarted

#3–Inspirational

Dominant and Interactive DIRECTOR pattern
- Accept competition and even aggression from self and others
- Appear to reject affection (on the surface)
- Fear seeming too soft and dependent

#4–Creative

A Cautious DIRECTOR pattern
- Want to change the way things are done; strive to accomplish the unusual
- Answer to own personal ideas and standards
- Under pressure, can become bored or blue

The Interacting Socializer Patterns

#5–The Promoter

An Interacting SOCIALIZER pattern
- Want and are motivated by popular approval from others
- Give both time and emotions free rein
- Fear loss of social acceptance and resulting loss of self-esteem

#6—The Persuader

A Dominant SOCIALIZER pattern
- Collect status symbols
- Convince others to pursue a common vision with enthusiastic optimism
- Under pressure, can become soft and rather easy to manipulate

#7—The Counselor

A Steady SOCIALIZER pattern
- Tendency to empathize and understand; this can be overused so that others take advantage
- Can become overly attached and trusting
- Under pressure, can become too intimate, and possibly gullible

#8—The Appraiser

A Cautious SOCIALIZER pattern
- Want to win and get results with flair
- Judge others by their ability to start activities, i. e., make things happen
- Under pressure, may become restless, aggressive, and impatient

The Steady Relater Patterns

#9—The Specialist

A Steady RELATER pattern
- Want acceptance, respect, and organization
- Follow established procedures and traditions
- Under pressure, tend to comply

#10—The Agent

An Interacting RELATER pattern
- Display loyalty and expect the same from others
- Want acceptance/approval; dislike aggression
- May overdo helpfulness and empathy

#11—The Achiever

A Dominant RELATER pattern
- Busy and industrious work style
- May do too much; have difficulty delegating
- Fear looking bad because somebody else did something wrong

#12—The Investigator

A Steady, Cautious, and somewhat Dominant RELATER pattern
- Prefer a logical approach
- Keep emotions on an even keel; don't outwardly express euphoria or rage
- Carry grudges, but often don't verbalize them

The Cautious Thinker Patterns

#13—The Objective Thinker

A Cautious THINKER pattern
- Naturally geared toward reasoning and logical thinking process
- Seek quality control
- Fear irrationality and loss of emotional restraint

#14—The Perfectionist

A Steady THINKER pattern
- Follow established rules, if they were formed by someone the Perfectionist respects
- Naturally use diplomacy and tact
- Dislike opposition and hostility

#15—The Practitioner

An Interacting and somewhat Steady THINKER pattern
- Have high aspirations and ambitions
- Cultivate self-control
- Dislike criticism, especially regarding the Practitioner's *expert* ideas

How You Can Help All 15 Classical Patterns Behave More Productively

When a person is being less effective or less productive than is possible, look first at the following list of the three behaviors recommended for increased effectiveness for that classical pattern. If one of these behaviors fits a requirement for greater success, suggest that behavior as a single action to help that person (or you) achieve his or her basic motivating goal. For example, help the Dominant Director (D) get results, the Interacting Socializer (I) get positive responses from others, the Steady Relater (S) get continuing stability, and the Cautious Thinker (C) get the reassurance that he or she has made a correct choice.

How Each Classical Pattern
Can Increase Their Effectiveness:

#1—Developers

- show more patience
- collaborate with others
- demonstrate empathy

#2—Results-Oriented

- demonstrate genuine concern for others
- verbalize reasons for their views non-judgmentally
- show more humility and empathy

#3—Inspirationals

- show genuine sensitivity to others
- facilitate and promote the success of others
- use a quieter, more systematic and thoughtful approach

#4—Creatives

- exhibit genuine warmth and caring for others
- remain tactful when under pressure or stress
- cooperate

#5—Promoters

- increase emotional self-control
- clarify expectations, reactions, events and outcomes more objectively
- follow through on tasks

#6—Persuaders

- objectively analyze situations, including facts and feelings
- more democratically respond to others' ideas
- provide personal attention and follow-up

#7—Counselors

- cultivate a sense of priority, thus avoiding procrastination
- monitor the tendency for over-tolerance
- attend and commit to realistic deadlines and constraints

#8—Appraisers

- show empathy, even when feeling disapproval or frustration
- develop added patience with themselves and others
- pace themselves: prioritize and recognize degrees of achievement

#9—Specialists

- share ideas, experiences, and insights with others
- develop long-term self-confidence by focusing on their strengths
- focus on critical, essential task priorities and sometimes on shortcuts

#10—Agents

- act more self-assertive and less indirect in communications
- be firmer when it is appropriate to say no or take a stand
- learn to respond to conflict as an opportunity for greater stability

#11—Achievers

- look toward longer term results in mutual collaboration with people
- respond to feelings and needs of others on each person's terms
- clarify priorities for long range personal development

#12—Investigators

- develop tolerance and sensitivity to the needs and difficulties of others
- learn to communicate in a warmer, more open, shared manner
- develop more open, exploratory approaches to their views

#13—Objective Thinkers

- learn to share insights and views with others
- accept imperfections and mistakes (their own and others')
- open themselves up more to facilitate collaborative relationships

#14—Perfectionists

- develop more open, accepting attitude toward different approaches
- learn interdependence through collaboration with others
- develop genuine, unconditional acceptance of themselves as human

#15—Practitioners

- learn to genuinely collaborate with others for the common benefit
- share discoveries and procedures with others
- learn to more appropriately delegate key tasks

More on How Each Pattern
Can Increase Effectiveness

Developers (Pattern #1) can further increase their effectiveness by developing three additional relationship-focused strengths: patience, collaboration with others, and empathy.

Three task-oriented characteristics which can help them are: attention to quality performance considerations, follow-through on details, and listening openly before coming to premature conclusions. People are likely to describe them as direct, daring, dominating, and demanding. Their motto is, "Watch out! Here I come!"

Results-Oriented (Pattern #2) people can further increase their effectiveness in relationship situations by demonstrating genuine concern for others, acting more patient, and showing more humility and empathy. In task situations, they can seek out others' views and ideas in goal-setting and problem-solving situations. They can verbalize the reasons for their own points of view in a non-judgmental manner. People often describe individuals with this behavioral pattern as forceful, direct, competitive, poised, convincing, and confident. Their motto is, "What's the bottom line?"

Inspirationals (Pattern #3) can build upon their current level of effectiveness in the context of relationships by showing genuine sensitivity to others.

In task situations, they can benefit by willingly facilitating and promoting the success of others in their own separate goal-focused or problem-solving efforts—even when there is no direct payoff for the Inspirational helper. A quieter, more systematic and thoughtful approach can increase their success with both tasks and people by keeping them on track and less susceptible to outside distractions and diversions. They are likely to be described as direct, daring, forceful, enthusiastic, sociable, charming, charismatic, and spontaneous. Often their motto is, "I'm going to help you whether you want it or not!"

Creatives (Pattern #4) can be more effective in their relationships by exhibiting genuine warmth and caring for others and by remaining tactful in their communications when under pressure or stress.

In task situations, they can benefit by demonstrating their desire to cooperate as part of the work team/unit and by exhibiting respect for the sanctions or norms which are important in that environment. They are often described by others as direct, innovative, pioneering, forceful, analytical, and calculating. They tend to be quite cautious about sharing their inner thoughts and feelings with others. In fact, when asked their opinion they are likely to respond by saying, "So, what do you think?" and then sidestep direct answers which define their point of view.

Promoters (Pattern #5) can enhance their effectiveness with people by (1) increasing their self-control and (2) clarifying expectations, reactions, events, and outcomes more objectively.

In task situations, they can benefit by developing further (1) control of time, (2) follow-through on tasks, and (3) a greater sense of priority management relative to what is more urgently needed or expected and what is not (rather than reacting to the person and the moment). People often describe Promoters as enthusiastic, sociable, popular, entertaining, spontaneous, and casual. Their theme might be summarized by their often-heard words, "Wow, do I ever have a deal for you!"

Persuaders (Pattern #6) can further increase their effectiveness in relationships by (1) objective analysis of situations, including the data from both facts and feelings and (2) responsiveness to others' perspectives as well as listening to the opinion of VIP's they tend to identify with.

When focused on task considerations, they can gain by (1) providing personal attention to task-directed service, including follow-up on key details and (2) ongoing renewal of their own energies by identifying more challenging assignments which provide longer term growth and more meaningful fulfillment. They are typically described by others as enthusiastic, sociable, popular, spontaneous, direct, dynamic, inquiring, and risk-taking. Persuaders like to think of themselves as super salesman of ideas and possibilities. The essence of that outlook is, "This is tailor-made just for you."

Counselors (Pattern #7) can become more effective with people by (1) being more straightforward with others in sharing their own expectations, ideas, or reactions. Their preference for the indirect, more subtle approach encourages others to consciously or unconsciously take advantage. "I'm flattered you want to borrow my purse when you go to Europe, Sally."

In addition, they can improve by (2) monitoring their tendency to be overly tolerant to the point of potentially being placed in rescuer or victim roles which are not in the interest of their own personal well-being. At the extreme, less than honest people can view the Counselor's soft-heartedness as easy prey. When enough is enough, Counselors can learn to put their rather reluctant feet down and set some realistic limits. "Sally, I'm going to need the purse you borrowed last summer by next week."

In task situations, they can benefit by developing their potential for growth in (1) taking the initiative to get tasks focused or accomplished. Their natural optimism may delude them into thinking they can finish a task much easier and quicker than they initially thought. Then they need to persevere until the job gets done. They can also bolster their natural characteristics by (2) attending to realistic commitments and constraints, including deadlines. "I can research this project at the library for two hours, five days a week, for ten days. Then, I can comfortably write it up by May 1." Counselors are typically described as warm, enthusiastic, personab'e, patient, friendly, and deliberate. They can perhaps best be understood through the saying, "All people need is a little bit of love (TLC)."

Appraisers (Pattern #8) can increase their personal effectiveness in relationships by (1) showing empathy to people when they experience feelings of disapproval or frustration, while also (2) developing added patience with both themselves and others.

They can benefit in task situations by (1) pacing themselves by clearly focusing on their priorities, monitoring the purposes of each priority, and recognizing realistic degrees of achievement and (2) involving themselves in follow-through can help assure them they can reduce the gap between idealized expectations and operating reality. Their motto is, "This is the answer!"

Specialists (Pattern #9) can increase their effectiveness with people by (1) sharing their ideas, experiences, and insights with others and (2) developing their long-term self-confidence, especially by attending to the genuine positive feedback they receive from others about their demonstrated strengths.

In task situations, they have the potential for growth through (1) more clearly focusing on the critical, most essential task priorities and the most important aspects of responding to each and (2) identifying and developing shorter shortcuts and techniques for achieving the same basic results required for a specific task. Specialists tend to be predictable, consistent, systematic, and moderate or low-keyed. Their approach to life might be summarized by their matter-of-fact statements like, "Here's the final product," or, in the social environment, "Here's what you asked me to do."

Agents (Pattern #10) could enhance their effectiveness in relationships by being (1) more self-assertive and less indirect in their communications with people and (2) firmer when it is appropriate to say no or take a stand for themselves in situations where their own well-being and self-worth are in jeopardy.

In task settings, they could (1) realize the valuable contributions which they make and the potential for even greater personal accomplishments and (2) learn how to respond to conflict as opportunities for greater stability and satisfaction among people through even, problem-solving actions, instead of their more natural view of conflict as a threat.

Agents tend to be patient, predictable, servicing, sociable, and mild-mannered. They give the impression of being concerned about others, whether they actually are or not. (This factor can be explained by a different motive—personal values—a separate and distinct dimension from behavioral type and style.) The classic line which captures their inner nature is, "How can I help?"

Achievers (Pattern #11) of the world can increase their effectiveness in personal relationships by their (1) willingness to compromise short-term victories for ongoing, increasingly longer term results through a spirit of mutual collaboration with others and (2) demonstrations of responsiveness to the feelings and needs of others in their groups on each person's terms, not just the way that fits the Achiever's preconceived notions.

In the task environment, Achievers can further benefit by (1) reducing their tendency toward either/or thinking and solutions, while stretching to try a more comprehensive, strategic approach to complex problems and situations and (2) clarifying their essential priorities in life (work and personal) for long range personal development, including exploring the most realistic options for attaining these results with the least cost to themselves and others. This approach will help them more than their natural *full steam ahead* style. Realistically, few people can live totally self-reliant lives without depending on anyone else, even this independence focused Achiever pattern. People of this pattern are most often viewed as more methodical, predictable, deliberate, persistent, competitive, self-reliant, and industrious. The theme of an Achiever's life can be summarized as, "My current objective is . . . "

Investigators (Pattern #12) can increase their effectiveness in relationships by (1) developing increased tolerance and sensitivity to the needs and difficulties which others experience, as well as (2) learning to communicate in a warm, more open manner which invites conversation, mutual exchange, and genuine cooperation.

In task settings, they can benefit by (1) developing more open, exploratory approaches to their view of situations. They can respond to problems in ways which may be less comfortable for them but more appropriate for satisfactorily achieving the desired outcomes and (2) genuinely becoming more personally involved with others in their work tasks in a spirit of shared problem solving and goal attainment. This would be different than their usual tendency toward a more adversarial, competitive approach. Individuals like this are frequently described as methodical, deliberate, persistent, cautious, restrained, analytical, and sometimes Direct or Controlling. You can readily identify them by their personally penetrating questions like, "How do you know that's true?" or, "Let's not let emotions cloud our thinking . . . "

Objective Thinkers (Pattern #13) can increase their personal effectiveness in relationships by opening themselves up so they can gradually identify trusting, collaborative relationships in their life environments. Then they can more readily and productively disclose and discuss their inner feelings, hopes, goals, apprehensions, and fears in a way that can transform their inner stress-producing energies into more productive, outer-focused actions.

In task situations, Objective Thinkers can benefit by sharing their insights and views with others when these are essential to understanding the real problem. They can also contribute realistic, logical suggestions that have a higher probability of making things better than the alternative(s), even if their solutions aren't perfect. By being less critical and demanding of themselves, they can better accept the reality and personal right to be incorrect, like all other human beings. Then they can accept the prospect of becoming imperfect friends, family members, co-workers, employees, or bosses. Objective Thinkers are most often described as restrained, logical, calculating, meticulous, and precise. You can identify them by comments like, "The facts of the matter seem to be . . . "

Perfectionists (Pattern #14) can increase their effectiveness in relationships by developing a more open attitude towards different approaches for satisfying the requirements in a situation. This would be better than sticking to their more perfect or classic textbook solutions, which may be resented or resisted by others. In terms of a situation's human realities, even the right solution may be wrong. In both their relationships and task situations, they can also benefit by developing their own interdependence through collaboration with others. They can also profit by developing independence from others in situations which require little mutual involvement or dependence.

In task situations, the Perfectionist's view of the world can truly benefit by developing further genuine, unconditional acceptance of themselves as human beings with inherent dignity and worth. They are entitled to such treatment by both themselves and others. This unconditional acceptance is separate from, not contingent upon, the quality and quantity of work they accomplish. Perfectionists are most often described by others as deliberate, methodical, detailed, precise, logical, restrained, and somewhat diplomatic. Their motto is, "If you are going to do something, you might as well do it right (correctly), or not at all."

Practitioners (Pattern #15) can become more effective in their relationships by learning to genuinely collaborate with others for the common benefit, rather than focusing on their own needs first or only. (By the way, Practitioners seldom disclose those needs to others). Along the path toward correctness, they may discover procedures that can be beneficial to others as well as themselves, so they can learn to share those discoveries with colleagues.

In dealing with task situations, Practitioners can further develop their potential by learning to more appropriately delegate key tasks. Practitioners are often variously described as inquisitive, diplomatic, cautious, somewhat sociable, enthusiastic, systematic, deliberate, and persistent. Their motto is, "The line of least resistance seems to be . . . "

Afterword

After reading *People Smart*, we hope that you will apply what you've learned to enrich all aspects of your life from your workplace to the social arena, including family experiences and romantic encounters. You now have the tools to create more positive relationships for yourself and others.

Mutual respect and commitment are the keys to understanding and getting along with people. Of course, degrees of respect and commitment vary from relationship to relationship. You probably don't feel as committed to your grocer or butcher as you do to your spouse, significant other, or best friend.? But using what you now know about People Smart concepts, you can learn to accept and even appreciate the differences in others.

Remember, people's strengths can be carried to the extreme at times. You can actually encourage them to act in more positive ways by consulting the appropriate charts and graphics in Chapters 5-12. Identify the person's behavioral style by using the inventory in Chapter 2, identify the environment, then use the visuals to help you enhance your relationship with that person.

Resources

Alessandra & Associates, Inc.

"PEOPLE SMART" can be the keynote or general session presentation at your next annual meeting! Dr. Alessandra has a remarkable intensity and an endearing charisma in his award winning PEOPLE SMART presentation. It is offered in a one to three hour format and is customized to satisfy your meeting objectives and theme. You are assured of a quality performance every time Dr. Alessandra speaks. That's a guarantee!

Alessandra & Associates also offers a vast library of resources built around the PEOPLE SMART concepts. These training materials include workbooks, books, audiotapes, videotapes and comprehensive training programs. For free information on our products and services, please contact us at: Alessandra & Associates, P.O. Box 2767, La Jolla, CA 92038, (800) 222-4383 (outside California), (619) 459-4515 (in California).

Life Associates

In the late 1960's, Dr. Michael O'Connor founded Life Associates. Its services emphasize both public and in-company train-the-trainer and management consultancy projects to further increase both personal and organizational performance and productivity.

LIFE's training resources consist of more than 100 off-the-shelf pre-packaged training workshops, seminars and related materials. It also provides custom-designed programs and their unique application in an organization's own setting.

LIFE's consulting resources involve high level personal consulting services, focusing especially on CEO/COO and key management staff, and application of PEOPLE SMART concepts to further enhance business success. It is a pioneer in the field of computer-based personnel and organizational assessment, management, and targeted development systems. For further information about LIFE's services contact: Life Associates, P.O. Box 41336, Plymouth, MN 55441, (612) 553-0400.

Carlson Learning Company

In order to help you personally acquire the knowledge and competencies involved in understanding and dealing with people, Carlson Learning Co. has created follow-up training resource materials for you to use—either individually or with groups.

These follow-up PEOPLE SMART concept materials include audiotapes, videotapes, workbooks, and self-assessment instruments. If you wish further information about these you may contact: Carlson Learning Company, Carlson Parkway, P.O. Box 59159, Minneapolis, MN 55459-8247, (612) 449-2856.

Index

C

Give the Gift of "People Smarts" to Your Friends and Colleagues!

ORDER FORM

YES, I want _____ copies of *People Smart* at $19.95 each, plus $3 shipping per book. (California residents please include $1.45 in state sales tax.) Canadian orders must be accompanied by a postal money order in U.S. funds. Allow 15 days for delivery.

___Check or Money Order enclosed
Charge my ___VISA ___MasterCard ___AmEx

Name_____ Phone_____

Address _____

Company_____

City/State/Zip_____

Card # _____Expires_____

Signature _____

Check your leading bookstore or call your credit card order to 800-222-4383 (from outside California) 619-459-4515 (in California)

Please make your check payable and return to:

Keynote Publishing Company
P. O. Box 2767
La Jolla, CA 92038